Artifacts of Orthodox Jewish Childhood

Personal and Critical Essays

EDITED BY

DAINY BERNSTEIN, PHD

Teaneck, New Jersey

Artifacts of Orthodox Jewish Childhoods © 2022 by its authors.
All rights reserved. No part of this book may be used or reproduced
in any manner whatsoever without written permission except in the
case of brief quotations embodied in critical articles and reviews.

Published by Ben Yehuda Press
122 Ayers Court #1B
Teaneck, NJ 07666

http://www.BenYehudaPress.com

To subscribe to our monthly book club and support independent Jewish
publishing, visit https://www.patreon.com/BenYehudaPress

Ben Yehuda Press books may be purchased at a discount by synagogues, book clubs, and other institutions buying in bulk. For information, please email:
Markets@BenYehudaPress.com

Cover image courtesy of Judaica wholesaler Rite Lite Ltd.

Set in Arno Pro by Raphaël Freeman MISTD, Renana Typesetting

ISBN 13 978-1-953829-25-2

Contents

Introduction   vii
    Dainy Bernstein

PART I: STUDYING THE ARTIFACTS OF ORTHODOX CHILDHOODS

A Childhood Siddur Around 1990   3
    Hillel Broder

The Anachronisms of Hasidic Yiddish Biblical Coloring Books   19
    Frieda Vizel

From Honey Cakes to Upsherin Cookies:
Jewish Mothers at the Beginning of Jewish Boyhood   29
    Wendy Love Anderson

A Passover Haggadah with
a Refreshing Appreciation of Violence   37
    Yoel Finkelman

Devora Doresh and the Case of the Frum Girl Detective:
Female Heroes in Ultra-Orthodox Jewish Children's Fiction   47
    Meira Levinson

Cultural Ambivalence Praxis
in Haredi Jewish Industrial Toy Design   69
    Shlomi Eiger

Diagramming Modesty   81
    Goldie Gross and Yehudis Keller

The *Shomer Negiah* Song: A Touchy Subject   95
Talia Weisberg

PART II: THE SONGS AND MUSIC OF ORTHODOX CHILDHOODS

Parody and Pathos: The Art of Country Yossi   107
Elli Fischer

Passing on the *Journey*   125
Hannah Lebovits

The Music of the *Marvelous Midos Machine*   133
Lonna Gordon

An Old Kind of Song   139
Miriam Moster

Pesach with Rebbe Alter   151
Miriam Bernstein

Lubavitch Summer Camp Songs   157
Schneur Zalman Newfield

Singing Our Sadness at Sleepaway Camp   161
Jessica Russak-Hoffman

PART III: ORTHODOX CHILDHOODS: PERSONAL ESSAYS

"This is the Greatest Show":
Bais Yaakov Production and My Orthodox Girlhood   167
Leslie Ginsparg Klein

Singing in the House of Jacob   177
Sarah Snider

A Zine Called *The Heresy*:
Angst and *Apikorsus* in a Modern Orthodox Day School   189
Sara Feldman, Abby Glogower, Sarah Gray

My Shul, My Place   219
Miriam L.

My Yechi Yarmulke *Chanan Maister*	225
The Golem, Goyim, and the Hasidic Imagination *Schneur Zalman Newfield*	231
Torah Shebe'al Peh *Devora Steinmetz*	237
Ephemeral Memories of Childhood Ephemera *Shamma Boyarin*	241
Bibliography	245
About the Authors	257

Introduction

Dainy Bernstein

Hang around on the internet long enough and you'll encounter at least one "only 90s kids will remember..." meme or listicle. They're filled with such memories as keeping a Tamagotchi alive, collecting Troll dolls, keeping track of Polly Pocket figurines, biting off pieces of candy necklaces and bracelets, rewinding VHS tapes, using pencils on cassette tapes, listening to The Spice Girls and Destiny's Child or 'N Sync and the Backstreet Boys...[1] Remembering childhood objects with nostalgia is not unique to 90s kids, though they are the first generation to have the technology and the avenues to both preserve and amplify their nostalgia for childhood objects. The artifacts of childhood are a crucial component of our development, no matter what decade we grew up in. In her preface to a collection of essays on childhood and material culture, Joanna Sofaer Derevenski explains that "[c]hildren perceive, react and add to the world through material culture as objects guide the child's experience."[2] The things we have access to and interact with in our youth directly affect the way we understand the world around us. The artifacts mentioned in the "only 90s kids will remember" listicles are worth remembering

---

1. For example, see Korin Miller, "40 Things Only 90s Kids Will Remember," *Women's Health Magazine*, August 2, 2019, https://www.womenshealthmag.com/life/g28471716/things-only-90s-kids-remember/.
2. Joanna Sofaer Derevenski, *Children and Material Culture* (Routledge 2000), xv.

because they define a generation, and because they can tell us about how children of the 90s understand the world.

But not all 90s kids have the same memories of their childhood artifacts. Every time one of those social media games is going around, where people share the most defining song from their adolescence, I love to spam everyone's Twitter threads and Facebook posts with Miami Boys Choir or Abie Rotenberg songs. Those are the defining songs of my generation, after all! I wasn't listening to any of the songs my non-Haredi generational fellows were listening to, because I wasn't allowed to listen to secular music. I don't have that "universal" experience of awkward 90s prom, and when I watch *10 Things I Hate About You* as an adult, I don't feel any emotional or nostalgic reaction to those 90s prom dresses. I had a few Troll dolls that I won as prizes at Bnos events, but while my friends and classmates had Tamagotchis and Polly Pocket sets, I didn't because my parents either couldn't afford or didn't approve of those toys for various reasons. The "universal" childhood and adolescent experience often talked about on social media is the white, American, Christian, middle-class experience. It's not representative of even the majority of American childhood and adolescence, and certainly not of American Orthodox Jewish childhood and adolescence.[3] Because of the relative insularity of the Orthodox world, with educational institutions, communal organizations, and publishing houses separate from mainstream American institutions, the experience of childhood for 90s kids in Orthodox communities is necessarily different from the one represented in "only 90s kids will remember" listicles.

In addition to differences in lived experience, the field of childhood studies is built on the acknowledgment that "childhood" is a social construct, that the concept of "childhood" is not a fixed biological truth but an idea that is built up through society's interpretations of age, development, ability, and gender, as well as through the lens of religion. In Judaism, there are opposing ideas of the child, sometimes

---

3. In childhood studies, the term "childhood" is often used to refer to both childhood and adolescence. I use the term "childhood" here to refer to the social constructs encompassing children and teens of all ages.

as a being subject to the Evil Inclination until the Good Inclination enters at the age of bar or bat mitzvah, sometimes as a being whose purity will bring Moshiach.[4] Depending on which view is dominant at a particular time or in a particular context, interpretations of halakhot relating to childhood are affected, as is the general treatment of children.[5] Other ideologies of childhood are influenced by socio-economic status. Is a child a being who needs to be taught a work ethic, or a being who needs to be nurtured? The answer to that can depend on whether the child was born into poverty or wealth. These ideas that shape the concept of childhood can all overlap and exist simultaneously, as well, which is why it is so vital to drill down to the tiniest details and acknowledge all the differences that affect ideologies of childhood if we want to understand how a society thinks of and raises its children.

And why would we want to understand how a society thinks of and raises its children? What's the value in pursuing that line of inquiry? Well, take the case of the 90s kids accepted as the default in memes and listicles: the objects from their childhood and adolescence certainly shaped their understanding of the world around them, but who gave them those objects? Who created those toys, made that music, perfected the technology that defined their interaction with the world? These childhood and adolescent artifacts were all curated by adults with specific ideas about what children and teens are, how children and teens should learn to interact with the world. Deborah Brandt, a leading scholar in literacy studies, argues that a child has access to literacy through literacy sponsors, and that these sponsors "deliver the ideological freight that must be borne for access to what they have."[6] If we understand all artifacts – texts, music, toys, etc. – as

---

4. See: Yossi Toiv, "Little *Kinderlach*," *Country Yossi and the Shteeble-Hoppers Volume 1*, 1983.
5. See Simha Goldin, "Jewish Society Under Pressure: The Concept of Childhood," in *Youth in the Middle Ages*, edited by P.J.P. Goldberg and Felicity Riddy, York Medieval Press, 2004, pp. 25–43.
6. Deborah Brandt, "Sponsors of Literacy," *College Composition and Communication* 49.2 (1998), 168.

Figures 1–4 an *Olomeinu* magazine cover; *Labels for Laibel*, a picturebook published by Hachai; *The Little Old Lady Who Couldn't Fall Asleep*, an Artscroll Middos Book; an *Uncle Moishy and the Mitzvah Men* videotape

tools in shaping a child's literacy, i.e., their understanding of how to "read" the world, it's clear that they all carry the "ideological freight" of the sponsor of literacy, i.e., the individual adult or institution who acts as the gatekeeper of the child's interaction with the world. If we want to understand how children develop an understanding of the world around them, we need to understand what ideological freight their literacy sponsors have attempted to pass on.

In my work on Haredi childhood, I study primarily textual sources like books and magazines, but I am interested in all the artifacts of Orthodox childhood that can tell us both about how Orthodox children of the 1980s and 1990s learned to read the world and about how Orthodox adults in the 1980s and 1990s viewed children. Orthodox Jewish kids and teens in the 80s and 90s learned to understand the world in a particular way because of their particular sponsors of literacy: Torah Umesorah's *Olomeinu* magazine, Hachai's picture books and Artscroll's Middos books, Torah Cards and Gedolim Cards, Uncle Moishy and Shmuel Kunda, and so on. Over the last few years, as I wrote my dissertation on American Haredi children's literature, I often used Twitter to share bits and pieces of the texts I was reading and the artifacts I was reminded of as I worked. Haredi childhood – and Orthodox childhood in general – is under-studied in the field of Jewish Studies,[7] and it does not appear at all in the field of Childhood Studies, so I found myself turning to #JewishTwitter and #FrumTwitter when I needed references, memories, or critical engagements with texts. Nostalgia abounded, as did fascinating insights among conversants from wildly different upbringings who shared some common childhood or adolescent experiences. No matter what any of us thinks or feels about our childhood and adolescent experiences, it's clear that we all have a lot to say about it, and that the things we have to say are smart, productive, and worth being heard.

Many of the items or ideas we discussed were beyond the scope of my dissertation and the book I'm currently working on, which focuses solely on textual artifacts. I wanted to include information about 613 Torah Avenue, Pirchei Choirs, Torah Island, Kivi and Tuki, etc., but

---

7. For a study of Hasidic childhood, see Ayala Fader, *Mitzvah Girls: Bringing Up the Next Generation of Hasidic Jews in Brooklyn*, Princeton University Press, 2009.

Figures 5–8 a *613 Torah Avenue* vinyl record cover; a *Pirchei Choir* vinyl record cover; a *Torah Island* CD cover; *When Zaidy Was Young*, a Shmuel Kunda Production CD cover

it's impossible for one person and one project to cover all of the items important to Orthodox childhoods. I joked on Twitter that I would love to have something I can cite for each of these artifacts, pointing my readers toward other people's descriptions and analyses of these cultural artifacts without having to include huge footnotes in my own work. That joke became serious very quickly, and I was delighted to have the chance to work on a collection of essays about key concepts and artifacts of Orthodox Jewish childhood, creating a resource for myself and others to use as we continue to delve into the experiences of Orthodox childhood, to build an understanding of how Orthodox adults think about children and childhood as well as an understanding of how Orthodox children learn to read and understand the world around them. This collection of essays is the result, proof that there is much to discuss with regard to artifacts of Orthodox childhood and that those who experienced Orthodox childhood have much to say.

This book is also proof of the richness and vastness of this potential field of study. One of the hardest editorial comments I had to make on multiple contributors' essays was: "I know this might feel like a universal Orthodox experience to you, but it's actually not universal beyond this small segment of Orthodox Judaism." Because while Orthodox childhood is itself already a very niche subject area, it can be divided into multiple even-more-niche areas: There's Modern Orthodox (ideologically combining the religious and the secular), Chabad / Lubavitch (adhering to ideologies of the Lubavitcher Rebbe with a focus on religious outreach), yeshivish (communities organized with the yeshiva at the center), chassidish (Hasidic communities following a Rebbe), Haredi (ultra-Orthodox but not Hasidic), and more. And of course, within each of those sub-divisions, there are even more sub-sub-divisions, because the experience of Modern Orthodox Jews growing up in the New York metropolitan area differs from those growing up "out-of-town," as Jessica Russak-Hoffman's essay demonstrates, and the experience of Chabad Jews in Crown Heights differs from the experience of Chabad Jews on *shlichus* across the country and around the globe, as Chanan Maister and Schneur Zalman Newfield's essays demonstrate. While chassidish childhoods may share the coloring books which Frieda Vizel discusses, the various chassidish sects and neighborhoods vary significantly in their childhood experiences. This volume is merely a taste, barely even scratching the surface of insights to be gleaned from the artifacts of various Orthodox childhoods.

At one point while editing this volume, I considered dividing the essays into sections based on which sub-division of Orthodoxy the author and/or artifact belonged to. I quickly abandoned that as it became clear that this was entirely unproductive, not only because the definitions of boundaries between various groups is contested by various essays: Some use the term "yeshivish" to differentiate between Modern Orthodox and Haredi communities, some use "yeshivish" to differentiate between Hasidic and Haredi communities, and some use "yeshivish" to differentiate between right-wing and left-wing Modern Orthodox communities. This is reflective of real-life usage, where even the word "frum," literally translating to pious, is subject to different definitions depending on which community the speaker identifies with.[8] More practically, while there may be clear differences between various experiences of Orthodox childhood, there is a significant enough amount of overlap between the artifacts present in each particular community and between the ideologies of childhood and modes of reading the world represented. The volume therefore groups essays from all parts of the Orthodox world together without differentiating between them. This does not mean that the volume argues for a universal Orthodox experience. Far from it. Rather, the organization should be read as an initial attempt to carve out Orthodox Jewish childhood as a niche field of study within the fields of Childhood Studies, Jewish Studies, and Material Culture. There is more to be gained from considering all these artifacts as a single set than as separate sets for the present moment as we begin to focus on Orthodox Jewish childhood as a distinct category. As we continue studying this area, future volumes will be able to dig deeper and split off into more nuanced studies of discrete Orthodox communities.

One of my greatest joys in working on this collection came from speaking with individuals who were hesitant to submit essays or proposals because they thought they were not expert enough or learned enough in the academic fields of material culture, childhood studies, or Jewish studies. Throughout the process of putting the volume together, from the moment of inspiration to the call for papers to the editorial process, my goal has been to bring in the voices of experts

---

8. Rather than attempt to standardize usage of these terms and others in the same situation, I have left the usage up to each author. This editorial choice captures the slippage of these terms as used in lived experiences and the ways they affect perceptions of insider and outsider in each community.

beyond academia – to center the voices of laypeople with personal experience of the artifacts and of Orthodox childhood. As a result, the essays in this volume are wide-ranging in their approaches to the topic of Orthodox Jewish childhoods, in their literary styles, and in their positioning within specific Orthodox Jewish communities. Transliterations of Hebrew and Yiddish words therefore vary from one essay to the next, as we wanted to preserve the pronunciation differences among communities.

The first section of this volume, "Studying the Artifacts of Orthodox Childhoods," consists of essays more heavily weighted to the academic than the personal. The opening essay, Hillel Broder's "A Childhood Siddur Around 1990," weaves together personal reflection and theoretical discussions of childhood and literacy. Using Walter Benjamin's German-Jewish memoir, *Berlin Childhood around 1900*, as an exemplar, Broder examines his own Modern Orthodox childhood siddur in great detail, from the cover decoration to the printed page and his memories of the siddur in classroom use. The result is an emotionally-laden and theoretically-driven rumination about the ways in which children are drawn into normative religious observance and textual literacy. Focusing on Hasidic childhood on the other end of the Orthodox spectrum, Frieda Vizel's essay, "The Anachronisms of Hasidic Yiddish Biblical Coloring Books," analyzes an artifact ubiquitous in Hasidic preschools and homes to demonstrate that the images and language in these coloring books directly affect the ways in which Hasidic children see their Jewish history and their non-Jewish contemporaries. Vizel's essay brilliantly lays out the concepts of Jewishness and of history as understood through Hasidic ideology and as represented in children's coloring books.

Drawing comparisons between medieval Jewish practice and contemporary Orthodox practice, Wendy Love Anderson's "From Honey Cakes to Upsherin Cookies: Jewish Mothers at the Beginning of Jewish Boyhood" analyzes the rituals surrounding the entrance of a Jewish boy into communal Jewish life. Her study spans centuries from the Middle Ages to the twenty-first century, relying on sources ranging from rabbinic books like Rabbi Eleazar ben Judah's *Sefer ha-Rokeach* to contemporary mothers' discussions such as those on the imamother.com website. Through an examination of the artifacts surrounding these rituals of Jewish boyhood, their development through the centuries, and the practices they are associated with, Anderson is able to trace the role of the mother in a Jewish boy's introduction to Jewish life, concluding that the mother is simultaneously present and absent in these boyhood rituals.

Yoel Finkelman's essay, "A Passover Haggadah with a Refreshing Appreciation of Violence," traces another tradition from its medieval to contemporary manifestations by contrasting Yoel ben Shimon's fifteenth-century illuminated Haggadah and a contemporary children's Haggadah edited by Baruch Chait and illustrated by Gadi Pollack. Finkelman situates the fifteenth-century Haggadah in its cultural context of rich Jews in the Italian Renaissance representing historical Jewish figures ahistorically (as the contemporary Hasidic coloring books discussed in Vizel's essays do), and contrasts this with the contemporary Haredi illustrations of Israelites and Egyptians matching a self-perception of being separate from the rest of the world. Commenting on the unusually graphic and violent illustrations in a Haggadah for children, he also gestures toward parenting debates about whether it's better to shield children from horror and tragedy or to portray the darker sides of legend and history, trusting that children will be able to cope and will be the stronger for it. While emphasizing that Chait and Pollack's Haggadah is not representative of contemporary Haredi children's books, Finkelman's essay demonstrates the ways in which Haredi ideologies of Jewish identity and history might influence children's materials.

Highlighting the inherent tension between normative and radical ideologies of Orthodox Jewish childhood and gender, Meira Levinson's essay, "Devora Doresh and the Case of the Frum Girl Detective: Female Heroes in Ultra-Orthodox Jewish Children's Fiction," discusses the brainy and adventurous detective who appears to break Orthodox gender norms. Levinson argues that while the Devora Doresh books are not quite feminist, they are radical in presenting an Orthodox girl who is not only given permission to use her intelligence and

Torah knowledge to solve mysteries – a role usually reserved for boys in both Orthodox and mainstream American books of the time – but is also not censored for getting into physically adventurous and dangerous situations in the process of solving mysteries. In addition to the crucial analysis of gender in Orthodox literature, Levinson's essay also clearly demonstrates the nuances of Orthodox ideology and the way it often creates paradoxes in childhood artifacts.

Shlomi Eiger's essay, "Cultural Ambivalence Praxis in Haredi Jewish Industrial Toy Design," continues this theme of tension and ambivalence through an examination of the interaction between industrial toy design and Haredi concepts of modesty and gender segregation. Using his personal experience as a designer of Haredi toy sets and as an expert in the theory of toy design, Eiger discusses the various halakhic interests of the Haredi markets and the ways in which these considerations are both helped and hampered by western secular production and market patterns.

The final two essays in the first section both focus on modesty standards for girls in Orthodox communities. Goldie Gross and Yehudis Keller, in "Diagramming Modesty," discuss the growing phenomenon of illustrations depicting the rules of modesty for teen girls and adult women. They trace the origin of the phenomenon, analyze the implications of male-authored modesty diagrams dictating women's bodily appearance, and contemplate the efficacy of intense focus on the body as a method of promoting modesty. In "The *Shomer Negiah* Song: A Touchy Subject," Talia Weisberg departs from examining normative artifacts like *tznius* diagrams, and instead focuses on a non-normative and potentially transgressive underground song, popular in Modern Orthodox girls' camps and schools, about the restriction of physical contact between boys and girls. Weisberg argues that the song, while ostensibly upholding the norm of restricting contact, subverts communal norms by creating a humorous girls-only song based on a popular song sung by the Miami Boys Choir. Similarly to Levinson's and Eiger's analysis of the paradoxes and tensions inherent in artifacts of Orthodox childhood, Weisberg's analysis demonstrates that transgression and conformity can co-exist in a single childhood artifact. The presence of paradox, tension, and ambivalence in cultural artifacts of Orthodox childhoods is in fact a common thread among all the essays in this first section, and the theme echoes throughout many essays in the rest of the volume.

Another theme that emerged as I gathered and organized contributors' essays was music. So many essays engaged with music, in fact, that music snagged an entire section of its own in this volume, "The Songs and Music of Orthodox Childhoods." The first essay in this section, Elli Fischer's "Parody and Pathos: The Art of Country Yossi," draws connections between the American songs on which Country Yossi's songs are based and the themes that emerge in the Orthodox parodies. Fischer deftly sketches a portrait of the people and places inhabiting Country Yossi's corpus of songs, arguing that these songs reflect a particular anxiety of the post-Holocaust generation attempting to bridge the gap between their old-world parents and their new-world reality.

Hannah Lebovits's essay, "Passing on the *Journey*," similarly examines the picture created by Abie Rotenberg's corpus, arguing that the vision of idyllic Orthodox existence was an aspirational fantasy not based on the realities of the time. Lebovits muses on the irony of her children becoming interested in Rotenberg's songs of an idealized version of Orthodox existence and wonders what the future holds as a new generation absorbs these ideas. Lonna Gordon's "The Music of the *Marvelous Midos Machine*" traces this same phenomenon, of sharing one's childhood music with one's own children. Gordon focuses on individual songs about character traits from the *Marvelous Midos Machine* series, arguing that each song is perfectly suited to the character trait it seeks to instill in children through its lyrics and tempo. Gordon explores how some songs allow the child healthy expression of negative feelings like anger while learning how to regulate their emotions, and she posits that the songs permeate communal Orthodox culture beyond use in children's environments because of these musical and emotional qualities.

In the next two essays, Miriam Moster and Miriam Bernstein turn to songs about Jewish holidays and their use of Hebrew, Yiddish, and

English. Moster continues the theme of parents looking back at the music of their childhood in "An Old Kind of Song," this time with a focus on the way popular Chanukah songs from the Miami Boys Choir and the Yeshiva Boys Choir actively negotiate boundaries between the Haredi world, the non-Haredi Jewish world, and the secular world. In contrast to Lebovits, who hopes her children might realize the idealized version of Orthodoxy represented in Abie Rotenberg's *Journeys* songs, Moster grapples over the tension between the desire to share a nostalgic piece of her past with her children and the desire to raise children who are more accepting of others than these Chanukah songs are. Bernstein's essay analyzes the songs of *Pesach with Rebbe Alter* and argues that the pattern of repetition between the adult Rebbe Alter and the child singers is crucial to the child's understanding of their place in familial rituals of Passover. Thinking about the album as an educational tool, Bernstein looks beyond the surface lessons of the Passover rituals and Jewish history to explore how the child listener would learn about their place in Jewish society and how they as a child should participate in these rituals.

The final two essays in the section on songs and music address the phenomenon of songs and music in summer sleepaway camps, though each one focuses on a very different environment. Schneur Zalman Newfield's essay, "Lubavitch Summer Camp Songs," continues Bernstein's examination of how certain songs instill values and teach children about their roles in Orthodox communities. Newfield discusses a few songs and demonstrates how each one presents the camper and singer with a vision of how he could occupy space and move in society. Jessica Russak-Hoffman, in "Singing Our Sadness at Sleepaway Camp," skillfully narrates the emotional effect of learning and performing popular Orthodox songs in a Modern Orthodox girls' camp, Machaneh Morasha. Through the story of learning and singing the popular song *"Yisroel,"* composed by Chumi Berry and sung by Dov Levine, Russak-Hoffman evokes the feelings she experienced, feelings of emo sadness and Jewish identity.

The third and final section of the volume, "Orthodox Childhoods: Personal Essays and Memoirs," includes critical analysis, but the essays in this section focus on personal artifacts and experiences rather than those shared by the Orthodox community as a whole. This volume attempts to define Orthodox childhood through its communal artifacts, always acknowledging the variations between various sub-groups of Orthodox Judaism, but individual experiences are an equally important part of the picture. Most of the essays in the previous two sections have used the personal and individual interactions with artifacts shared by the community as tangential to their theses; the essays in this final section zero in on the personal and only briefly gesture outward in discussions of how their personal experiences might inform our understanding of Orthodox childhoods. More emotional and visceral, these essays are filled with insights into real Orthodox children's lived experiences.

Leslie Ginsparg-Klein's essay, "'This is the Greatest Show:' Bais Yaakov Productions and My Orthodox Girlhood," uses Ginsparg-Klein's own personal experiences with Bais Yaakov productions to make claims about Orthodox girlhood more broadly, a topic she studies and has written about for peer-reviewed journals. She argues that while there are many flaws in the way production has historically been handled, especially in regard to the way high school girls perform plays about the male life cycle or adult characters, an all-female space for creative expression is a valuable part of Orthodox girlhood. Sarah Snider's essay, "Singing in the House of Jacob," explores another example of a song-infused Bais Yaakov, emotionally and effectively arguing against a dominant mainstream perception of Orthodoxy – and especially Orthodox girlhood – as repressed, silent, and gloomy. On the contrary, Snider illuminates the many instances when the halls of her Bais Yaakov school were filled with songs of joy, songs of sadness, songs of learning, and songs of rebellion, similarly to "The *Shomer Negiah* Song" discussed by Weisberg in this volume.

In "A Zine Called *Heresy*: Angst and *Apikorsus* in a Modern Orthodox Day School," three childhood friends recall a zine they created and distributed as they grappled with the injustices they felt in their Modern Orthodox school and community. Sara Feldman, Abby Glogower, and Sarah Gray painstakingly review the pages they created as teenagers, rightfully treating their own work as a cultural artifact[9] which can shed light on how the Modern Orthodox school and community functioned, as well as how some students struggled to find their place. Miriam L., in "My Shul, My Place," similarly tracks her struggle with finding her place as an Orthodox Jewish girl through the multiple shul experiences of her childhood, adolescence, and young adulthood. She takes us on a journey through the many different shuls she attended, beginning with the "shul" of her mother teaching her how to recite Shabbos *tefillos*, on to the shul where she was made to feel her gender was an obstacle, and finally to a shul where she could take her place as a core member of the congregation and embrace her passion for participating in communal Jewish practices.

Chanan Maister uses his *Yechi* yarmulke, his kippa embroidered with the Hebrew phrase meaning "May our master and teacher, the king Messiah, live forever," as a touchstone for exploring the attitudes of Chabad communities surrounding the death of the Lubavitcher Rebbe and the controversial belief that the Rebbe would rise again as the Messiah. Tracking how he was treated in various settings while unwittingly wearing a controversial garment, Maister illuminates the way ideology creates community, insiders, and outsiders. Schneur Zalman Newfield, in "The Golem, Goyim, and the Hasidic Imagination," similarly contemplates the creation of Lubavitch identity, but he reaches outward to examine how Orthodox children's stories about the legendary Golem of Prague affected his perception of his Black non-Jewish neighbors in Crown Heights. Both of these essays narrate a child's perception of self and others, convincingly demonstrating how childhood artifacts can shape a child's understanding of the world around them.

Finally, the last two essays provide snapshots into childhood artifacts that influenced the authors' Jewish development and ideas well into adulthood. In *"Torah Shebe'al Peh,"* Devora Steinmetz tells the story of her official exclusion from the male realm of studying

---

9. The zine is now housed in the Special Collections Research Center at the University of Michigan, where it will be preserved in the archives.

Talmud in her Modern Orthodox co-ed middle-school classroom, and her unofficial inclusion in the form of a supportive teacher and helpful male classmates. Steinmetz's essay, like Weisberg's essay on the *Shomer Negiah* song and Snider's essay on singing in the halls of Bais Yaakov, highlights the importance of artifacts that push the boundaries beyond the accepted and authoritative artifacts.

In "Ephemeral Memories of Childhood Ephemera," Shamma Boyarin settles into a space of clouded memory, contemplating the effects of a childhood artifact long gone and likely unrecoverable. A perfect end to a volume about artifacts from a time in one's life often colored by mis-memory, Boyarin's essay wonders about the purpose of a popular story printed in a pamphlet for children and distributed via the community shul. In attempting to square his memories with his current knowledge of history and Jewish thought, Boyarin's essay is a poignant reminder of the corners and crevices in our minds filled with memories so ephemeral yet so powerful, and of the understanding of our present lives waiting to be gleaned from clearing out the attics and basements of our childhoods to examine the artifacts they store.

Part I
*Studying the Artifacts
of Orthodox Childhoods*

A Childhood Siddur Around 1990

Hillel Broder[1]

My Shilo siddur was my first prayer book. I was six, the year was 1990, and it was celebrated in a first grade assembly attended by teachers and parents, covered and adorned by my own hand, and subsequently used daily through the fourth grade of my Modern Orthodox day school in suburban Maryland. This siddur was my entry into the language and choreography of normative prayer, and as the first Hebrew book in my possession, it served as an early, if not first, Hebrew primer.

As formative and as critical as my initial experiences with this Siddur were, it lay dormant in my parents' basement – and in my subconscious – for nearly thirty years. A few years ago, inspired by my own son's first grade siddur party, I retrieved it, mostly out of admiration for its apparent and unlikely preservation, and promptly shelved it, mostly out of concern that this relic of my childhood would be neglected by the rougher hands of my children. It continued to rest for the past two years, along with my interlinear Metsudah and encyclopedic Artscroll prayer books, a collection accumulated over my teenage and young adult years.

---

1. This essay is dedicated to my first grade teacher, Mrs. Debbie Kipperman of blessed memory, who first introduced me to my siddur.

It remained out of use until the spring of 2020. Amid the months of lockdown that ensued during the Covid-19 pandemic, my prayer practice shifted from formal, communal prayer with an adult congregation to a lively and sometimes messy round of praying with my nursery-aged children, where we would all don prayer shawls and sing through the greatest and most memorable Jewish songs of today's early childhood classrooms. With the world around us shuttered, and with my children's Jewish day school classrooms entirely online, we retreated to a tired living room that became, nearly every morning, our synagogue.

I pulled out all the stops to sustain and energize their religious life of prayer: we sang, danced, and clapped our way through the prayers that we knew. I set familiar prayer tunes to folk guitar picking and cymbal shaking. And I stocked our "shul" with our prayerbooks on hand at home, pulling what I had off the shelf, including my long-neglected Shilo siddur as my go-to text. After all, this was my prayer origin story, the foundation of all of my later prayer education and experiences to come. And after all, it had served as a child's first siddur, one that would surely speak to my young children, now homebound. If anything, I thought, it was a fitting contribution to this shared moment of forced regression. What I discovered – and recovered – was far more complex.

* * *

The Shilo siddur was first compiled and published by Professor Zevi Scharfstein in 1932. Scharfstein was an American-based Jewish historian of the nineteenth-century cheder and the nascent twentieth-century American Jewish educational system. He published the siddur as part of his greater pedagogical mission, spearheaded by his founding of the Shilo publishing house: to disseminate Hebrew-language materials to the Talmud Torahs, Hebrew schools, and few but popular Jewish day schools of his day. His siddur was one of the first of many modern Hebrew curricular materials produced by Shilo, which was one of the first American-Jewish educational publishing houses.

Contemporaneously, and on the other side of the Atlantic, the

German-Jewish critic and philosopher Walter Benjamin was thinking through the artifacts and experiences of his childhood, a childhood nearly a century older than mine. As an adult student of Benjamin's eclectic thought about memory and modernity, I can't help but read my early and then subsequently adult experiences of the Shilo siddur through Benjamin's lens. So it is quite serendipitous that in that same year of the Shilo siddur's publication, 1932, Benjamin composed a brief aphoristic memoir of his childhood, *Berlin Childhood around 1900*, refracted through the objects and spaces that populated his earliest years. Benjamin was forty at the time of this composition of recollections; I was thirty-six when recalling my childhood artifact through Benjamin's lens. Close enough.

In this work, Benjamin's recollections are magical, sometimes fearful, and nearly always surreal. His childhood observation of a glistening rain on an otter, in the Berlin Zoo, became the sensation of calm he experienced while sheltered at home; the quiet hunt of a butterfly transforms his own child's body into that of a monarch, becoming the butterfly, while the butterfly recedes from its own animality, anthropomorphized in the child's imagination with a newfound human cunning and will. A rare commentary, embedded in a riff on a nursery rhyme, emerges as a brief key to his exercise in memory:

> Early on, I learned to disguise myself in words, which really were clouds. The gift of perceiving similarities, is, in fact, nothing but a weak remnant of the old compulsion to become similar, to behave mimetically. In me, this compulsion acted through words. Not those that made me similar to well-behaved children, but those that made me similar to dwelling places, furniture, clothes. I was distorted by similarity to all that surrounded me.[2]

Children who see correspondences, who notice, verbalize, or even perform affinities between themselves and the natural world, Benjamin says, are accessing the lost art and ancient ability of the mimetic

---

2. Walter Benjamin, *Berlin Childhood around 1900*, (Harvard University Press, 2006): 97–98.

faculty. As Nicola Gess has argued,[3] Walter Benjamin's interest in the psychology of children was far out-shadowed by his fascination with the materials and artifacts of childhood, an interest that seems to haunt nearly all of his writing on the subject. These objects and spaces not only anchor a child's memories, but also shape and form his early experiences of reading as a nearly mystical but anthropologically ancient practice.

In Benjamin's unpublished essays on the mimetic faculty, this non-verbal mimesis of early childhood accesses the ancient ability to "read what was never written." The ancients practiced non-verbal mimesis in reading anything from entrails to the stars, or through the practice of the art of dance; children, similarly, perform such primordial non-verbal mimesis by becoming the world that they "read:" they play "at being not only a shopkeeper or teacher, but also a windmill and a train." Turning towards reading – first runes and hieroglyphs, then language – "may be seen as the highest level of mimetic behavior and the most complete archive of nonsensuous similarity."[4]

For Benjamin, it is the early child speaker and reader who can still surface mimetic correspondences in language. The interest was not only retrospectively personal – "it was contemporaneously familial." Benjamin logged, recalled, and systematically archived the language play, games, and distortions of his young son Stefan in a notebook that spans nearly a decade (1922–1932). In a letter to Gershom Scholem, he describes this very notebook as the manuscript of a future publication – his son's "opinions and thoughts" ("opinions et pensées") – that documents the "unusual words and expressions"[5] of a child's play in language, one that showcases language not as semiotics but as, even

---

3. Nicola Gess, "Gaining Sovereignty: On the Figure of the Child in Walter Benjamin's Writing," *MLN* 125.3 (2010), 682–708.
4. Walter Benjamin, "On the Mimetic Faculty," *SW*, Vol. 2.2: 1993, 722. Benjamin scholars read this 1933 essay as a secularization, reconsideration, and possible revision of his earlier essay "Doctrine of the Similar."
5. Walter Benjamin, *Correspondences*, eds. Gershom Scholem and Theodor W. Adorno, trans. Manfred R. Jacobson and Evelyn M. Jacobson, University of Chicago Press, 1994, 288.

after thousands of years of evolution, still preserving an "archive of nonsensuous similarities, of nonsensuous correspondences."[6]

And the interest was not only in the playfulness of a child's spoken language. It was also in the language games that reached into the graphic nature of a text's orthography, layout, and typography. Benjamin's childhood memoir includes a fixation on the calligraphy of the signature of a postcard artist, one that assigns meanings to her last name, Pufahl, as follows: "the 'p' at the beginning was the 'p' of perseverance... 'f' stood for faithful... 'l' at the end, it was the figure of lamblike piety."[7] In his manuscripts, Benjamin's spatial and even graphic reorganization of language affords new correspondences. Language is distorted and then put to sleep, in the image of an embryo printed with the words "Sleep my Sleepiken sleep, sheep my sleepikin sheep." In other essays on Krauss and Kafka, Benjamin retains the graphic nature of language, utilizing ellipses to illustrate dialectics at work.[8]

* * *

I will confess, now, that I was never an original artist. As Benjamin suspected about the mimicry of children, I too suspect the same about my childhood self. Indeed, I can only recall looking at and listening to the world around me and doing my best to mimic it. I also suspect now that most of the children in my class were in the same boat, barely self-conscious, mimicking our parents, older siblings, and favorite cartoons. But as the oldest in my family, my paradigms, let alone self- and other-awareness, were still developing. Many of my early academic successes lay in both my diligence and my precision when assimilating others' ideas and paradigms – I did my best to most thoroughly execute my emulations. My early education in becoming a dual-linguistic, Hebrew reader of Jewish prayer was dominated by the uniquely mimetic nature of my siddur project and education – which

---

6. Walter Benjamin, "Doctrine of the Similar," *SW* 2.2, 697.
7. *Berlin Childhood*, 67.
8. Ursula Marx, Gudrun Schwarz, Michael Schwarz, and Erdmut Wizisla, eds., *Walter Benjamin's Archive*, trans. Esther Leslie, (Verso 2007), 237–247.

is, namely, a story of becoming. By extension, one of my earliest works of mimesis, still in my possession, is the cover of my Shilo siddur.

When we were tasked with decorating the cloth cover with crayons by my first grade Hebrew teacher, I looked around the room, and I reviewed internally what I knew how to draw. I saw some of my classmates, perhaps more artistically inclined or practiced, drawing borders of wavy clouds and grassy foundations, with prickly suns extended and shining. I observed others drawing outsized Israeli flags, no doubt copying the large Israeli flag that adorned our chalkboard. Though I certainly can't trace its origin, I myself knew how to draw a square house with a triangular roof, and I knew how to draw myself as a stick figure. So naturally, having observed everyone and having made no real conscious decision at all, I incorporated all that I observed and knew into my siddur's cover, including a house with an elongated twist of smoke coming out of the chimney, a kippa-clad stick-figure self-portrait seated on a stick-figure swing set, a comprehensive landscape bordering its entirety, and Israeli flags adorning it all. My name, in Hebrew, was stenciled on the side (fig. 1 & 2).

At the time, my cover stood out amongst my peers' for its clutter. Now, I think, it speaks to the complexity of the moment, and the clutter of what was to follow: ideologically, the moment demanded a statement of both personal and religious identity, one that was both uniquely expressive and somehow communally or universally true. I wouldn't have known that at six years old, but I knew the materials in my life that seemed to represent a stable religious identity: my home, my kippah, the Israeli flag. The inclusion of multiple scenes on both covers, as well as a bordering motif, speaks to my childhood's religious impulse of obsessive inclusivity: cover it all, and as I would learn from this siddur, say it all, lest I miss something important. These correspondences of identity – of my classroom Israeli flags adorning my home, of my collector's impulse to include, or even hoard, all available images – were not symbolic. They were, mimetically speaking, images that overwhelmed my senses and identity. More than anything else, when I held this Siddur, I was the skull-capped child, I was the pride of the Israeli flag, I was the heat of the sun shining on the scene, and I was the comforting smoke of my projected Jewish home.

My ambition to encapsulate my religious identity, to foresee the clutter of my ideology, foreshadows my experience of reading – mimetically, mostly, but also linguistically – the book contained therein. The text of the prayer book itself was a daunting challenge to master, both visually and linguistically. But the first text that we had to master was our Hebrew name, stenciled by our teacher on paper, practiced to perfection by our own hand, and then copied onto the spine by our own hand. Here, the square block lines of my Hebrew – especially the double *lameds* of my first name – were a revelation to me, reaching like lightning bolts, zig-zagging across the spine. There are no soft, circular edges of cursive Hebrew; my Hebrew name, in its all-caps and sharp edges, becomes as sharp and focused as the edges of the squared Israeli flag and its embedded star, as crystallized as my faith in everything I had to become.

As a child learning to simultaneously read Hebrew and pray, to learn Hebrew as we prayed, to fall into this foreign language, as Scharfstein had likely envisioned, as an American Jew of the twentieth century, I was told to point to the place, to count the numbered lines, and to mimic the text's rhythms. Historically speaking, if this book's place truly was to teach prayer, it was an overwhelming introduction to the task. If it was to serve as a Hebrew primer for those religiously devoted to prayer, well, it functioned as a read-along textbook. No doubt for me and my classmates – as well as the generations that preceded and followed – it served both purposes. We were both early students of the language *and* beginning to learn the work of prayer. Neither seemed to support – or forgive – the other, and so those who succeeded, including myself, devised a mimetic approach to prayer, and to this prayer book in particular.

* * *

In Benjamin's childhood archive, it is his earliest experiences of school library books – their overwhelming materiality, the uncanny

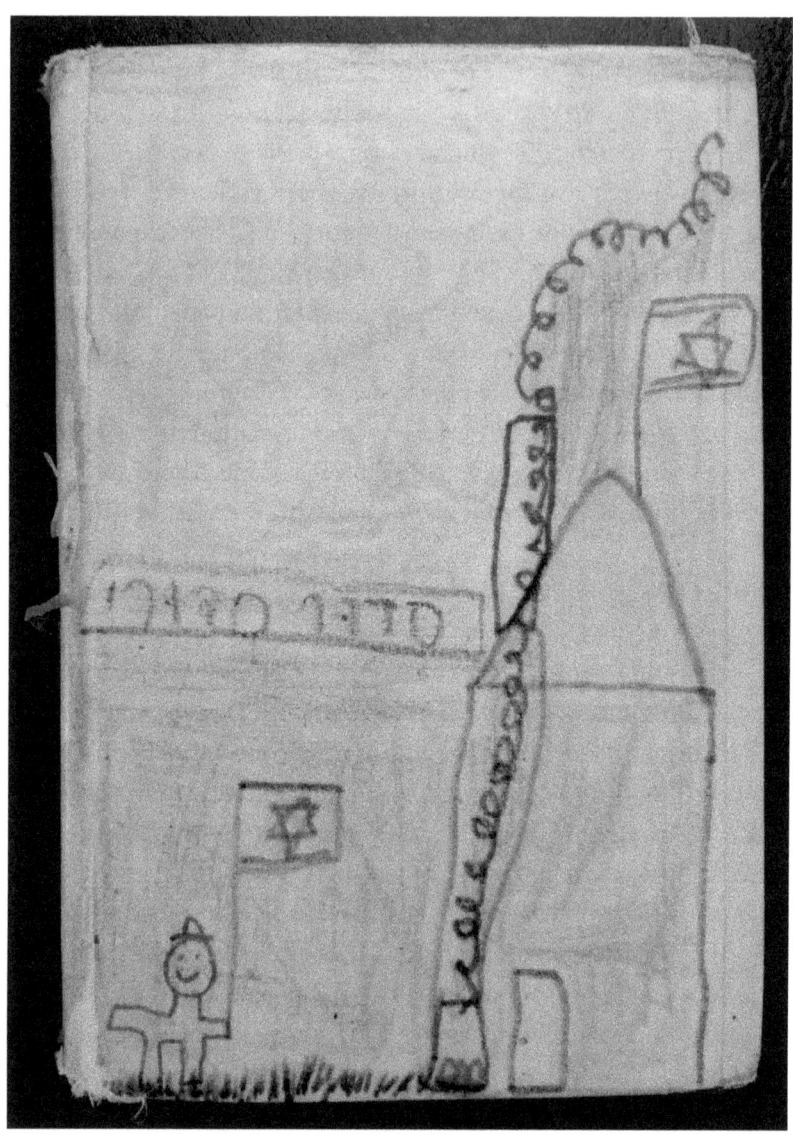

Front and back covers of Hillel Broder's Shiloh siddur

resonance of their stories with pre-linguistic sensations – that envelop his child-self. These books possess an irreducible materiality: their pages "bore traces of the fingers that turned them;" the corded fabric constituting the binding "was dirty;" the spine was misaligned, with the two halves of the cover "slid[ing] out of place by themselves." The

A Childhood Siddur Around 1990

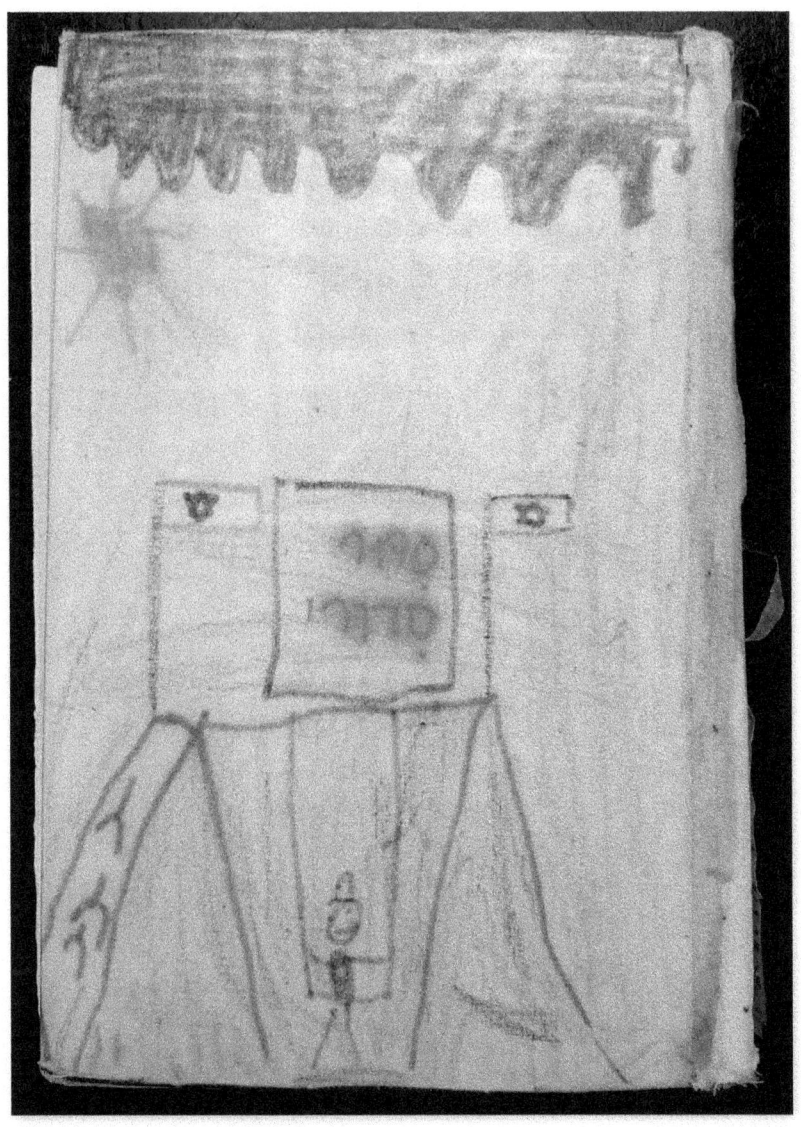

edges of the book form "ridges and terraces." And hanging on its pages "like Indian summer on the branches of the trees, were sometimes fragile threads of a net in which I had once become tangled when learning to read."[9] Benjamin's earliest memory of a library book has

---

9. *Berlin Childhood*, 58.

a history that precedes him; it is worn out and distorted by others' hands, and it threatens to entangle him – to engulf him, perhaps, as he emerges as a young reader.

It is the reading process itself in which Benjamin's childhood mimetic faculty is fully awakened. In particular, his reading of "distant lands" offers both internal organization and an elusive coherence, akin to the transience of bands of snowflakes:

> While reading I would cover my ears. Hadn't I already listened to stories in silence like this? Not those told by my father, of course. But sometimes in winter, when I stood by the window in the warm little room, the snowstorm outside told me stories no less mutely.
>
> What it told, to be sure, I could never quite grasp, for always something new and unremittingly dense was breaking through the familiar. Hardly had I allied myself, as intimately as possible, to one band of snowflakes, than I realized they had been obliged to yield me up to another, which had suddenly entered their midst. But now the moment had come to follow, in the flurry of letters, the stories that had eluded me at the window. The distant lands I had encountered in these stories played familiarly among themselves, like the snowflakes. And because distance, when it snows, leads no longer out into the world but rather within, so Baghdad and Babylon, Acre and Alaska, Tromso and Transvaal were places within me.[10]

Here is the moment, perhaps, where the non-verbal mimetic faculty falls into language. It might also be read as the moment of recollecting non-verbal, non-sensuous mimesis when linguistic mimesis arises. For Benjamin, the silent stories told by one band of snowflakes offer glimpses of coherence before "something new" breaks through "the familiar." In the controlled process of linguistic reading, the bands of stories seem to play "familiarly among themselves," so that Benjamin can organize the text – arbitrarily by alphabet – within himself.

* * *

---

10. Ibid, 59.

Revisiting and using my Shilo siddur, it became clear to me as a Jewish educator that it is itself a complex piece of work, one that is cluttered in layout and ambition. No doubt Scharfstein envisioned it as a central ur-text, one that would not play second fiddle to his Hebrew and Bible companions. While it is no longer printed or sold by Shilo, what remains in product descriptions by online sellers are brief statements lauding the text's clarity and longevity – its usefulness for the young reader. And indeed, somehow, despite its vacillating layout and wild typography, it remained the centerpiece of nearly fifty years of day school prayer induction ceremonies, usually dubbed "Siddur Plays" or "Siddur Parties" for their performative and celebratory rituals put on before a gushing parental audience. No doubt it had cornered the market and had found some resonance in the modern Hebrew education of the Jewish day school movement. Yet navigating it, even as an adult, is no easy task – though it does come with its mimetic rewards. So when I opened it with my children, I was struck (again) by its layout and font. What returned, first and foremost, were the mimetic impressions – and correspondences – of my childhood self.

It is impossible to shake the presence of my first Hebrew and Judaica teacher when holding and opening the siddur. More than God, we were terrified – and in awe – of her. After all, she held the ability for us to see our own success or failure in what was going to be a daunting venture. She orchestrated our movements – stand up, sit down, now the boys, now the girls. And while I can't recall her voice or even her face, I can trace a profile in my memory of a sturdy, aged woman, with an Israeli accent and powerful fingers, whose favor was earned through our strong, usually vocal performances, and which was recognized by her sharp pinches on our cheeks. Learning prayer in the Shilo siddur was really learning Jewish literacy more than anything else. We were entirely hypnotized by the form that language took in this wild book.

The morning service begins on page 7, but what is most pronounced is the bold, large-type font that the opening prayer, *Ma Tovu*, seems to occupy. Of all of the font sizes in the book, this is just under the largest. As a child, and even now, I was never sure what this meant. Did it mean that I should say it loudly, as we did every morning in our first grade classroom, bordering on a high-pitched shout? Did it mean that we should say it with greater emphasis or focus, as if this were a primary prayer, and the smaller-type ones were secondary? Whatever the intention, the effect was one in which I – and I'm sure many of my peers – fell into the words' shapes and forms. The falling that we experienced was not a gentle one: the words seemed to shake us, to demand that we start the day with a bang. So while the words on the page are muted, sitting in silence, their dramatic opening was nothing short of a daily early morning alarm blare.

Indeed, in reabsorbing some of my earliest impressions, it is the letters' sizes which are what was most seared in my memory, reopening this siddur nearly thirty years later. No doubt it was thirty years ago that I learned to mimic the prayer-song of my teacher and those around me, committing the sensation of sounds and words to memory before I matched them to written words. At some point, the shapes on the page took on these sounds, but they seemed to still carry – then and now – an excess of associations beyond their articulation or semantics.

Figure 3-4 Ashrei and Shma in the Shiloh siddur.

What followed the opening prayers and songs in first grade – *Ma Tovu, Adon Olam, Yigdal* – was a series of blessings. The briefer blessings were placed in that same large font, but the longer, winding ones were in a smaller, secondary font, one that I came to associate with tedium and speed. It was almost as if those smaller fonts had to take the same quantity of spoken time given their physical allocation on the page, though then and now I'm still not quite sure how or why I privileged one font over the other. The smaller one seemed to be more forgiving – it didn't require a loud shout or anything truly dramatic. The blessing that the girls said – "*she'asani kirtzono*" (that I was made according to His will) – was similarly dwarfed visually by the boys' blessing, "*she'lo asani isha*" (that I wasn't made a woman). The boys remained silent as the girls whispered their visually muted blessing, perhaps training us for the delicate balance of difference Modern Orthodoxy attempts in a co-educational environment.

If the opening blessings and prayers were the first of four or five "movements" of daily, morning prayers, it would seem that the primary ones – the ones which our teachers trained and rehearsed with us – were those in the larger font. The "highlights" of the second phase of prayer, "*Pesukei d'Zimra*" (verses of praise), opened with "*Baruch She'amar*" (Blessed is the One who Says), continued with "*Ashrei*" (Fortunate), and ended with "*Yishatabach*" (He will be praised). These were all said aloud in a sing-song, one that easily preceded any actual reading of the verses. I noted as much with my first grader, who had just received his Siddur. He, too, could easily recite these prayers with reference to pages but without anchoring himself in any obvious reading practice or finger pointing.

He was surprised to note, as I was surprised then, that the lines were numbered in increments of five. This seemed helpful, in theory, for the instructor calling out the place, but it was a feature mostly ignored by our primary instructors. I only recalled its presence when, as a young adult, I started to study poetry seriously in Norton anthologies. Only then did a distant memory rise, the familiar numbers silently hanging in the margins of my siddur.

Visually, for each of these prayers, I was reminded more than anything else of the coherence and organization they lent to both an overwhelming and sometimes confusing incipient experience. Even as we were taught nothing of the text's meaning, and even as the prayer's messy layout did not have a clear beginning on the page (the *Kaddish* that precedes it has the same font and extends to the opening line of the prayer), I was able to track the recurring word – *Baruch* – of *Baruch She'amar* in its place at the opening of each line and anchor myself in that repetitive versification. If anything, perhaps Scharfstein envisioned children everywhere noticing that visual repetition at the start of each line, an organization that is not typical in the block-paragraph scheme of today's "adult" prayer books. Similarly pronounced and obviously highlighted is the alphabetical organization of *Ashrei*, each line progressing through the Hebrew alphabet, each line opening with a letter slightly outsizing its line (fig. 3). While our teacher (in my recollection) did not draw attention to that organization, my association with this prayer, in praying again with this siddur, is one of coherence and meaning built through the orderly sequence of these title letters.

The alphabet is similarly highlighted in the opening blessings of the third phase – the blessings and recitation of *Shma* (fig. 4). It makes me wonder, in fact, if the author and organizer of this siddur desired that the child notice the Hebraic alphabet – its repetition, its organizing structure – more than anything else. *Shma*, of course, takes the large font, with the opening verse written in the largest font of the entire prayerbook. This drew our visual attention, as if we might get lost in all that precedes and follows it; with no direction, instruction, or obvious cue, it vied for our attention, easily capturing and drawing us to its arbitrary location at the back and bottom of a page.

The peak of prayer – the fourth phase, *Shmone Esre* – was first said communally, when taught, and then later said in silence. It was certainly confusing to navigate in the Shilo siddur, as the entire prayer took on the large font, with the exception of the closing *"Elokai Netzor"* after-prayer, which we, therefore, skipped. I recall how my classmates sometimes confused parts of *Kedusha*, the segment included in the adult repetition, with the prayer itself – the text was simply embedded in the silent prayer, with no clear direction otherwise. A "vav" that was contained in a half parenthesis before the closing of the third blessing likewise confused, and some of us no doubt included it in our personal recitation. It was only as an adult that I can infer its place as optional and only included when the "Havdalah" is included in that prayer.

What followed *Shmone Esre*, as a young child, was the *Alenu* prayer, which for us was like reaching the finish line of our daily marathon, an exercise that we found trying and even exhausting, and that often left some of us behind, though they were certainly not unpunished for doing so. The first paragraph of this final prayer, in large font, was sung ceremoniously and victoriously; the second paragraph, in smaller font, was a breathless exercise through which we sprinted to the finish. Both took on equal weight and needed to occupy the same time scale.

* * *

Looking back, the Shilo siddur is no doubt a complex childhood artifact, one that I embraced as an ideological foundation, a cornerstone and necessary rite of passage for my entry into a normative community. Even as I embraced it, it presented me with a multiplicity of experiences, introducing me to its jarring world of text, sound, and associations. Most important, perhaps, was the absorption the siddur of its childhood reader. I didn't recite the siddur's text; the siddur's text was a rabbit hole through which I not only mimicked but became a praying ritual.

Praying with my children during our extended lockdown was a sort of recovery of such an immersive experience, and in light of Benjamin's recollections, the timing was one in which I could see my own childhood through the eyes of my children. Together, we became the sounds and rhythms of this daily ritual, and with the guidance of the Shilo siddur, we seemed to become the prayer book itself.

The Anachronisms of Hasidic Yiddish Biblical Coloring Books

Frieda Vizel

For years, I have collected coloring books – specifically Hasidic Yiddish children's coloring books that tell Biblical stories. I have tens of these thin large books with their black outlines and blank white spaces that wait to be colored. I own the *A Hilf Far'n Kind* (A Help for the Child) series, *Di Torah Dertzylt Mir* (The Torah Regales Me) series, and the series by one Brondvein from Israel, which does not have a name but is recognizable for its bright solid-colored covers. I collect these children's books because I feel compelled to see, with adult eyes, the stories that were so innocent in my youth. When I was a child in the Hasidic village of Kiryas Joel, I spent hours coloring a single flowing stream in turquoise and cerulean and blue-green. Despite all the time and focus I dedicated to these pages, I saw in the images only the lovely reflection of my own artistic creations. I would bring the pages home from school at the end of the week and proudly show them off. But with mature eyes, I see different things. I see that these books introduce children to a foundational perspective of the world, of history, of Judaism, that is shockingly anachronistic.

The Coloring Books

The coloring books that illustrate the story of the Bible are probably the most important piece of religious education for very young

Hasidic children. Every home owns these series, and from the time a Hasidic child begins school, which is usually before age three, the child's curriculum consists of spending each week on the *parsha*. For Orthodox Jews, the *parsha* – the weekly portion of the Torah – is not only relevant during synagogue services but is also studied by students of all ages. Children have various programs to learn, read, dramatize, analyze, and moralize, and they work on crafts that visualize the Biblical stories. For example, in the weeks of early October, following the completion of the annual cycle of the *parsha* during the High Holidays, a new cycle commences, and the students study Genesis. The first week is devoted to the story that God created the world ex-nihilo. First, the students learn the story. A particularly good kindergarten teacher will tell it in a way that will capture the children's imaginations. She might turn off the lights and let the suspense of this darkness build, so that thirty little faces will sit on the floor with their eyes bulging, waiting for her to exclaim "Let there be light!" and flip on the light switch. The class will then spend the rest of the week on projects to depict this. Maybe they'll stick star stickers on a round paper plate and paste a yellow moon on the side to portray the fourth day of creation. And as part of all this, for some hours of the week, the children will color the pictures of this story on photocopies from the famous biblical coloring books. This they will do every year, for five or ten years. Even when they outgrow crayons, they'll ooh and ahh at the artwork of their little siblings, and later at the masterpieces of their own children.

Since Hasidic children do not watch television or read comic books, there is very little visual storytelling. There are picture books with stories that teach lessons in interpersonal behavior, and there are some collectors' books about nature. But the only coherent visual rendering of a story of the world comes from these coloring books. The books play a deep and subliminal role in shaping the Hasidic child's very consciousness. The drawings are all hand illustrated. Some are badly drawn, and the pictures look deformed, which was very funny to us as children. Other versions, especially the illustrations by a Mrs. Acker in Canada, are sweet and handsome and admired by all. But the narrative itself was not viewed as the work of an author or artist but as the Torah, as God's word. It was presented as simple fact of life. I now see that these books imparted to the young deep mythologies, ideas about history that were foundational to the Hasidic resistance to modernity. It quietly imparted to us messaging of what it was to be a Jew, as well as a meta-narrative of history that is entirely ahistorical.[1]

The Concept of a Jew

The Hasidic movement began in Eastern Europe at the dawn of modernity. As is recounted in *Hasidism: A New History*, the remarkable expansion of Hasidism happened during "the Century of the Enlightenment and of the American and French Revolutions."[2] Hasidism thus developed as a modern phenomenon, in reaction to it and to counter it: "As Hasidism confronted modernity, it transformed itself from a movement of spiritual and communal renewal to a conservative bulwark of tradition."[3] The Hasidic resistance to the Jewish Enlightenment and pressures of modernization often focused on outer appearances, specifically clothing. In the nineteenth century, the Russian government sought to forcefully modernize the Jews, with, among other decrees, the Dress Decree, which forbade the traditional dress, and "[t]he Hasidim called on the public not to give in to the temptation of modern dress and to preserve the traditional garb, which now came to have symbolic meaning."[4] And so, the clothing, the artifacts, the symbols that became so important to Hasidism were the fashions of early modern Eastern Europe.

In Hasidic coloring books, all Jews are depicted as if in this mythical, frozen moment in time, at the dawn of modernity. Not only do contemporary Jews or the Hasidic tzaddik look like this, but all

---

1. For more on the concept of ahistoricism in Jewish art history, see Yoel Finkelman's essay in this volume. See also: Jacob Neusner, *The Idea of History in Rabbinic Judaism*, Brill, 2003.
2. David Biale, et al. *Hasidism: a New History*, Princeton University Press, 2020.
3. ibid. 15.
4. ibid. 547.

the "good" Biblical characters, beginning with Adam himself, look like nineteenth-century Ashkenazi shtetl Jews. According to these illustrations, when God said, "Let there be man," man came about with side-curls styled with proper gel, with a respectable beard, with a kaftan and belt. Adam, Noah, Abraham, Isaac, Joseph, the Jewish kings, the Jews of Persia during the Purim story – all of them look just like this.

For an example we can look at the story of Eve and the forbidden fruit. We learned in school that Adam and Eve were naked in the garden. In Christian and secular art, this iconic moment is associated with the fig-leaf, which symbolizes the stark nakedness of the first couple. One such illustration is the 1526 painting by Lucas Cranach, *Temptation in Eden*. The couple here is white and young and naked, surrounded by luscious greens and wildlife. They look neither particularly Jewish nor prudish. In the Hasidic coloring book version, Adam and Eve are both clothed before they have a chance to recognize their nakedness after eating from the tree (fig. 1). Adam has a beard, side-curls, and a *shtreimel* of sorts. Eve arrives in a modest long dress with her hair tied in two braids, the *tzepelakh* that young Hasidic girls wear, and by the next page she is already in the headscarf of a married woman.

And this continues throughout. All Jewish historical figures look like disciples of the Baal Shem Tov (seventeenth-century Rabbi Levi Yitzchak from Berditchev) and customers of G&G Designer Men's Hasidic Suits. This makes a deep impression on children who then imagine that all Jews look one distinct way – the Hasidic way. They think that to be a Jew is for a man to have side-curls, a long beard and a kaftan. To be a Jewess is to wear lengthy robes and to modestly cover one's hair after marriage, to have many children, and of course, to have a distinctly demure demeanor. In this dualistic rendering, children also learn that gentiles wear a uniform of jeans, baseball caps, t-shirts, and sideburns. The message that children internalize is not only that Jews look Hasidic, but also that those who don't look Hasidic are not Jews. There is a total collapse of all forms of Judaism, both contemporary and historical, into Hasidism. I see the effects of this play out on the walking tours I lead through Jewish Brooklyn, where I work as a

The Anachronisms of Hasidic Yiddish Biblical Coloring Books · 23

Figure 1 Adam and Eve in the Garden of Eden before sinning, as portrayed in Hasidic coloring books.

tour guide; the Hasidic children who pass by my tour groups think that the group is all "goyim," solely because they don't look Hasidic. I've even been called a goy myself by a wide-eyed child who yelled out, "Mammi, the goy speaks Yiddish." The parents came over to me and apologized profusely. I had not taken offense, could never have taken offense, because I understand why the child thinks so. After all, I left the fold and now sport my own jeans and t-shirts and very little of that signature demureness. I fit the goy side of the binary. Visual lessons are powerful.

Language complicates the problem: in Yiddish, a "yid" speaks Yiddish and observes Yiddishkeit. In English, these concepts are expanded into two words, Yiddish and Jewish. The language is Yiddish, and the people are Jewish. But for Hasidic children, the line between Yiddish and Yid does not linguistically exist, so they believe that to be a Yid (Jew) one must speak Yiddish and express Yiddishkeit (religious Judaism). A fellow ex-Hasid once told me that an Uber driver asked him where his accent was from. "I answered him," he recalled, "that I used to be Jewish." It was a strange answer that obviously did not explain his accent to the driver. After all, people who are Jewish have many accents across America. But the friend, who was an adult at the time but still very new to his post-Hasidic journey, had meant to say that he used to be a Yid – by which he meant the Yid who spoke Yiddish and who looked like the Yidden from the coloring book. He meant to say that he was Hasidic, but he did not yet know the distinction because he had internalized a lifetime of Jews as Hasidim.

The Concept of History

The greater effect of these depictions is that they erase history for Hasidic children. The past – world events, inventions, changing fashions – is missing. There are no turning points with the start of agriculture, civilization, cave art, tools, the wheel, writing, money, printing, domesticated animals, weapons, medicine. None of this forward motion exists. In the rendering of Biblical events, everything is set at about a few hundred years ago, with simple modern houses and furniture, animal-driven transportation, shopping markets, weapons of arrows and batons, clothing and linens (not running water – it's always the age of wells).

Adam, as soon as he is cast out of the Garden of Eden, dives right into agriculture, tending to many neat rows of crops and a large flock of sheep. His first tool is not a jug or an arrow chiseled from stone as history and archeology suggest; rather, it's a state-of-the-art shovel that looks like it could have come from Home Depot. Later, but still in the dawn of time, Noah sits inside his abode with lovely curtains, studying the Torah with his sons (fig. 2). Meanwhile, outside his window, the population of the other side of this binary, the people who look like 'goyim,' have two-story homes with chimneys and storefronts with little awnings – a perfectly modern setting in which they steal and beat each other.

The Anachronisms of Hasidic Yiddish Biblical Coloring Books · 25

Figure 2 Noah learns Torah with his sons in their home with non-Jews visible outside through the window.

There are gems of anachronism sprinkled everywhere. It's as if everything is in a simple Russian village, but for the strange pops of modernity. In Abraham's father Terah's shop of idols, Terah bags the clay god for a customer in a nice shopping bag with his logo on it. In another instance, one of the evildoers of Sodom steals a scooter. Esau gets his fill of soup from Jacob while stretched out on a recliner. And when the matriarch Rebecca's covetous brother runs off to steal some jewelry, he is shown to be the evil character, outfitted with a pretentious ring of keys and what looks like a Nokia car phone from 1999 (fig. 3).

These pictures reflect only what the artists knew and imagined. It's clear that these pictures are not influenced by contemporary ideas of what an ancient Egyptian might have looked like, what an ark might

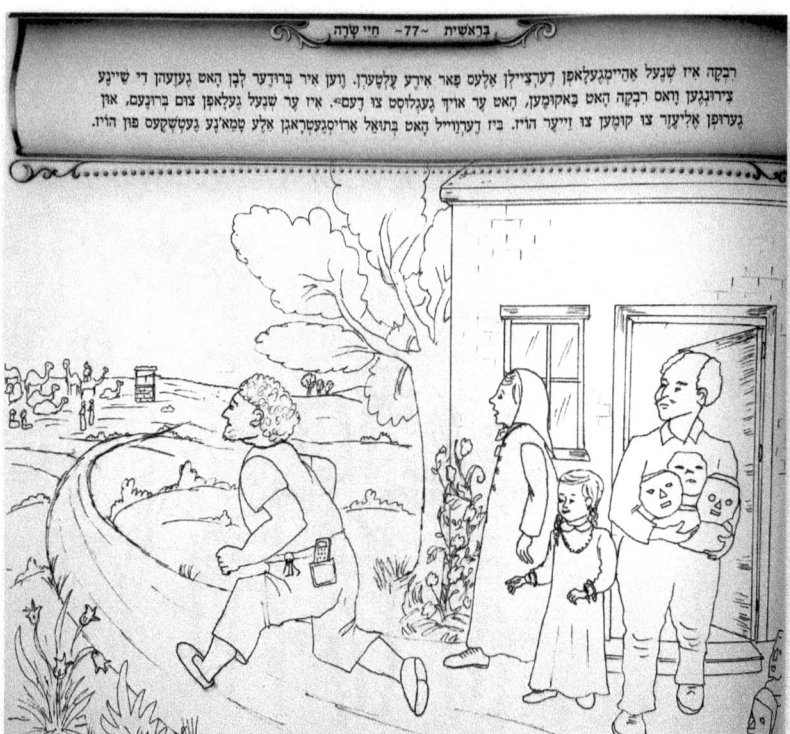

Figure 3 Rebecca's brother Laban rushes off to steal.

have looked like – the National Geographic version of the past. And the artists' naïveté is not benign; it is a cultivated ignorance that limits the scope of the story. Since Hasidic children do not learn about evolution and are taught to view the Bible as literal history, they have no perception of history as a series of events that propel new ones, discoveries that create new technologies, or wars and trade that create new cultures. The Hasidic student might memorize the names and dates of important people and places during state-mandated secular studies, but so long as it's all decontextualized from its setting, it does nothing to illuminate the past.

This is hard to unlearn. When I was a young mother with a son who was already starting to color some of these pages himself, I read Bill Bryson's 2003 book *A Short History of Nearly Everything*. It felt like an epiphany and a paradigm shift. I realized then that there was a timeline, that it was no use to know that there was a King Alexander and a Christopher Columbus if I could not understand the relative culture and what came before and after. So I set out to try to put the story together. It was as if I had a million fragments that I needed to sort into a single puzzle, with many more millions of missing pieces as well as extra pieces. Every time I came across some new information, I put it inside an endless Excel spreadsheet that I titled "timeline." At the time, it felt like I could never collect enough information. But looking at it now, I am struck most by how much irrelevant information I collected. The skill to know what's important and what is not depends on a larger understanding of the underlying story, and that was a story I would have to read again and again until I fully knew it.

Part of my self-education has been cracking open these coloring books. I've even colored some pages myself. The narratives I see in the pages now are much more important, impactful and eye opening. I can see the powers that little playthings like toys and books have over growing minds. Children's artifacts tell us what to see, what not to see, and how to see things. We like to imagine ourselves rational beings with minds made up of our own direction, but so much of our consciousness is shaped by the cultural messaging embedded in the backdrop of our lives. I cannot go back and undo the messaging, nor can I always choose what messaging to be exposed to. But I have found it meaningful to revisit the coloring books of my childhood, and to see them with a wiser eye. This time, I see a story of indoctrination, mythology, narrative-making and blind spots. I also see creative eagerness and sweet innocence. This story gives me the comfort of understanding that was so absent before.

From Honey Cakes to Upsherin Cookies: Jewish Mothers at the Beginning of Jewish Boyhood

Wendy Love Anderson

Sometime before 1230, Rabbi Eleazar ben Judah wrote in his *Sefer ha-Rokeach* (*Book of the Perfumer*) about a "custom of our ancestors" that, like many such customs, had never been recorded.[1] He described a ritual in which young boys were initiated into Torah study on the first morning of Shavuot: the father transported his son, covered in a cloak, from his own home to his teacher's house or to the *beit midrash*, where the boy was placed on his teacher's lap to recite the Hebrew alphabet from a tablet and eat a series of symbolically sweet and tasty foods. First the boy licked honey from the letters on the tablet; then he received a honey cake and a peeled hardboiled egg inscribed with verses from Isaiah 50:4–5[2] and Ezekiel 3:3[3] respectively, which he was

---

1. I am using the translation of Ivan G. Marcus in his "Honey Cakes and Torah" chapter of Lawrence Fine, ed., *Judaism in Practice: From The Middle Ages through the Early Modern Period* (Princeton: Princeton University Press, 2001), 122–3.
2. "The Lord God gave me a skilled tongue, to know how to speak timely words to the weary. Morning by morning, He rouses, He rouses my ear to give heed like disciples. The Lord God opened my ears, and I did not disobey, I did not run away" (translation from sefaria.org).
3. "As He said to me, 'Mortal, feed your stomach and fill your belly with this

only permitted to eat once he had recited the verses, word by word, after his teacher. "Let no one deviate from this custom," the Rokeach warned, and closed his description with no fewer than five Talmudic and midrashic sources emphasizing the centrality of custom itself.

About eight hundred years later, the Imamother.com website (tagline: "Connecting Frum Women") features several message threads from mothers looking for a different series of symbolically sweet and tasty goods for their young sons' initiation rituals. "Where can I get upsherin cookie cutters in Monsey?" asked a 2010 thread. Another thread from the same year solicited decorating advice: "I've baked a ton of alef-beis sugar cookies for my sons [sic] upsherin next week. They are yummy but I'd like to make them a bit fancier. Does anyone have ideas?" By 2021, with *"upsherin* cookie cutters" an easy Amazon or Google search away for most of Imamother.com's posters, the latest messages are inquiries about catering: "Looking for recommendation for a bakery in bp/nearby that does the upsherin sugar cookies (tizizit and kippa) w royal icing and a name. Not crazy expensive."[4] Whether today's *upsherin* cookies are shaped like Hebrew letters, calling back to the older Ashkenazi ritual, or like the tzitzit and kippah that are the uniform of Orthodox Jewish boyhood, they too have become a "custom of our ancestors."

Between the inscribed honey cakes of the thirteenth century and the custom cookie cutters of the twenty-first, there is a very important story about Jewish boys and their mothers. Of course, the Jewish boys are much more visible than the mothers in all these rituals. The "Kosher Cook" brand sells one assortment of cookie cutters that are clearly and prominently labeled with the words "JEWISH BOY!" They include the shapes of the first three Hebrew letters, a kippah/yarmulke,

---

scroll that I give you.' I ate it, and it tasted as sweet as honey to me" (translation from sefaria.org).

4. Posts from https://www.imamother.com/forum/viewtopic.php?t=135988 (the first two) and https://www.imamother.com/forum/viewtopic.php?t=430250. Spelling and punctuation are reproduced faithfully from the original posts.

Jewish Boy! Cookie Cutter set. (Image courtesy The Kosher Cook Company Sales Department.)

a pair of scissors, and a *tallit katan*. If a cookie cutter could have a gender, every item in this brightly colored box is gendered male – even though the likely cutter (and decorator) of these cookies is surely not a young boy. She disappears behind the JEWISH BOY! label. In fact, her disappearance is one of the main features of the ritual.

Missing Mothers and Substitute Sweets

The medieval sources make the constitution of Jewish boyhood through the exclusion of or separation from the mother clear and unambiguous. In the medieval Ashkenazi ritual, as Ivan Marcus points out, "the child leaves his natural mother at home and enters the culture of a new symbolic mother–the male Torah teacher, who is portrayed as the nurturing mother of a newborn child."[5] The Rokeach specifies that the teacher is acting in accordance with Moses' role as nurse to the Israelite people (Num. 11:12) and with the prophet Hosea's metaphor in which God dandles or pampers Ephraim (Hos. 11:3), both examples of male-associated figures taking on maternal roles. The ritual's association with the giving of the Torah at Sinai further ensured that women would be not only displaced but also excluded: the Rokeach's ritual took place at sunrise on the first morning of Shavuot, the moments in which the Israelites were given the Torah. When thirteenth-century manuscripts of the *Mahzor Vitry* describe essentially the same school-initiation ritual, now with the addition of fruit to the honey cakes/loaves and the eggs, they do not require that it be held on Shavuot, but they do specify that "a virgin kneads the dough [for the cakes/loaves]."[6] The *Mahzor Vitry* then offers a detailed explanation for this requirement, based on its author's understanding of how the Torah was given, and to whom:

> Why is only a virgin permitted to knead the dough? We have found that the Torah stipulated that no one discharging semen could be present when the Torah was given, as it is written, "Be ready for the third day [do not go near a woman]" (Exod. 19:15). For this reason, they said: Let a pure virgin knead for a pure boy.

Here, in an all-male ceremony, even the possibility that the boy's mother might have provided the honey cakes is foreclosed! Even as the medieval ceremony moved away from Shavuot, its association with the giving of the Torah – and the exclusion of the boy's mother – remained strong.

By the fifteenth century, the medieval Ashkenazi initiation rite for young boys disappeared from Jewish textual tradition, as attention shifted to the relatively new and seemingly more

---

5. Ivan G. Marcus, *Rituals of Childhood: Jewish Acculturation in Medieval Europe* (New Haven, CT: Yale University Press, 1996), 15.
6. Marcus, "Honey Cakes and Torah," 125.

developmentally-appropriate ritual of Bar Mitzvah. However, some elements – perhaps even some practices – must have survived, although exactly how and where is not clear.[7] An entirely different "ancestral" custom, involving cutting young boys' hair for the first time on their third birthday, surfaced in the kabbalistic circles of sixteenth-century Ottoman Palestine, where Sephardi, Ashkenazi, and Mizrachi or Musta'arabi Jews mingled; by the nineteenth century, and especially in Hasidic circles, this haircutting ceremony (*upsherin* or *ḥalaka*) had been combined with the surviving custom of encouraging the three-year-olds to lick honey from a page or slate with Hebrew letters on it, thus formally beginning their Jewish education. Modern *upsherin* became a blended ritual, featuring a boy's haircut followed by his initiation into Jewish learning.

Different forms of this two-part *upsherin* ritual continued to grow in popularity over the course of the twentieth century. Today many Israeli boys from Hasidic and some other Haredi Orthodox communities receive their first haircut on Lag b'Omer at the Meron tomb of Rabbi Shimon bar Yochai, holding aleph-bet flags and bags of candy, but even more honeyed letters and other sweets appear months later, in a communal ritual on their first day of school. Anthropologist Yoram Bilu observed the Meron *ḥalaka* ceremonies during the 1980s and 1990s: "the inner courtyard of the shrine where the ritual takes place is separated by an opaque railing into a men-only arena and a female gallery. The women watch the ceremony through tiny peepholes in the

---

7. On this, see Marcus, *Rituals of Childhood*, 18–23 (hypothesizing a parallel medieval Sephardic/Mediterranean tradition of school initiation) and Yoram Bilu, "From Milah (Circumcision) to Milah (Word): Male Identity and Rituals of Childhood in the Ultraorthodox Community," *Ethos* 31:2 (June 2003): 172–203, especially 187: "the historical continuity between the medieval ceremony and its present-day successor is quite oblique, although elements of the ritual surfaced throughout the centuries in various localities.... It appears safe to conclude that, rather than an invariable ritual sequence from time immemorial, the powerful convergence of the haircutting and school initiation ceremonies around age three, particularly as crystallized in the Hasidic milieu, is a fairly modern phenomenon."

railing or from the balconies above the courtyard, which are also gender segregated."⁸ The second part of the ritual, including honey cakes and eggs, is conducted in school buildings where "the mothers are relegated to the classroom's backyard. They watch the ceremony from the outside, pressed against the grilled windows of the class."⁹ Here, the exclusion of the women is structural, in both senses of the word. Bilu argues that the Israeli ḥalaka ritual has developed in this way precisely in order to separate young boys from their mothers and re-enact their transition into a distinctly male identity. Although women (indeed, mothers) are probably involved in preparing the honey cakes and candy bags, their baked goods are countered by their visible, physical exclusion from the all-male ritual space, from which a long-haired toddler emerges transformed into a short-haired boy. Under these conditions, a "Jewish Boy" cookie-cutter set seems redundant.¹⁰

How the (Upsherin) Cookie Crumbles

In the Orthodox world outside Meron, *upsherin* remains overwhelmingly a boy's ritual – but one at which the boy's mother is typically present. Especially in the United States, the blended *upsherin* ritual which combines haircutting and honeyed letters/sweets at a boy's third birthday celebration is increasingly dominant in Orthodox life.¹¹ Many *upsherins* are held in the child's home, but others take place in synagogues, in other event spaces, or at a friend's or relative's larger

---

8. Bilu, "From Milah (Circumcision) to Milah (Word)," 184.
9. Ibid., 186.
10. Of course, any Israeli family who wishes to purchase such cookie cutters can buy them from their American manufacturers!
11. A handful of Hasidic groups cut the boy's hair at age two, and in some Sephardic communities the haircut takes place at age five, separate from the school initiation; however, these are relatively small minorities of the worldwide Orthodox Jewish community. On these and other variations in contemporary *upsherin* observance, see Bilu, "From Milah (Circumcision) to Milah (Word)," 183–185, and Amy K. Milligan, "Hair Today, Gone Tomorrow: Upsherin, Alef-Bet, and the Childhood Navigation of Jewish Gender Identity Symbol Sets," *Children's Folklore Review* 38 (2017), 11–14.

home. Depending on family preference and community norms, the scale of the event can vary widely, from a modest gathering of half a dozen immediate family members to a catered meal for a hundred friends and relatives. *Upsherin* celebrations are even filtering into some non-Orthodox families of Jewish boys (and, more rarely, Jewish girls[12]), but they remain a predominantly Orthodox childhood tradition.

One crucial aspect of the contemporary Orthodox *upsherin* is the extent to which it not only affirms but actively performs the gendered roles that pervade many other aspects of Orthodox Judaism. Folklorist and gender theorist Amy K. Milligan notes that in its American context, *upsherin* "functions just as much as a ritual to mark a change for the boy as it does a community ritual, affirming the gendered roles and expectations of Orthodox Jewish life for all in attendance."[13] Whether at home or in the synagogue, an American *upsherin* does not merely transform an androgynous toddler into a tiny, kippah- and tzitzit-clad male; it also reinforces the public participation of men and boys in Jewish ritual, while women and girls remain on the sidelines.

However, the sidelining of mothers in the *upsherin* ritual runs up against a very different expectation when it comes to American (or more generally "Western") children's birthday parties, which is also one element of the contemporary *upsherin*. In the contemporary culture of American motherhood, to which Orthodox families are not immune, mothers are expected to be present in their children's lives at all times, and especially at special events. Children's birthday parties are a striking example: over the past decades, as they have become more commercialized and more elaborate, mothers are still typically expected to manage these rituals of social consumption: preparing or ordering the cake, assembling gift bags, purchasing appropriate décor, keeping track of the guest list, and so forth.[14] It is no wonder that the

---

12. A recent overview of feminist reinterpretations of *upsherin* can be found in Chapter 3 of Amy Milligan, *Jewish Bodylore: Feminist and Queer Ethnographies of Folk Practices* (Lanham, MD: Lexington Books, 2019).
13. Milligan, "Hair Today, Gone Tomorrow," 16.
14. On the mother's role as social agent in the commercialized birthday party,

women of Imamother.com feel pressure to plan the perfect *upsherin*, down to the perfect cookies.

It is also no wonder that *upsherin* cookie-cutter sets do their best to telegraph male identity, despite their implication in maternal cookie baking and party planning. Even versions of these cookie cutters that do not include the "Jewish Boy!" label still scream "Jewish Boy!" to an Orthodox viewer: the Hebrew letters might pass unremarked in an era when Hebrew literacy is no longer as gendered as it was in the thirteenth century, but the kippah and *tallit katan* are unmistakably part of a male-only uniform. Meanwhile, the scissors hint at not only the featured haircut but also the *other* significant ritual of Jewish male childhood, brit milah.

Human biology dictates that every living child must ultimately separate from its mother, whether through childbirth, weaning, or both. The gendered roles and spaces of Orthodox Jewish culture further complicate this transition for boys, since following and identifying with their fathers and other male caretakers necessarily entails leaving their mothers behind. But the mothers do not disappear; they leave their mark even on ceremonies designed around their absence. Beautifully decorated *upsherin* cookies, like the inscribed honey cakes of their medieval Ashkenazi prototype, symbolize the simultaneous presence and absence of mothers in the creation of Jewish boyhood.

---

see Alison J. Clarke, "Making Sameness: Mothering, Commerce and the Culture of Children's Birthday Parties," in Lydia Marten and Emma Casey, eds., *Gender and Consumption: Domestic Cultures and the Commercialisation of Everyday Life* (England: Ashgate, 2007), 79–96.

A Passover Haggadah with a Refreshing Appreciation of Violence

Yoel Finkelman

The Passover Haggadah is not only the most published book in Jewish history; it is also one of the most illustrated. That's not surprising. Passover's emphasis on collective memory, on children, on founding myths of the Jewish People, and on freedom lends itself naturally to illustrations that imagine the past, with its Jewish protagonists and the significant others with whom they interact. Moreover, the emphasis in the Passover ritual on educating children focuses on passing along a sense of identity and belonging to the youngest Jews, who may not know how to read. Illustrations offer a great opportunity to impart to participants, especially children, a sense of who they are and who they are not.

I am particularly interested in this essay in how one contemporary Orthodox illustrator, Gadi Pollack, presents the story of the Exodus in *The Katz Passover Haggadah* published in 2003.[1] The Haggadah, which appears in English, Hebrew, and Spanish editions, is part of R. Baruch

---

1. Baruch Chait, *The Katz Passover Haggadah: The Art of Faith and Redemption*, Illustrated by Gadi Pollack (Modiin Illit: B & B Septimus Educational Materials, 2003).

Chait's series of folio-size children's books, *Halamdan Hakatan* (the Little Scholar), which also includes a brilliant book on the thirty-nine categories of prohibited work on Shabbat, as well as two books on character traits which I, at least, find overly didactic.

With the possible exception of some of the Haggadot published by survivors immediately after the Holocaust[2], the artwork in *The Katz Haggadah* does more than others to emphasize the horror, suffering, misery, and pain suffered by both Israelites and Egyptians in the story of slavery, plagues, and eventual redemption. I find this oddly refreshing. Brutally honest presentation of reality, with all its problems, is something I strive for in my own parenting, despite the fact that this seems out of line with modern western and Haredi notions of protecting children. Unlike my previous work on Haredi popular literature,[3] I want to avoid making generalizations here, and I do not see this as a case study of a broader phenomenon. There is something idiosyncratic here but fascinating nonetheless. In order to make sense of Pollack's Haggadah artwork, I propose to compare it to that of a much more influential and famous Jewish artist, the Renaissance scribe and illuminator Yoel ben Shimon.

Yoel ben Shimon

Yoel ben Shimon, active in the second half of the fifteenth century in Germany and Italy, had his hand in some of the most famous illuminated Hebrew manuscripts, including the famed Rothschild and Washington *Haggadot*. In several of his illustrated *Mahzorim* and Haggadot, he paints a similar scene, though I will focus on the one in *Mahzor LeMinhag Roma*.[4] This Haggadah occupies several pages of a longer fifteenth-century *Mahzor* of the Italian rite. Most of

---

2. See, for example, Yosef David Sheinson and Zvi Miklos Adler, *Mosaf LeHaggadah Shel Pesach* (HaHistadrut HaTzionit Ahidah VeNahem BeGermaniah, 1946). For more, see the blog post by Chen Mallul of the National Library of Israel: https://blog.nli.org.il/en/exodus-from-europe/ (viewed April 2021).
3. Yoel Finkelman, *Strictly Kosher Reading: Popular Literature and the Condition of Contemporary Orthodoxy* (Boston: Academic Studies Press, 2011).
4. Yoel ben Shimon, *Mahzor LeMinhag Roma*, Italy, ca. 1450, JER. NLI. 8 4450,

the pages are covered in a striking (but fading) Italian semi-cursive hand, and a handful of pages are elaborately decorated, particularly the page from the Haggadah in the accompanying image and another page depicting the giving of the Torah at Mt. Sinai, depicted in the prayers for Shavuot.[5]

In this image (fig. 1), an Egyptian army on the right side of the opening chases fleeing Israelites, depicted on the left side of the opening. Moses leads the Israelites toward a splitting Red Sea, guided by a pillar of fire, while a pillar of cloud protects the Israelites from Egyptian arrows. The two sides of the image are roughly parallel. The castle on the right and the split sea on the left frame two groups of people, facing in the same direction. Some heads and faces are visible, while others are hidden by the crowd, creating an impression of a large group.

The Egyptian army is all male (the smaller people appear to be adults drawn small rather than children). The army is also well armed: they wear armor and helmets, and they travel with horses and a dog. Pharaoh, depicted with a gold crown, has round, rosy cheeks, and seems more like a person on a pleasant ride in the countryside than someone in the midst of battle.

The Israelites are a more diverse group, including men, women, and children. They are armed, but less well than Pharaoh's army. They are not particularly prepared for battle – the few spears they have are resting on shoulders of Israelites in the background, whose faces are not depicted. The Israelites are dressed not in armor but in fine clothing and headwear. They carry the silver and gold vessels they have taken from the Egyptians, but they have no horses or dogs. Moses leads, looking up to heaven (perhaps to God) and carries the staff which symbolizes divine assistance. The place of children in the image

---

https://www.nli.org.il/en/books/NNL_ALEPH000042898/NLI. (Image courtesy of the National Library of Israel.)

5. The artist and commissioner of this manuscript chose to invest a great deal in the decoration of a handful of pages, rather than spread less elaborate decorations over many pages, which is more typical, particularly of illuminated Haggadot.

Figure 1 A page from *Mahzor LeMinhag Roma*, Italy, circ. 1450, Jer. Nli. 80 4450. Picture courtesy of National Library of Israel.

is critical, since *"vehigadeta levincha"* [and you shall tell your children, Exodus 13:8] is so central to Passover, and the Talmud explains much of the Seder ritual as an attempt to interest children.

But much is missing from this image, particularly any sense of fear or tragedy. The Egyptian army does not look like the weakened remnants of a powerful force that had been ravaged by ten plagues. Nor do they seem terribly worked up. Aspects of the Israelites' travels from Egypt are absent. There is no sense of rush or urgency, so central to the Biblical narrative and to the baking of unleavened bread, perhaps the most central symbol of the holiday. Moreover, the Israelites are not wearing traveling clothes as the Biblical verses describe. They are protected by God's pillars, but absent is the crying out to God in the face of the approaching Egyptian army. Perhaps the thing I find most striking about this image is the utter lack of expression on the faces of virtually anybody, Israelites and Egyptians, who are neither fearful nor vengeful.

In summary, this illumination depicts the Exodus from Egypt with virtually no violence or danger, no fear or urgency. What danger does exist is depicted as well under control by God's protection. Moreover, the Israelites are depicted as upper-class Italian Renaissance figures dressed in the latest fashion rather than as refugees. This is a depiction of a completely celebratory Exodus, for a community that feels like it belongs (or wants to belong) in the comfortable upper-class Italian Renaissance environment. No doubt the family that could afford to commission such a manuscript, on parchment, from such a well-known artist and scribe, had the money and socio-economic status to see themselves as part and parcel of the elite, and they certainly saw themselves in this celebratory image.

These themes are not surprising in the history of illustrated Haggadot which, following European artistic tradition, almost always depict the events of the Exodus anachronistically, imagining them as occurring to people dressed in the latest European fashion. And often, illustrations in manuscript and early print Haggadot put a mostly smiling face on the events, depicting slavery as less than terrifying, slaves as well-dressed and fed, plagues in stylized ways that avoid the horror. In short, Yoel ben Shimon helped to blaze what is today a well-trodden path in emphasizing in illustrations the freedom side of the dialectic between slavery and freedom, focusing more on redemption than suffering in the Passover liturgy.

It reminds me of contemporary children's songs that depict the ten plagues in a cheerful, silly way (think: "Frogs here, frogs there, frogs were jumping everywhere"), or the plush toys my family keeps with our Passover supplies, each one symbolizing a different plague. We throw them at one another during the Seder. Yes, we seem to say, there is something violent, deadly, bloody, and miserable about both the Israelites' experiences and that of their Egyptian enslavers, but with enough creativity and good cheer (and a few cups of wine), we can paper over it to engage the children. At least in a contemporary context, part of the papering over the violence and terror of the story of the Exodus relates to the twentieth-century notion of children as delicate, who need protection not only from actual suffering itself (or sexuality, for that matter), but even from encountering those themes depicted directly or indirectly.[6]

---

6. Peter Stearns, *Anxious Parents: A History of Modern Childrearing in America* (New York: New York University Press, 2003).

This notion of protection is baked even deeper into contemporary Orthodox notions and practices of childhood, particularly in the more right-wing Haredi versions, which emphasize the danger of encounter with the threatening "outside" world. As a minority in a larger and attractive western culture, Orthodox Jews invest a great deal in maintaining their boundaries and protecting believers, young or old, from what is perceived as the threats of that culture. These two contexts – a Jewish tradition of downplaying suffering in depictions of the Exodus in illustrated Haggadot, and a desire to protect children – make the depiction of horror, suffering, bloodshed, misery, and pain in a contemporary illustrated children's Haggadah all the more surprising.

Gadi Pollack's Katz Passover Haggadah

Pollack is one of the most popular and imaginative Orthodox illustrators today. Born in Odessa, he became an accomplished artist and graphic designer in his home country before moving to Israel and adopting an Orthodox lifestyle. While Rabbi Chait stands behind this particular Haggadah as editor, most of the artistic work is Pollack's.

A four-page foldout depicts conditions under Egyptian slavery. Night spreads over the Israelite dwellings in Egypt, and the oversized page is covered almost entirely in dark blue and black, making most of the scene almost invisible (fig. 2). But a handful of torches illuminate a few scenes, mostly of Egyptian taskmasters whipping Israelites, the throwing of Israelite babies into the Nile, and Israelite families (men and women!) escaping into hiding. When the foldout is folded up again, the child reader is faced with an elderly Jewish man with his eyes closed (in prayer?), while an Egyptian taskmaster with a look of hateful passion on his face beats him bloody (fig. 3). He wears a grey and white cap, reminiscent, no doubt intentionally, of prisoners in Holocaust concentration camps.

On the next page, Pharaoh bathes in a tub of blood (!) (echoing *Shemot Rabbah* 1:34), while an elderly Israelite with his back bent sits on the floor (fig. 4). A torch perched on the old man's head provides the only light. The darkness makes it impossible to tell if this old man is

A Passover Haggadah with a Refreshing Appreciation of Violence · 43

Figure 2 An oversized pullout page in Chait and Pollack's Katz Haggadah depicting Egyptian cruelty to Israelites.

Figure 3 An Egyptian beats an Israelite (Pollack).

Figure 4 Pharaoh bathes in blood while an Israelite crouches nearby (Pollack).

identical to the one on the previous page, but they are certainly similar. Faux hieroglyphics on the wall tell the story of the enslavement of the Israelites, including the feeding of Israelite babies to crocodiles.

Depictions of Egyptians do not shy away from their suffering, either. Dehydrated Egyptians search desperately for something to drink during the plague of blood, and vultures circle a deathscape of dead animals and undernourished humans in the illustration of the plague *dever*. Horses and chariots are tossed to a violent death after the splitting of the sea, as are a few already-emaciated Egyptian soldiers.

An appendix to the Haggadah cites references for each detail of the illustrations, suggesting that a young person (male or female?) might look into the original text of the Biblical verses, ancient Midrashim, or medieval commentaries to understand how the illustrations borrow from and interpret the textual tradition. More, these short explanations for the illustrations even mention the sexual aspects of the story, which one might expect to be absent from a Haredi children's text. The first in a numbered list of commentaries on the illustration of Egyptian bondage emphasizes that "Jewish women were prevented from going to the Mikvah,"[7] with an assumption that at least some readers understand what that means. A similar hint describes consequences of boils for Egyptian couples: "The Egyptians suffered with boils that prevented them from being with their wives."[8] (It seems that only men qualify as full-fledged Egyptians.)

Part of the explanation for this radical departure from the tradition of positive depictions of the Exodus stems from something that to my mind consists of a refreshing attitude toward children. There is no need to sugarcoat reality for children, who are capable of facing real challenges, and in any case already know that the world can be an unpleasant place. Hiding the darker sides of things can even alienate some young people, who understand that adults depict the world as more cheerful than it is. Things that one cannot talk about are often a great deal more frightening than beasts with names.

Perhaps I am reading more into Pollack's illustrations than he intended – but the Haggadah hints that the artist and publishers understand what they are doing. They state outright that "this Hag-

---

7. p. 105, based on *Shemot Rabbah* 9:10.
8. p. 111.

gadah is unusually graphic."[9] But even if I am over-reading, what of it? (The author is, after all, dead – metaphorically, of course. Pollack should live and be well.) But Pollack's audience of children and parents will not be damaged by facing sacred history, including its most frightening episodes, with their gory and bloody suffering contained in that history.

Granted, for all its innovation, these illustrations fit neatly into other aspects of a Haredi worldview. Haredim present the lachrymose theory of Jewish history as their own, though of course it comes together with divine protection and the inevitable salvation of the select few who remain faithful. Some of the lessons of this lachrymose history are: the outside world is not to be trusted, Jews can only rely on God, and sacrifice and suffering are part and parcel of Jewish experience. As R. Chait puts it in the opening sentences of his introduction to the Haggadah: "What is the secret of Jewish survival throughout the centuries of merciless pogroms, barbaric persecutions, and endless inhuman terrorization? It is their faith in God!"[10]

The Exodus story has occupied our collective minds for thousands of years – not only because it is our foundational myth – but also because it has all the elements of a good adventure: heroes, heroines, villains, tension, violence, action, blood, and war. It's healthy to focus on those, too.

---

9. p. 5.
10. p. 8.

Devora Doresh and the Case of the Frum Girl Detective: Female Heroes in Ultra-Orthodox Jewish Children's Fiction

Meira Levinson

In the universe of Orthodox Jewish children's fiction from the 1980s and 1990s, books featuring female protagonists and characters tended to focus on domestic themes: friend drama, growing up, or events at school and at home. The *Devora Doresh* books, by Carol Korb Hubner, however, are a notable exception. Devora was frum[1] – and she solved crimes. The *Devora Doresh* books are significant in that they feature an Orthodox Jewish girl having adventures of the kind that were otherwise normally limited to either Orthodox Jewish boys or non-Jewish girls.

In some ways, *Devora Doresh* portrayed Orthodox Judaism in a similarly didactic manner as did series such as Leah Klein's *The B.Y. Times* and Miriam Zakon's *The Baker's Dozen*: they portrayed an Orthodox Jewish female protagonist who unquestioningly observes

---

1. Orthodox Jewish and observant of Orthodox Jewish law.

The Haunted Shul, 1979; *The Whispering Mezuzah*, 1979; *The Tattered Tallis*, 1979; *The Twisted Menora*, 1981; *The Silent Shofar*, 1983.

Orthodox Jewish law and whose life mostly consists of conservative gender roles. Devora's mysteries center on Jewish themes, as is evident through their titles ("The Twisted Menora," "The Tattered Tallis," "The Whispering Mezuzah") and Devora uses Torah to solve the mysteries. Yet Devora preferred to get her skirts dirtied in creepy cobwebbed tunnels rather than pursuing the tamer pastimes of her female counterparts in other novels. This felt exciting and personal to me as a young reader – I felt seen, because *Devora Doresh* reflected my own preferences, as the girl who always preferred to create haunted houses in the garage with the neighborhood boys to fussing over clothing or makeup. Simultaneously, the mere fact that *Devora Doresh* depicted an Orthodox Jewish female protagonist was exciting to readers like me, who were not used to seeing characters from similar backgrounds appear in novels.

The *Devora Doresh* books were not mainstream novels by any means – they were published by Judaica Press – and it would be decades before an Orthodox Jewish female tween superhero protagonist appeared in mainstream children's literature (her name is Mirka, and she made her debut in 2010 in the *Hereville* graphic novels[2]). But their genre sets them apart in some ways from other Orthodox Jewish publishing house novels aimed at girls, as Marci Lavine Bloch notes in her *Jewish Book Council* review of the series reboot.[3] Given that the first *Devora Doresh* book was published in 1979, at a time when Haredi children's books altogether were rare, this depiction of a female protagonist who is both frum and an amateur detective is even more notable.

This essay intertwines critical readings of the *Devora Doresh* books with an exploration of the ways in which these stories can potentially affect child readers, especially female Jewish readers. While Devora was far from a radical feminist role model, she was a pretty rare female protagonist within the realm of Orthodox Jewish children's literature for two key reasons: First, Devora spends most of her time actively seeking mysteries and adventures. She solves crimes and uses her wits to think quickly on her feet and save herself and others, sometimes from acute danger. Second, the books foreground and emphasize Devora's scholarly Torah knowledge and learning – to the point where even adult male rabbis laud her as a scholar. I argue that both aspects of Devora stand out from other female depictions within Haredi children's books circa 1979–2000. This is not to say Devora is unique. For one thing, Hubner actually went on to write more Haredi mystery books featuring a female detective protagonist – the *Leah Lamdan*

---

2. Barry Deutsch, *How Mirka Got Her Sword* (New York: Amulet Paperbacks, 2012).
3. Marci Lavine Bloch, "Devora Doresh Mysteries 2," *The Jewish Book Council*, 2012, https://www.jewishbookcouncil.org/book/the-devora-doresh-mysteries-2.

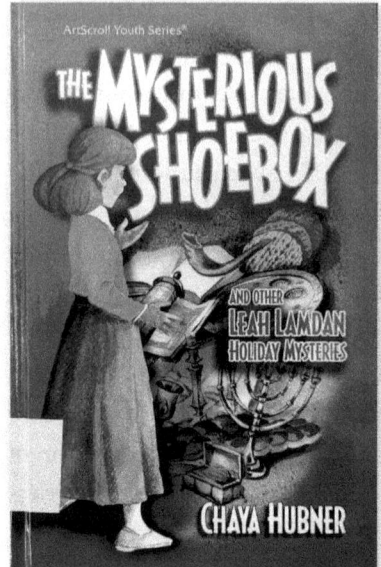

A Mystery from Afar and Other Leah Lamdan Holiday Mysteries, 2007; *The Mysterious Shoebox and Other Leah Lamdan Holiday Mysteries*, 2008.

series – under the name Chaya Hubner, rather than Carol Korb Hubner. The *Leah Lamdan* books are thematically similar to *Devora Doresh*: both feature a frum female detective who solves mysteries using Torah. The scope of this essay, however, is limited to examining the *Devora Doresh* books.

Devora may not have been unique, but she stands out as rare in her Torah prowess, her focus on solving crimes, and the sheer action and dangerous scrapes that form the backbone of her stories. This was true in 1979. My sense is that it still holds true despite a burgeoning scene of Haredi children's book publishing. While this does not indicate any feminist agendas on the part of Hubner, it does still serve to depict for child readers a wider range of possible female – and Orthodox Jewish female – roles, skills, and empowerment. Regardless of author intentions, these strong, repeatedly emphasized depictions of Devora open the door for child readers to come away from their reading experiences with messages of frum female empowerment.

Devora Doresh and Haredi children's book publishing in the 1970s–1990s

The *Devora Doresh* series is a compilation of short stories featuring Devora Doresh, a middle school-aged girl[4] living in a Haredi community in Brooklyn, who solves mysteries using her vast knowledge of Torah and Jewish history. "Doresh" is Hebrew for "seek, consult, inquire of."[5] This is actually called out within the stories themselves: Chaim, Devora's eight-year-old younger brother, says, "With a last name like Doresh, […] what else could my sister do? Doresh is the Hebrew word for 'investigator.'"[6]

Yoel Finkelman describes how "Haredi novels borrow literary genres and formulas from the general bestsellers and fill them with Haredi characters and values."[7] Similarly, the *Devora Doresh* series reads like a frum version of *Nancy Drew* or *Encyclopedia Brown*. In a review of the 2006 reprint for *The Jewish Book Council,* Bloch writes that Devora is quite clearly the "Orthodox Jewish version of Nancy Drew."[8] Hubner, a lover of mystery novels, explained to me that her dream was, indeed, to create a Jewish version of mainstream children's mystery novels popular at the time, such as *Nancy Drew, Hardy Boys,* and *Cherry Ames.*[9]

When *Devora Doresh* was first published in 1979, very little existed

---

4. In perusing the stories, I have yet to find a mention of her actual age. We do know she's in middle school.
5. Brown, Driver, and Briggs, *Brown-Driver-Briggs Hebrew and English Lexicon,* 205.
6. Carol Korb Hubner, *Devora Doresh Mysteries,* Judaica Press, 1979: 8.
7. Finkelman, *Strictly Kosher Reading,* 45.
8. Bloch, "Devora Doresh Mysteries 2," 2012.
9. Hubner, phone correspondence, May 2021. It was interesting to me that Hubner described these series – i.e., series such as *Nancy Drew, Hardy Boys,* and *Cherry Ames* – as "clean," referring to the non-racy nature of the content (of the original series for *Nancy Drew* and *Hardy Boys,* at least). This is in contrast to what Dainy Bernstein describes other Haredi reactions were to series such as *The Babysitter's Club* and thus I found Hubner's perspective fascinating (see Bernstein, *Reading the World,* 16).

in the realm of Orthodox Jewish children's literature.[10] When I say "Orthodox Jewish" children's literature, I really mean Haredi and Chabad, because there wasn't much Modern Orthodox Jewish children's literature – at least to my knowledge – aside from a few notable picture books such as *A Hanukkiyah for Dina* (1980), which depicted an observant, seemingly Modern Orthodox Jewish family, although this is not made explicit in the text.[11] Hubner notes that at the time she wrote the first *Devora Doresh* books, the landscape of Orthodox Jewish children's fiction was a virtual desert. Feldheim Publishers still hadn't yet published any children's titles; *Savta Simcha and the Incredible Shabbos Bag*, their first children's book, was published in 1980.[12] Hubner describes going from one Orthodox Jewish bookstore to the next with the manuscript for "The Haunted Shul," her first Devora Doresh story, and was laughed out each time. The bookstores and publishers published *sfarim* (Jewish religious books), not children's books, she told me. The message she heard repeatedly was

---

10. Hubner, phone correspondence, May 2021; see also Bernstein, *Reading the World*, 13–14.

11. I say that this picture book depicts a Modern Orthodox Jewish family due to the information presented via the illustrations: Dina's father and grandfather are clean-shaven, the men and boys all wear kippot (yarmulkes) that are fairly small and rest on top of their heads – while it's impossible to tell, from the black and white illustrations what texture/fabrics the kippot are meant to be, they resemble, from their shape and size, more the style of kippot *srugot* of the Modern Orthodox community, as versus, for example, larger kippot that might designate more yeshivish styles (e.g., see the rendering of kippa size on the covers of many of the contemporary kids' books from Judaica Press, the publishers of *Devora Doresh* [https://www.judaicapress.com/collections/jp-kids]. Aside from *kippa* illustration, Dina's whole family lights *chanukiyot* with blessings (so they are observant of mitzvot), yet Dina wears pants (she is depicted as being around toddler age) and her mother is illustrated as not covering her hair, although she does cover her hair for lighting the Chanukah candles. Note, though, that the term "Modern Orthodox" does not appear within the book's text; the family's specific denomination is not made explicit.

12. Dainy Bernstein, "Reading the World: American Haredi Children's Literature 1980–2000" (English dissertation, New York: The Graduate Center, City University of New York, 2021), 1.

that "no customers would want it, no one would buy it." There were a handful of other Orthodox Jewish children's books out at the time, but not many.[13] When Hubner arrived at Judaica Press, she told me, the publisher laughed just like the other booksellers, but his adult daughter happened to be in the back room, and he said he would ask her opinion. A few days later, two months before Chanukah, he called back and said, "My daughter said these will sell." Judaica Press marketed *The Haunted Shul* as something parents could purchase as a Chanukah gift for children. A few days after Chanukah, Hubner was told it sold out and that they wanted a reprint (although she acknowledges she doesn't know how many copies were in that first printing). Hubner recalls that she and her publishers were all in shock. They simply hadn't expected that a children's fiction book would be so popular. Hubner's publisher asked if she had any other manuscripts, and she gave him *The Whispering Mezuzah*.

The industry began picking up soon after the first *Devora Doresh* books were published. Yaffa Ganz's *Savta Simcha* books were published beginning in 1980, and, as Dainy Bernstein describes, additional Haredi publishing houses followed suit with children's titles.[14] In the 1990s, two series, *The B.Y. Times* and *The Baker's Dozen*, appeared on the scene.[15] As Bernstein describes, these series were very popular. *The B.Y. Times* is about "a group of middle school girls who begin a school newspaper in their Bais Yaakov, the generic name for an Orthodox girls' school," and *The Baker's Dozen* is about a large Haredi family and their daily lives.[16] Both series are set in the same (fictional) New York City suburb; characters occasionally appear, or are referenced,

---

13. Hubner, phone correspondence, May 2021
14. Bernstein, *Reading the World*, 1
15. There very well may have been other titles featuring female protagonists, and geared toward similarly-aged female readers, published in the interim; I specifically reference these two series here and throughout this essay simply because they were and are extremely popular series within the realm of Haredi children's literature, and reached a broader audience beyond the Haredi community.
16. Bernstein, *Reading the World*, p. 16

The first books in the B.Y. Times and Baker's Dozen series, 1991 and 1992, respectively.

across the two series. Both series had the same creator, Miriam Stark Zakon; the *B.Y. Times* was published under the name Leah Klein "so as not to have one author's name dominate Haredi book covers." The *B.Y. Times* was meant to be a Haredi version of *The Babysitters Club* (sans boyfriends), and had a similar appeal to young female readers, even some who hailed from non-Orthodox Jewish backgrounds, as Mara Wilson recalls.[17]

For me as a child reader, seeing any Orthodox Jewish female character (in contexts outside of picture books) was always impactful. Whether in *Devora Doresh* or in more domestic-themed books, such as *The B.Y. Times* or *The Baker's Dozen*, it was affirming to see aspects of my own religious and cultural life reflected back to me from the pages of a book. As Wilson explains, "They were Jewish, so they were

---

17. Mara Wilson, "The B.Y. Times: The Orthodox Jewish Answer to The Baby-Sitters Club." *The Toast*, March 5, 2015, https://the-toast.net/2015/03/05/the-b-y-times-jewish-answer-baby-sitters-club/.

like me. They were in the tribe. They understood." As a girl growing up Modern Orthodox, my reading choices were bifurcated: either I could read secular, mainstream books, which sometimes depicted Jewish characters (e.g., works by E.L. Konigsburg), but usually these characters weren't Orthodox Jewish; or I could read novels published within Haredi or Chabad contexts.

I read *Devora Doresh* alongside *The B.Y. Times*, *The Baker's Dozen*, and many other stand-alone titles from assorted Haredi and Chabad publishers. And while I enjoyed most of them, I felt a stronger pull towards Devora as a protagonist. I was that kid who preferred to spend her time either reading or exploring our creepy, cobwebbed crawlspace over more "girly" pursuits. There were definitely moments within *The B.Y. Times* and *The Baker's Dozen* that spoke to my – and other readers' – more tomboyish cravings. *B.Y. Times* characters like Nechama Orenstein, the resident tomboy and athlete, and Shani Baum, the strong-willed leader of the paper, create space for less stereotypically feminine portrayals. And there are moments of suspense across both series. Batya Ben-Levi spends most of *The B.Y. Times #4: War!* in and out of bomb shelters; and Tikva Baker, one of the Baker quintuplets, captures counterfeiters in a secret tunnel beneath their house in *The Baker's Dozen #2*. However, Devora's stories are firmly rooted in the mystery genre, which allows them more pervasive suspense, adventure, and high stakes than merely the occasional suspenseful episode in the more domestic-themed novels. *Devora* also stood out in other ways that felt more relatable to me. I grew up with a father who cooked and cleaned just as often as my mother did; the idea that a girl would be chastised for not having supper ready for her father, like Shula Goldman is in *The B.Y. Times #4: War!*, was pretty foreign to me.[18] Devora and her mom perform plenty of domestic duties – but

---

18. Klein, *B.Y. Times #4, War!*, 50–51. It should be noted that the context here is that Shula's younger brother is critically ill in the hospital; both parents are depicted as being by their son's side outside of work, and thus Shula is responsible for making dinner. Yet the depiction of her father's disappointment in her, and Shula's self-inflicted air of tragedy as her father is forced to open a can of tuna and prepare tuna salad for dinner, seems a little extreme. Granted,

these are shared, in part, by the men, as discussed further below. I enjoyed *The B.Y. Times* and *The Baker's Dozen*, but the domestic and interpersonal themes, such as friendships, family drama, or community service, were simply less exciting to me than were Devora's mysteries and adventures.

Subversive Gender Roles in Devora Doresh: Devora as Detective and Hero

What's fascinating about Devora is that, unlike the other female protagonists of other frum series, Devora spends her free time not immersed in domestic duties, friendship drama, or extracurriculars such as the school newspaper, but rather solving crimes and, at times, getting into danger (though usually not on purpose). Within the world of Haredi children's books, this was, and still is, rare. There are other mystery-genre Haredi children's books. For instance, Galila Ben-Uri's *The Missing Crown* (1988) and its companion books feature Orthodox Jewish boys in Toronto who help Israeli detectives solve international smuggling (and other) mysteries, and *Gemarakup* (1990) has been compared to a frum Encyclopedia Brown.[19] But those series feature male protagonists and, frequently, male side characters.[20] *Devora*

---

the narrative tone is filtered via Shula's perspective, and emphasizes her guilt for wasting time on her emotions as versus preparing dinner, but the scene is still depicted as a daughter remiss in both her familial and halachic duties. The religious framing of it – as Shula "giving herself...*mussar*" – is especially striking (as versus, say, simply depicting an instance of a parentified child writ large).

19. Bernstein, *Reading the World*, 38. Funnily enough, Devora is once referred to as "Gemara Kup" in "The Missing Papers," the first story in *The Devora Doresh Mysteries #1* 2006 reprint, and thus contemporary readers' introduction to Devora. It should be noted that these stories, which were originally published 1979 – 1981, actually predate Zakon's *Gemarakup* (1990). It's also notable that, after this story, Devora is not referred to by this term.

20. Although I can't speak for every book in both series, many do not include any female child characters working alongside the male characters (e.g., a frum parallel to Sally from Encyclopedia Brown), which makes sense given separate social spheres of boys and girls within Haredi communities.

Doresh stands out in that the mysteries are just as action-packed as the books mentioned above, but the protagonist is female.

Devora is a student at Yocheved Junior High School and has started a detective business on the side. I say "business" but it's notable that she never charges, despite printing up business index cards.[21] The fact that she doesn't charge nods to the fact that Devora started her "bureau" in order to help her neighbors find lost objects. Devora's business cards describe her business as a "Lost and Found Bureau," with the line, "Will help you find anything you lose." In the story "The Missing Papers," which is the first story in volume one of the 2006 reprint (so, in essence, contemporary readers' introduction to Devora), the narrative tells us that Devora's "'Lost and Found' bureau had been the result of her eagerness to be helpful. She had already helped many families in her neighborhood find things they had lost – some of them quite valuable."[22] In this way, Devora's detective work can be viewed as an outgrowth of the *hessed* (community service or charity) types of activities in which Haredi female protagonists participate across girls' series such as *The B.Y. Times* and *The Baker's Dozen*. But her venture grows when she starts solving bigger crimes (although she does still solve small mysteries, like missing belongings, as well) and becomes a regular consultant of the local police – even, at one point, of the FBI. Sergeant O'Malley, from her local precinct, is her very own Lestrade.[23]

Devora solves mysteries ranging from finding a family's secret compartment location containing crucial certificates (in "The Missing Papers") to foiling Communist spies (in "The Gold Bug" and "The Russian Connection") to actively intervening when (Caucasian, North American) terrorists are torturing a kidnapped mole and trying to

---

21. Hubner, *Devora Doresh Mysteries*, 8–9.
22. Hubner, *Devora Doresh Mysteries*, 8.
23. Similar parallel characters include: Nancy Drew's dad, the Hardy Boys' dad, and Encyclopedia Brown's dad – they're all people who are either police, or associated with crime cases (Nancy Drew's father is a lawyer and he brings her some of his cases), who bring unsolvable mysteries to outside, child/teen consulting detectives.

The original Devora Doresh stories repackaged in new editions, 2006.

poison the waterways between Canada and the United States (in "Convention to Catastrophe"). The mysteries always end up tying in to Devora's Torah studies: either something she is learning at school (e.g., related to a Jewish holiday that's occurring), or prior knowledge she coincidentally recalls within the story plotline (e.g., halacha, legends, or episodes from Jewish history). Devora uses her Jewish studies knowledge to solve the mysteries.

In many ways, Devora presents a traditional depiction of female gender appearances and roles, dressing according to norms within Haredi communities. Devora's friend Shira is described as "always dressed in the latest fashions, but she never wore anything that was not tzniyusdik – modest and ladylike as befitting the Orthodox Jewish girl she was," and "Devora, too, wore only tzniyusdik dresses, not quite as fancy as Shira's but always crisp and neat."[24] Devora accepts as a given the overall gendered roles within the home, and she conveys

---

24. Hubner, *Devora Doresh Mysteries*, 136–7.

unquestioning faith and acceptance of halacha in general, as well as halachic gender divides. Thus, Devora does not outwardly present as either a tomboy or as a character attempting to push gender boundaries within her community. Yet, in Devora's pursuit of mysteries and adventure, she embodies what Michelle Ann Abate attributes to Nancy Drew: an "adventurous personality, bold temperament and daring nature."[25] As Abate describes regarding Cherry Ames, Devora is more of a "feminine tomboy than a gender-bending one," but can still be viewed as a "behavioral tomboy" due to her "performance of an array of difficult and often even dangerous tasks."[26]

As a child, I loved that Devora's adventures had real stakes. In "The Twisted Menora," for example, she finds herself accidentally trapped and injured in a secret tunnel underneath an old synagogue; and yet, despite being injured and scared, she calms herself down by thinking:

> There must be a way out of here, [...] This tunnel was probably like the tunnel in the Touro synagogue her teacher had described. One of the oldest shuls in the country, the building was constructed with a tunnel underneath the bima so that the congregants could escape in case of a surprise attack by the Indians.[27]

Devora then goes on to recall "another tunnel she had learned about in school," the "cave of Zedekiah." Devora thinks:

> When Jerusalem had fallen to Nebuchadnezzer, King Zedekiah made a tunnel all the way to Jericho by traveling through a cave under his castle. If so, and if the tunnel she was in was anything like the other two – why then, there must be a way out! If she would only walk far enough she would have to find it.

---

25. Michelle Ann Abate, *Tomboys: A Literary and Cultural History* (Philadelphia, PA: Temple University Press, 2008), 140.
26. Ibid., 156.
27. Hubner, *Twisted Menora*, 35. The reference to "Indians" as aggressors is racially problematic; my sense is that the series does not stand out from mainstream racial depictions in contemporaneous children's literature.

Using this logic, Devora persists and finds her way to a second exit (as well as a geniza along the way). There, she discovers another character being held prisoner. Despite her injured ankle, Devora rescues the woman, knocks out the antagonist, and leads the protagonists to safety. While Devora's extrapolation from the Touro synagogue makes sense contextually, her application of the King Zedekiah story is far from foolproof logically (she had no reason to expect this tunnel would mirror that one). That said, her cool logic in the face of injury and with her back to a corner (literally), her courage in putting her own life in danger by leaving her hiding place to prevent the large adult male antagonist from hurting his victim, and her apparent physical prowess in swiftly knocking said criminal unconscious (although this is depicted as partially due to the momentum of her pushing him from behind) are all impressive feats, especially for a young Haredi tween who apparently hasn't learned any martial arts or self-defense.

Both the high stakes and Devora's bravery in "The Twisted Menora" are not anomalies within the collections. Across a number of other stories, the stakes are life or death (either for Devora or for other characters), and Devora makes similar brave choices to endanger her own life in order to save someone else. Another example is "Convention to Catastrophe," when Devora knows she's risking the wrath of a criminal who is in the process of torturing someone. While she doesn't know yet that this criminal is a terrorist specifically, she realizes he would have no qualms in hurting or even killing her, yet she puts her life in danger to help the kidnapped torture victim. She doesn't help him escape; rather, he asks her to pass a piece of paper along to the FBI and she does so. Devora knows she endangers her own life – and possibly those of her classmates who are with her – by taking the paper, but her sense of duty prevails. In this story as well, her quick thinking on her feet (and the power of recalling the Biblical depiction of the Israelite encampment in the desert – obviously) enables her to trick the terrorists with an elaborate ruse, and to save everyone.[28]

All of this is not to say that Devora doesn't spend free time engaging

---

28. Hubner, *Devora Doresh Mysteries #2*, 95–103.

in activities similar to those of Shani Baum or the Baker girls – activities such as *hessed* projects, domestic chores, or, of course, learning. Devora is depicted as doing all these things to some degree. She's depicted, at times, as helping cook and clean, and doing community service activities such as tutoring Russian girls in her school in English, or doing art projects with children in the "children's home." And, by and large, characters in the *Devora Doresh* books conform to conservative, traditional gender roles: mothers who are mostly stay-at-home housewives, managing children and domestic duties, while fathers either learn or work.[29] Yet *Devora Doresh* at times blurs conventional gender boundaries, such as when the narrative depicts men doing domestic labor. For example, in "The Whispering Mezuzah," everyone prepares for Sukkot together. While the women cook, "the men cleaned up the house [...] Rabbi Doresh, his left arm in a sling, vacuumed the living room carpet with his right hand while Uncle Shlomo ran a mop across the hallway linoleum."[30] In another story, a male artist gently challenges a father's mentality that his son's artistic interests are not "manly" by emphasizing that being sensitive, showing emotions, and being an artist are legitimate expressions of masculinity.[31] Overall, while the books do not challenge gender norms to a large degree, these small moments do challenge some conservative approaches towards gender roles and affect, thus bolstering Devora's gender-bending via unconventional activities and adventurous disposition.

---

29. It's also important to note that, for example, in the *B.Y. Times* books, women often do have jobs too, although the jobs depicted are somewhat limited in scope: e.g., assisting a husband's dental practice, teaching nursery school, teaching girls in the middle school, selling *sheitels*. While it's common in certain Orthodox Jewish communities for women to support the family financially while men learn in yeshiva, the fathers/husbands in *The B.Y. Times* and *The Baker's Dozen* are mostly depicted as having jobs as well.
30. Hubner, *Devora Doresh Mysteries*, 60.
31. Hubner, *Devora Doresh Mysteries*, 131.

Devora as Torah scholar

Devora also stands out from her female counterparts in other Haredi children's novels because of Hubner's emphasis on Devora's extensive Torah study and knowledge. Almost every *Devora Doresh* story incorporates details of some aspect of Devora's Torah study: of facts, concepts, and/or values Devora learns from school, family, or community members. Usually, Devora specifically uses these facts, concepts, and/or values to solve the mysteries. If a story opens with Devora learning something in class, or casually discussing Torah concepts or mitzvot with family or friends, you can be sure that it will directly relate, later on in the story, to the mystery at hand, and aid Devora in her ability to brilliantly solve the mystery.

While the connections between Devora's studies and the mysteries' solutions are occasionally a bit of a stretch, the potential messaging for young readers here is fascinating to me. The ostensive purpose, as Hubner confirms, is to convey the idea that Torah applies everywhere in life – even in as seemingly unrelated an area as solving crimes. Additionally, though, this strong emphasis on Devora's scholarly Torah skills – albeit stemming from the "using Torah to solve mysteries" narrative structure – ends up conveying a strong sense of Devora as a *talmid chacham* (an esteemed Torah scholar). Granted, this is mostly limited to Torah subjects within the domain of study allowed to women in Haredi communities – areas such as Torah, midrash, halacha, and Jewish history and legends. In one story, "The Counterfeiters," Devora does reference Gemara, albeit an *aggadatah*.[32] For the most part, however, Devora stays within the domain of Torah subjects permissible (within Haredi communities) for female study.

Even with that caveat, though, the dominant impression readers receive of Devora is that of a preteen girl who is seriously dedicated to Torah study, who has a sharp critical mind and extremely strong

---

32. Hubner, *Devora Doresh Mysteries*, 165. *Aggadatah* refers to the more midrashic, story-like episodes within the Talmud, versus more legal-oriented sections.

memory, and whose analytical and associative cognitive skills allow her to accurately apply her Torah studies towards the seemingly unrelated contexts that occur via the mysteries. Devora is depicted as unusual in this regard, compared to her female classmates and relatives – unusual not in the sense of her love of learning, but regarding her brilliance. Both Devora's friends and her female relatives, such as her mother, are depicted as enjoying learning. Devora's mother teaches her children halacha alongside Devora's rabbi father, such as when she explains that one can live in a house without a kosher mezuzah "as long as you intend to get some proper ones at the first opportunity [...] If a person intended to do a mitzvah but was prevented from doing it by circumstances beyond his control, it is considered as if he actually did it."[33] Yet Devora is depicted as having cognitive skills – memory, close observation skills, and analytical thinking skills – that exceed those of her peers and many adult characters. This is not to say that any of these side characters, adult or child, are depicted as dumb or clueless, or even as simply not interested in studying (as with Gemarakup's sidekick "Slugger"). As mentioned before, Devora's peers also love learning: her father is a rabbi and scholar, and Sergeant O'Malley is portrayed as an intelligent police officer who excels at his job. In "The Gold Bug," we learn that O'Malley used to work for the FBI before switching to a job with the local police force for a better salary.[34] And Devora's Torah knowledge is definitely not depicted as exceeding that of her father or other venerable rabbis. Both Devora's father and O'Malley are depicted as supremely competent in both

---

33. Hubner, *Devora Doresh Mysteries*, 29.
34. Hubner, *Devora Doresh Mysteries*, 88. The specificity of this particular detail regarding O'Malley's choice to leave the FBI for the local precinct stuck out to me. Hubner said that when she was writing this particular story, which dealt with interactions between the FBI and the local Brooklyn precinct, her editor told her to "call up a policeman or FBI agent" and find out which one is a better place to work. So Hubner did – she went outside (in Brooklyn), looked around, saw a policeman, and asked him. The policeman answered that there were pros and cons of each workplace, and he laid those out for her, which she then incorporated into the story (Hubner, phone correspondence, May 2021).

their jobs; what Devora brings to the table is the fusion of Torah and deductive reasoning.[35]

The effect of this repeated emphasis, story after story, of Devora's mental prowess and the respect she garners from the adult authorities in her life, including Haredi rabbis and other Haredi adult men, is that Devora emerges as a potentially strong endorsement for women's Torah study. Everyone is astounded at Devora's deductive skills, memory, and her brilliance in seeing connections between Torah and the mysteries. Occasionally, characters express surprise at Devora's youth (e.g., characters initially dismissing her as too young to be of any help on a given case).[36] But the mere fact of her gender doesn't cause anyone to doubt her Torah skills.

For me, as both a child reader and an adult reader, this was striking. I don't recall fixating on it as a child reader: I happened to attend Modern Orthodox schools that taught girls Gemara starting in middle school, and I belonged to a synagogue community that endorsed this. My cousins, who actually introduced me to *Devora Doresh*, are Lubavitch, a community which has a history of approbation of women's

---

35. There is also something to be said of the necessary narrative trope at play here for the stories to function: that of the child hero/protagonist who succeeds where the adults can't, which in part is simply a function of being the protagonist, and of the (usually necessary) vantage point for child readers. In this regard, Devora is similar to the child protagonists of Ben-Uri's series. The adults in Ben-Uri's series are also either wise Torah scholars (or Torah role models, e.g., the *shammash* at their shul) or brilliant detectives, but since the child protagonists are the center of the story, they play an inordinately (and, at times, unrealistically) large role in solving the mysteries, and are depicted as just as competent – and often entrusted with just as dangerous jobs – as the adults. Sometimes this is justified within the text, but often these plot elements are simply presented immersively, as if this is normal – which, again, is in line with many child hero/protagonists across mainstream adventure dramas as well (e.g., mysteries but also fantasy, science fiction, etc.).

36. For example, in "Kidnapped," one adult character laments, "We're fools to rely on a young girl's memory" (Hubner, *Devora Doresh*, p. 275, 2006 reprint); or in "Mystery of the Secret Code," when the client shouts, upon being introduced to Devora, "This is just a child! It's a real waste of time!" (Hubner, *Devora Doresh*, 143).

Torah study. Devora's prowess in Torah study, therefore, didn't surprise me per se, despite the fact that it was clearly distinct from portrayals of female protagonists across other Haredi books aimed at girls. As a child, I was more struck – and immediately hooked by – Devora's action-packed adventures, which I do remember noticing as radically different from her female counterparts in other Haredi novels. I seem to not be alone in my childhood reader reaction. In response to a question I posted on the private Facebook group Orthodox Ladies United in Fandom, whose membership numbers in the thousands, 34 members responded that they remembered reading the *Devora Doresh* books as kids.[37] Twenty-four of these women specifically mentioned enjoying or loving the books; seven specifically pointed to appreciating, as children, the fact that Devora was a frum, female detective. A number of these commenters noted that this struck them as distinct from other female-marketed Haredi books focusing on friend dynamics. Devora's kickass detective work, tomboyish scrapes, and suspenseful stakes are all what group members recalled from their childhood impressions, as well as her scholarly prowess. Members compared Devora to a "superhero," a "Jewish Nancy Drew," and "female Encyclopedia Brown;" one member, Miriam Leah Gruenbaum, mentioned that "one or two of the stories gave me the spooks," a sentiment shared by another commenter (both still enjoyed the books).

My own experience as a child reader was that *Devora Doresh* subtly reinforced the values that I, personally, already happened to be learning: that girls could and should learn Torah just as much as boys. It should be noted that this in part aligns with Hubner's intentions – after all, Hubner's goal was to show that everyone should be learning Torah, and that Torah is valuable in all parts of our daily lives, even in modern life. I do not, however, argue that Hubner was trying to equate female Torah study with male Torah study. In fact, when I asked her why she

---

37. Note that this was not a survey that went out to all OLUF members, but rather a single post, and some of those who happened to see it responded. The OLUF page has a high volume of posts per day and it is likely that many members missed the post.

chose a female protagonist for her mystery adventures instead of a male one, she explained that she'd thought, well, who would have the time to go running around solving mysteries? Boys were supposed to be sitting and learning Torah! But girls had free time. Thus, I definitely don't claim that the impression I received from the books as a child reader was necessarily the message Hubner intended in this regard.

Yet this normalization of female Torah study was, in fact, a message I took away, albeit one reinforced by my own Modern Orthodox Jewish context. I would argue that the extreme emphasis on Devora's Torah study, reinforced by the repetition that stems from the structure of short stories (and thus, as readers read through each book, they're encountering repeated emphases of different instances of Devora applying her Torah knowledge to each mystery at hand) and by the adult (often male rabbinical) validation of her prowess, at least opens the possibility for child readers – especially female readers – to walk away with an empowering message of female capacity for Torah study. Given the general emphasis on male Torah study within Haredi communities as well as in many other Jewish communities, this strikes me as significant.

This is not to say that other Haredi books aimed at female readers, such as *The B.Y. Times* and *Baker's Dozen*, never include examples of female characters studying (or simply discussing) Torah or halacha. Occasionally some halachot enter into the plot – e.g., *lashon hara* with *The B.Y. Times* – but in these books, the female characters' studies, even *limudei kodesh* (Judaic studies), aren't the focal point that they are for Devora. In series such as *The B.Y. Times* and *Baker's Dozen*, domestic and relationship-based themes are the main narrative focal points, and the occasional action/adventure lies more on the periphery, across the series writ large.[38] With *Devora Doresh*, the narrative emphasis is flipped: the focal points are the action, adventure, and Devora's detective work, and domestic activities occupy the periphery.

---

38. *The B.Y. Times #4, War!* might be considered an exception here, since a main plotline centers on Batya experiencing the Gulf War in Israel.

Conclusion

Devora Doresh is rare in its depiction of an Orthodox Jewish female protagonist. Devora stands out from other Haredi female protagonists due to her crime-solving exploits, the fact that she spends most of the narrative focused on mysteries and adventure, and that domestic activities, while present, are more marginal than are her adventures. She also stands out due to the stories' emphases on her vast Torah knowledge, general Judaic-scholarly prowess, and her quick wits and ability to think on her feet in the face of danger. All of these factors cause Devora to stand out, in these regards, from her female Haredi counterparts in other Haredi children's novels. This was true at the time of *Devora*'s original publication, and this rarity seems to still be the case in the 2000s; in her 2012 review, Bloch notes that "there are few mystery options for girls who prefer to read about Jewish characters and values."[39] Devora was far from a radical feminist role model, but she did, ever so slightly, push against the boundaries of gender norms in terms of what was more commonly depicted of Orthodox Jewish girls in Haredi fiction.

---

39. Bloch, "The Devora Doresh Mysteries 2," 2012.

Cultural Ambivalence Praxis in Haredi Jewish Industrial Toy Design

Shlomi Eiger

In 2016, I attended a meeting with a Haredi entrepreneur from Jerusalem who was on a quest for a designer to develop a new toy for Haredi Jewish children. He presented me with a mix of miniature dolls from various non-Haredi brands to model a Haredi wedding. Some of the dolls were adjusted to the event's dress code with added cloth and makeshift paper clothes and accessories. Objects such as the chuppah and the bride's veil were improvised to mimic the actual event. According to the Haredi entrepreneur, this improvised toy is a typical way for Haredi children to play with dolls not initially designed for their needs.

The children's needs to play with the stories and scenery from their cultural world inspired this entrepreneur to establish a doll brand to accommodate their needs. The brand, called Kids Play, invites children to play with sets consisting of dolls and accessories imitating day-to-day Haredi scenery. This brand is part of a contemporary trend of Haredi children's toys and games designed from within the community,[1] partly due to a diffusion of secular consumer culture into

---

1. Laura Leibman, "Children, Toys, and Judaism," *The Bloomsbury Reader in Religion and Childhood* (Bloomsbury 2017), 299.

the Haredi community and its attempts to accommodate this diffusion with appropriate products that match the community's values.²

Haredi consumer culture consists primarily of stores from within the community, which serve as gatekeepers, preventing secular consumer culture from infiltrating the community. However, Haredi society in Israel is surrounded by secular consumer culture, which inevitably seeps in. This exposure to secular consumer culture leads to new leisure cultures, abundance, and pleasure-seeking that sprout in Israel's various Haredi communities. On the other hand, in the twenty-first century, the Haredi community in Israel sees halakhic extremism leading to a growing distance from the secular population in Israel and tighter rules regarding gender and modesty. These two counter-processes meet in the Haredi toy and games industry, inspired by secular products yet designed within the community and for the community.³

The diffusion of secular consumer culture, along with other secular cultures, into Israeli Haredi society creates what Zikherman calls "cultural ambivalence" (שניות תרבותית in Hebrew). He uses this term to describe the tensions in modern Haredi society in Israel between preserving the community's values and increasing exposure to secular cultures. The developing trend of Haredi toy design within the community exemplifies the community's rejection of the surrounding culture on the one hand; on the other hand, it uses secular styles of design and production to correspond with the community's values.⁴ The intersection of rejection and internalization of western secular cultures creates a culturally ambivalent product.

Children's importance in religious communities, their material culture's importance in preserving religious values, and religious communities' common objections to toys and free play makes religious toys a fascinating topic. Judaism's particular relation to the human

---

2. Chaim Zicherman, *Black Blue-White: a Journey to Israeli Haredi Society* (Tel Aviv: Yedioth Ahronoth-Sifrei Hemed, 2014), 99, 111.
3. Leibman, 99.
4. Zikherman, 262–3.

body and its image, both in rituals and in modesty and gender, creates a unique complexity in Haredi children's toy design. This essay will show how the toys and the processes leading to their creation serve as agents for Haredi values and messages. It will also present the obstacles and complexities stemming from these toys and how their design and production processes negotiate these obstacles. This negotiation mirrors the "cultural ambivalence – Western and Haredi"[5] of Haredi Jews living in Israel, a western-oriented country.

As I am a toy designer and was involved in the entirety of the design and production process for Kids Play,[6] this essay will take a practice-based stance. It will use material-culture research methodologies, which view objects and their design and production processes as active agents in culture, rather than passive products of it.[7]

The Ambivalence of Toys as Agents of Communities' Values

Besides cultural ambivalence, an additional ambivalence exists in this product, merely from being a toy. This ambivalence stems from the inherent gap between parents, the consumers, and the intentions and aspirations they are trying to instill with the toys, and their children, the customers, and how they play with the toy and experience it.[8] This

---

5. Ibid.
6. I have been working closely with the brand since 2016 as a design and production manager. Hence, I was involved in the internal discussions regarding the product's development.
7. Martin H. Wobst, "Style in Archaeology or Archaeologists in Style," *Material Meanings: Critical Approaches to the Interpretation of Material Culture*, ed. Elizabeth S. Chilton (Salt Lake City: University of Utah Press, 1999), 118–132; Miriam T. Stark, "Technical choice in Kalinga Ceramic Traditions," *Material Meanings*, 24–43; Ian Hodder, "Human-thing entanglement: towards an integrated archaeological perspective," *Journal of the Royal Anthropological Institute* 17 (2011A), 154–177.
8. Miriam Forman-Brunell and Jenifer Dawn Whitney, eds., *Dolls Studies: the Many Meanings of Girls' Toys and Play* (New York: Peter Lang Publishing, 2015); Dan Fleming, *Powerplay: Toys as Popular Culture* (Manchester, UK:

ambivalence is equally present in secular and religious toys, as both wish to expose children to the community's values.

Most religious content and ideas demand abstract thinking, which does not always suit children's cognitive abilities. Material culture and performance practices like drawings, illustrations, dance, music, and food can bridge this gap. Religious rituals and education use these elements as representational tools for more complex ideas and use stimulation of the senses to assist the learning process.[9] Therefore, on the one hand, toys may serve as an educational tool in religious communities. On the other hand, some toys use free-play methodologies and are not controllable, allegedly risking education goals.[10]

In addition, toys' association with leisure may generate suspicion and antagonism in religious communities.[11] This suspicion creates audit mechanisms for toys and games in religious communities.[12] In the process of auditing toys, Haredi communities may restrict or ban some toys' distribution and other commodities if they see them as interfering with community values.[13] However, a parallel process of designing toys occurs as well, where the community designs toys aligned with its values.[14]

The scenery in Kids Play's sets acts as an agent for the community's messages and aspirations for its children: messages like Shabbat observance, respect for parents and grandparents, the Torah's sanctity, and

---

Manchester University Press, 1996); Nikki Bado-Fralick and Rebecca Sachs Norris, *Toying with God: The World of Religious Games and Dolls* (Waco, TX: Baylor University Press, 2010); Sharon Brookshaw, "The Material Culture of Children and Childhood: Understanding Childhood Objects in the Museum Context," *Journal of Material Culture* 14.3 (2009), 365–383.

9. Tali Brener, "Children in the Synagogue and in Life Rituals in Early Modern Ashkenaz: Childhood Studies Contribution to Israel's History," *Zion* 78:B (2012), 197; Bado-Fralick 163.

10. Bado-Fralick, 157.

11. Gary S. Cross, *Kids' Stuff: Toys and the Changing World of American Childhood* (Cambridge, MA: Harvard University Press, 1997), 232.

12. Bado-Fralick, 157.

13. Zikherman; Bado-Fralick, 157.

14. Bado-Fralick, 157.

the importance of family. Besides the Haredi values, the toys convey messages of consumer culture and plenty. The plenty manifests in the product in the shape of leisure activities, gifts, and accessories. Religion, tradition, and family orientation do not inherently object to plenty and consumerism. However, Haredi society's values of making do with little and avoidance of consumer culture take a spiritual and practical part in this society's preservation.[15] The scenery therefore encompasses both Haredi values and opposition to Haredi values.

Haredi Toys: Intersections and Prohibitions

Kids Play, which is part of this growing industry of Haredi toys, started its distribution in 2020. The brand consists of nine sets of miniature dolls and accessories. Each set illustrates a different Haredi life theme and consists of the theme's appropriate figures and accessories. Some of the themes are religious, like Shabbat dinner and challah baking, and some are secular, like riding a bicycle or attending a birthday party. Categorically, Kids Play is part of a vast genre of toys used for free play in miniature scenes of people, accessories, furniture, and sometimes animals. One of the brand's characteristics is that it can interface and integrate into free play with other brands from the same category. Hence, these Haredi toys can interact with objects that were not designed for a Haredi consumer.

"Thou shalt not make unto thee any graven image" (Exodus 20:4–6)

Human-shaped dolls intersect with the Second Commandment according to Haredi interpretation, "Thou shalt not make unto thee any graven image, or any likeness [of any thing] that [is] in heaven above, or that [is] in the earth beneath, or that [is] in the water under earth" (Exodus 20:4). A more specific prohibition on creating objects in human shape can be found later in the text, "Thou shalt not make of me a God of silver; neither shalt thou make gods of gold" (Exodus

---

15. Zikherman, 246.

20:20), which, according to the Gemara in Tractate Avodah Zarah, refers particularly to material representations of humans and astronomical objects.

However, there is virtually no mention of toy dolls in Early Modern Hebrew literature.[16] Israel Ta-Shema reasons that toy dolls' absence from the literature is due to their absolute categorization as three-dimensional human figure representations, and therefore, they do not require particular debate. According to Ta-Shema, one Talmudist that provides a provision for toy dolls is the Maharit (Joseph di Trani, 1568–1639), who excludes human figures meant for play or education from the original prohibition. Rabbi Moshe Cohen presents an additional debate on human figure making. He presents a few Talmudists arguing that the prohibition on human figure making is only relevant to a complete, detailed visualization of the human figure, which he presents as the "necessary impression."[17] Therefore, a human figure with omitted details, like many toy dolls, complies with the halakhic rule.

Even if they do not primarily refer to children's toys, these debates are essential for industrial toy doll production in the Haredi community. Even though toy production within the Haredi community is allowed, it is a relatively new trend, part of a more remarkable change in the Haredi economy and consumerism, representing modern Haredi society. The debates about whether toy dolls fall under the prohibition of making idols is therefore immediately relevant for this new phenomenon.

"The king's daughter is all glorious within" (Psalm 45:14)

Apart from the halakhic question concerning idolatry, designing human dolls raises halakhic and cultural issues around the human body.[18] Haredi women's modesty codes materialize in sartorial habits

---

16. Israel M. Ta-Shema, "On Birthdays in Israel," *Zion*, (2001), 24.
17. Rabbi Moshe Cohen, "Doll Toys and Landscape Pictures Depicting Astronomical Objects", *Tehumin* 33 (2012), 467.
18. Forman-Brunell 2015; Judy Attfield, "Barbie and Action Man: Adult Toys for Girls and Boys," *The Gendered Object*, ed. Pat Kirkham (Manchester, UK: Manchester University Press 1996), 80–90.

blurring the body, including long clothing with simple patterns, tight buttoning of shirts, heavy skirts, long stockings, and more. Another component of sexual modesty in Haredi society is strict gender partition and the exclusion of women from Haredi products like commercials, illustrations, and the public sphere. Therefore, Kids Play and other Jewish doll brands' gender symmetry is rare in Haredi products. These toys' gender symmetry is an outcome of the dolls' production, which will be discussed shortly.

Halakhic Rules Mitigated by Western Toy Production Practices

Although manufactured toys are primarily identified with children in contemporary western culture,[19] industrial toy production and development processes include various factors that are not directly linked to the children who are about to play with them. These factors can be linked to financial aspects, technical aspects, or even debates about a toy's value from an adult perspective. Therefore, these factors inform a toy's physical characteristics and affect the design and the final toy produced for the child.

Despite the perception of western toys as having an idyllic, domestic, and gentle nature, their industrial production process involves powerful machinery and many professionals' hands. Kids Play's dolls and accessories are made of plastic and produced in contemporary modes of plastic production. Like most toys in the contemporary western toy industry, this product is produced in China by a local factory. Miniature toys start their lives as heavy steel blocks, which then go through molds milling. This process is one of the most expensive steps in the development of plastic products. The mold cavities will later be injected with melted plastic to create the desired shape following the mold milling (see figures 1 and 2). Due to high costs in producing products with multiple pieces, including miniature dolls and accessories, each mold has as many cavities as possible to facilitate the most efficient production of each toy.

---

19. Brookshaw, 368.

76 · Studying the Artifacts of Orthodox Childhoods

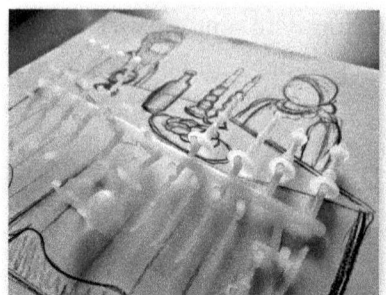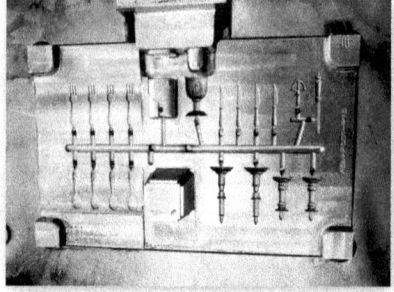

Figures 1–2 Mold Milling: The attributes of the religious idea and the religious ceremony are translated into the material. Photo: Shlomi Eiger

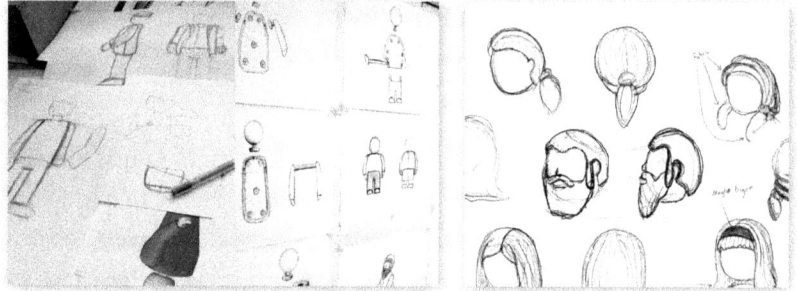

Figures 3–4 Designs with clean lines and minimal facial and textural details. Photos: Shlomi Eiger.

This western-oriented industrial process solves some of the halakhic problems presented above. The discourse about the prohibition of making a human figure is immensely focused on distinguishing between the *making* and *using* the figure when the *making* of it is forbidden.[20] The fact that this toy – like most plastic toys today – is made in China in a local factory and that the makers are not Jewish resolves the halakhic issue of making the toy, making it permissible for Haredi children to play with the human figures. The dolls' minimalist design and the elimination of some physical elements serve the halakhic rule as well, even if not intentionally. Kids Play dolls are designed with clean lines, simple shapes, and minimal facial and textural details (see figures 3 and 4). These design elements mark the doll as merely symbolizing a human rather than being a material

---

20. Cohen, 467–8.

Cultural Ambivalence Praxis in Haredi Jewish Industrial Toy Design · 77

Figure 5 The body and traditional clothing are united into one mechanical structure. An encounter between industrial, mechanical, and halakhic considerations. Photo: Shlomi Eiger

representation of one. Therefore, the "necessary impression"[21] is not created. These characteristics were not designed originally to satisfy Haredi taste, but in the case of Kids Play, these characteristics gain a new meaning of serving the halakhic rules.

The dolls' minimalist design also bridges the Haredi modesty rules for two reasons. First, Kids Play's miniature doll design combines the doll's body and garment; the dolls do not have a body separate from their clothes (see figure 5). This solves the majority of modesty issues. Unlike other doll types, like Barbie dolls, children can only expose the Kids Play doll's face and hands. Second, the doll's minimalist style creates a suggestion of a person without providing explicit physical features. This minimalist style serves the Haredi modesty code as well.

The industrial production process also negotiates gender issues. Due to constraints of the production method which has an equal ratio of male and female cavities in each mold, any set that includes a male character forces the company to think about and produce another set that includes a female character. The result is a toy brand where women are represented more than usual in the society in question (see figures 6–8).

---

21. Cohen, 467.

78 · Studying the Artifacts of Orthodox Childhoods

Figures 6–8 The Shabbat set includes an equal representation of genders. The study set includes only a male doll, and the kitchen set includes only a female doll. Gender roles are maintained, but gender representation across sets is higher than usual in Haredi society. Photos: Omar Friedman.

Lastly, another feature representing the brand's cultural ambivalence is the product's marketing content. The toy is described as being based on pure Jewish values on the one hand and as one that meets strict international standards on the other. On the one hand, it refers to high international standards of production and quality, which were crucial components in the development process. On the other hand, it conserves the values of the community and differentiates them. The brand's ambivalent nature is realized in many more of the product's features. Features like the non-Hebrew logo, the ability for the dolls to be playable with other western toys, the packages' graphic design, and some of the color and fashion choices in the dolls' design coexist with the product's Haredi nature. This coexistence personifies the cultural ambivalence in Haredi culture in Israel today.[22]

---

22. Zikherman, 99, 11.

Conclusion

Toys' agency to convey educational messages, Haredi society's relation to toys, dolls and play, and the new trend of toy design within the Haredi community were the starting point of this research. Modern Haredi society's unique traits juxtaposed with industrial toy constraints present the toys designed within the Haredi community as multi-faceted objects. These objects hold messages and discrepancies mirroring the cultural ambivalence of Haredi society in Israel today. This essay sought to provide a practice-based perspective and analysis of children's material culture, and to demonstrate how western technical choices and industrial toy production processes serve the product's religious and traditional message. It also demonstrates how contemporary design style and its secular nature may serve Jewish and even halakhic ideologies. The product is therefore a hybrid between modern Haredims' desire for western consumer culture, representing qualities like safety and good taste, and Haredi society's objection to this culture. This conjunction conceives a hybrid, culturally ambivalent toy that echoes the conflicting trends characterizing the society that creates it.

Diagramming Modesty

Goldie Gross and Yehudis Keller[1]

One of the most fundamental elements of an Orthodox Jewish girl's education is tznius, modesty. Tznius, as it is taught today, encompasses nearly every aspect of a girl's life, from the tone of her voice to the length of her skirt to where and how she is permitted to chew gum.[2] An overarching aim of the rules of tznius is to imbue Jewish girls with a sense of modesty. However, this is being done in increasingly immodest ways by imposing ever-more-stringent rules and regulations over minutiae of women's dress far beyond halachic (Jewish law) requirements. One pedagogical tool used in Jewish girls' schools and other settings that surpasses standard tznius requirements are tznius diagrams, instructive drawings demonstrating how to dress tzniusly.[3] While they are instituted to promote adherence to

---

1. The authors would like to thank, for their help in realizing this paper: Chaya Halberstam for helping think through the initial idea, Emmanuel Bloch for sharing otherwise inaccessible resources, Chaim Warshaw for the sources on tznius, and Rivkah Avins Pardue for sharing her unpublished thesis related to this topic.
2. Pesach Eliyahu Falk, *Oz Vehadar Levusha* (Nanuet, NY: Feldheim Publishers 1998), 46.
3. Ed: Linguistic note: The adjectival and adverbial forms of tznius (or tzniut) are usually created by adding a Yiddish suffix or Hebrew prefix: "tziusdig" or "be-tzniut," respectively. While "be-tzniut" flows more easily in English text, this usage is not reflective of the specific community in which tznius diagrams arose and continue to proliferate. "Tzniusdig" is an adjective and would re-

the rules of tznius and appear to be a benevolent phenomenon and an effective pedagogical tool, their history is rooted in misogynistic ideology about the intellectual capabilities of women, and their distribution may do more harm than good to their intended audience of Orthodox women and girls.

Tznius diagrams, a relatively recent phenomenon, are part of a larger trend of increasing modesty. Along with the codification of the rules of tznius and the erasure of women from ultra-Orthodox media (two quantifiable indicators of changing values), they promote strict tznius adherence as a response to perceived secularization in the western world. Indeed, photos found in yearbooks, family albums, magazines, and newspapers from years past paint a different picture than what one sees today when walking down the streets of ultra-Orthodox Brooklyn neighborhoods.[4] Books and pamphlets devoted to tznius dress codes and diagrams explicitly state that they are necessary because of immorality found in the culture in which religious communities are located.[5] This is tied to a general shift to the right in Orthodoxy that sociologist Samuel Heilman notes is a reaction to the "perceived decline of American culture beginning in the late 1960s and 1970s," when second-wave feminism, the sexual revolution, and unrest and radicalism among America's youth drew large numbers of Orthodox individuals from the fold.[6]

---

quire an additional suffix to make it an adverb, but this is not compatible with common usage, where the term is used as both adjective and adverb. The authors have therefore chosen to use only the English suffix "-ly" for accuracy and ease of comprehension.

4. Read, for one example of changing standards, Leslie Ginsparg Klein, "The Troubling Trend of Photoshopping History," *The Lehrhaus*, November 17, 2016, https://www.thelehrhaus.com/scholarship/the-troubling-trend-of-photoshopping-history/.

5. Language about this can be found, for example, in Reuven Brauner, trans., *Dress in Accordance with the Halochoh* (The Rabbinical Committee to Uphold the Honor of Jewish Sanctity n.d.), https://tznius.tips/dress-according-to-halacha.html, 3; Pesach Eliyahu Falk, *The Tznius Handbook: Educational Diagrams for Women and Girls (Pamphlet)* (n.p. 2010), 2.

6. Samuel C. Heilman, "Jews and Fundamentalism," *Jewish Political Studies*

In the realm of modesty, the shift to increased religiosity reached a peak in 1998 with the publication of a 706-page book detailing hyper-minutiae of tznius law called *Oz Vehadar Levusha* (with the English title *Modesty: An Adornment for Life*) written by Rabbi Pesach Eliyahu Falk. This book, possibly written as a more immediate response to the hypersexualized culture of the 1990s (manifested in Demi Moore posing nude and pregnant on a 1991 issue of *Vanity Fair*; the 1996 performance of Eve Ensler's *The Vagina Monologues*; Bill Clinton's affair with Monica Lewinsky, made public in early 1998; and the debut of Viagra that same year), helped move tznius from a general sense of modesty to a strict set of particular rules that govern the way women dress.[7] *Oz Vehadar Levusha* has had widespread influence in parts of the Orthodox world; as of 2006, approximately 45,000 copies of *Oz Vehadar Levusha* were sold.[8] This means that about 8% of the American Orthodox population owns a copy.[9]

In addition to Rabbi Falk's book, Emmanuel Bloch, in an essay about the development of what he terms "halakhic dress codes," counted over twenty books in five languages that "unequivocally qualify" as such compendia.[10] These books, several of which were expanded from pamphlets, are largely written by men for women, in

---

Review 17.1/2 (2005), 187; "A Portrait of Jewish Americans" (*Pew Research Center*, October 1, 2013), https://www.pewforum.org/wp-content/uploads/sites/7/2013/10/jewish-american-full-report-for-web.pdf, 50.
7. Rina Goloskov, "Modesty or Travesty? Understanding the Symbolic Annihilation of Women in Orthodox Jewish Media" (Master's Thesis, Towson University 2019), 8.
8. Pesach Eliyahu Falk, *The Tznius Handbook: Educational Diagrams for Women and Girls*, (Nanuet, NY: Feldheim Publishers 2010), 5.
9. Based on numbers from the Pew Center's "Portrait of Jewish Americans" survey, which estimates (using a restrictive definition of Jewish identity) that there are around 5,700,000 Jews and that 10% of them are Orthodox. "A Portrait of Jewish Americans," 10, 26.
10. Bloch has since discovered more than twenty additional books on this topic, published over the years. Emmanuel Bloch, "Immodest Modesty: The Emergence of Halakhic Dress Codes," *Studies in Judaism, Humanities, and the Social Sciences* 1.2 (2018), 25–32, https://journals.academicstudiespress.com

contrast to the usual female-to-female tznius pedagogy practiced in religious schools.[11] When used in an educational setting, these books promote the use of "schooling as the main method by which [rabbis and community leaders] [transmit] their values and prescriptions to the next generation of girls," often through their female teachers.[12] Several of these books contain what we term "tznius diagrams."

Tznius diagrams, illustrations of how to dress tzniusly, break down the wealth of information codified about the rules of tznius into digestible drawings. These drawings usually juxtapose women or woman-like figures wearing proper and improper dress with differentiating captions, often alongside text explicating the rules of tznius that the images reference. Studies show that this is an effective teaching tool: cognitive psychology proves that combining diagrams or photos with text has better learning outcomes than if one learns with either diagrams/photos or text alone.[13] Students also tend to think that any learning that combines multiple media formats is more effective than learning through one type of media, and this multimedia heuristic usually makes students subconsciously spend more time learning multimedia material and helps them retain the material at higher rates than if they learn with only one type of media.[14] Thus, distributing tznius diagrams to students may indeed be an effective teaching tool,

---

/index.php/SJHSS/article/view/102, 29; Emmanuel Bloch, email messages to author, March 10 and May 26, 2021.

11. Emmanuel Bloch, conversation with author, Zoom, March 15, 2021. For more on differences between text-based and mimetic learning and tznius, see Rivkah Avins Pardue, *Renewing Tradition Through Text: Tznius In 20th Century America* (Thesis, Barnard College 2021).

12. Leslie Ginsparg Klein, "'No Candy Store, No Pizza Shops, No Maxi-Skirt, No Makeup': Socializing Orthodox Jewish Girls Through Schooling," *The Journal of the History of Childhood and Youth* 9.1 (2016), 140.

13. Richard E. Mayer, ed., *Cambridge Handbook of Multimedia Learning*, 1st edition (Cambridge University Press 2005).

14. Michael J. Serra and John Dunlosky, "Metacomprehension Judgements Reflect the Belief That Diagrams Improve Learning from Text," *Memory* (Hove, England) 18.7 (October 2010), 698–711, https://doi.org/10.1080/09658211.2010.506441.

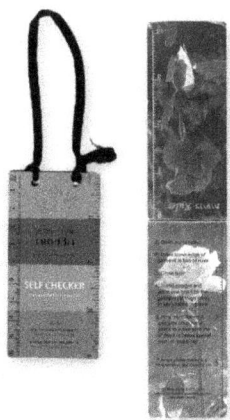

Figure 1 Two tznius rulers. (Photo courtesy Samuel Bialostozky.)

and many schools use them. In a survey distributed by the authors, 23 women of 44 total respondents recall receiving the diagrams in an educational setting as early as the first grade and throughout elementary and high school.[15]

Aside from being distributed individually to students, tznius diagrams are also put up as communal reminders of how to dress appropriately in schools and shuls, and they are hung as guides for buyers in some Jewish women's clothing stores. Diagrams designed for student distribution and communal display are either purpose-made or taken from pamphlets or books that fall under Bloch's definition of "halakhic dress codes." Furthermore, tools such as the tznius ruler have been developed to ensure that one's clothing complies with the rules of modesty (fig. 1).

Tznius diagrams are drawn in a variety of ways. They are often scanned line drawings or digital creations, and usually feature minimal shading and few details to better focus on the topic at hand. There are two distinct types of tznius diagrams: those that seek to eliminate

---

15. Eight of the respondents who said that they received tznius diagrams in an educational setting received them in elementary school, six received them in high school, and five received them in both elementary and high school. The remaining four respondents did not indicate when they received the diagrams. Additionally, the authors recall receiving them beginning from the sixth grade.

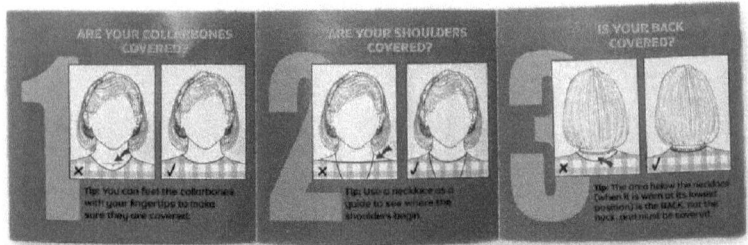

Figure 2a Neckline chart featuring faceless women.

Figure 2b Neckline chart featuring headless women. Photo originally published on A Mother in Israel (http://www.amotherinisrael.com/exclusive-official-haredi-guide-to-modest-necklines). Image link broken as of April 2021. The webpage was saved to an Evernote Notebook before the image link broke, where the image is viewable: http://bit.ly/modestnecklines.

anything feminine about their subjects by drawing women exclusive of their faces or heads, or by androgenizing their bodies (figs. 2a, 2b, 2c, and 2d); and, far rarer, those that represent women as they are, with faces and bodies intact.

While likely incidental, the outcome of using images in the first category can be considered pedagogically strategic, as "seductive details" (details added to learning materials to increase learner interest) often

Figure 2c Hair guide featuring women missing facial features. (Excerpt from Reuven Brauner, trans., Dress in Accordance with the Halochoh (The Rabbinical Committee to Uphold the Honor of Jewish Sanctity, n.d.), https://tznius.tips/dress-according-to-halacha.html.)

Figure 2d Shirt guide featuring primarily androgynous figures. (Excerpt from Shmuel Kats, Kedoshim tihyu: halakhot va-halikhot ba-hevrah uvi-tenu'ot no'ar (Jerusalem).)

confound a learner's understanding of their material.[16] This is supported for learning that is exclusively text-based and also for learning that combines text and illustrations.[17] In the case of tznius diagrams,

---

16. Ruth Garner, Mark G. Gillingham, and White C. Stephen, "Effects of 'Seductive Details' on Macroprocessing and Microprocessing in Adults and Children," *Cognition and Instruction* 6.1 (1989).

17. Suzanne Hidi and William Baird, "Strategies for Increasing Text-Based Interest and Students' Recall of Expository Texts," *Reading Research Quarterly* 23.4 (1988), 465–83, https://doi.org/10.2307/747644; Patricia Mohr, John A.

seductive details may be facial features or the realistic form of a woman. This makes drawings of featureless women dressing in accordance with the rules of tznius potentially effective at conveying how to properly follow these complex rules, as this type of diagram does not contain details that would distract the learner.

However, although this category of diagrams may have pedagogical value, such diagrams objectify women and girls by reducing the female body's role to that of an object bearing objects (clothing) that have the potential to arouse men. This serves a similar function to what Tova Hartman calls regressive discourse concerning tznius, which "[strips] women of even the most basic bodily integrity, constructing them as a collection of parts."[18] Unfortunately, no trait aside from a woman's role

---

Glover, and Royce R. Ronning, "The Effect of Related and Unrelated Details on the Recall of Major Ideas in Prose," *Journal of Reading Behavior*, 16.2 (1984), 97–108, https://doi.org/10.1080/10862968409547507; Larry L. Shirey and Ralph E. Reynolds, "Effect of Interest on Attention and Learning," *Journal of Educational Psychology* 80.2 (1988), 159–66, https://doi.org/10.1037/0022-0663.80.2.159; Suzanne E. Wade and Robert B. Adams, "Effects of Importance and Interest on Recall of Biographical Text," *Journal of Reading Behavior* 22.4 (1990), 331–53, https://doi.org/10.1080/10862969009547717; Shannon F. Harp and Richard E. Mayer, "The Role of Interest in Learning from Scientific Text and Illustrations: On the Distinction between Emotional Interest and Cognitive Interest," *Journal of Educational Psychology* 89.1 (1997), 92–102, https://doi.org/10.1037/0022-0663.89.1.92; Shannon F. Harp and Richard E. Mayer, "How Seductive Details Do Their Damage: A Theory of Cognitive Interest in Science Learning," *Journal of Educational Psychology* 90.3 (1998), 414–34, https://doi.org/10.1037/0022-0663.90.3.414.

18. Tova Hartman, *Feminism Encounters Traditional Judaism: Resistance and Accommodation* (Waltham, MA: Brandeis University Press 2007), 46. Hartman notes that "one of the main sources of resistance to egalitarian shifts within Modern Orthodox synagogue life is found in the discourse of *tzniut*." She goes on to specify that this includes issues of *mechitza* (a barrier between men and women in synagogue) and *kol isha* (which prohibits men from listening to women sing). Hartman also includes the phrase "*kol kevudah bas melech penima*," which roughly translates to "all honor of the daughter of a king (understood to mean a Jewish girl in today's context) is within." The primary motif on the cover of *Oz Vehadar Levusha* is a crown; on the spine and back cover of the book this phrase is underneath.

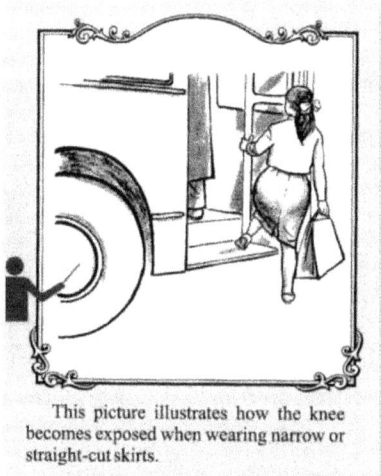

This picture illustrates how the knee becomes exposed when wearing narrow or straight-cut skirts.

Figure 3 Woman boarding a bus to show how the step affects her skirt. Excerpt from Reuven Brauner, trans., Dress in Accordance with the Halochoh (The Rabbinical Committee to Uphold the Honor of Jewish Sanctity, n.d.), https://tznius.tips/dress-according-to-halacha.html.

as clothing-wearer is apparent in these images. Occasionally, women in these drawings conduct activities, but they are for the sole sake of showing readers how these activities affect the positioning of their clothing (fig. 3). Drawings as such make women a function of tznius instead of incorporating tznius into the everyday life of a woman or girl – a missed opportunity to build an aspirational model of a modest career woman, a girl engaged in community service, or figures in line with community ideals of motherhood and religious piety.

This problematic interpretation of the symbolic meaning of these diagrams is tied to their misogynistic origin. Indeed, the basis for the use of diagrams to illustrate how to dress tzniusly is fraught with misogynistic ideas about the mental capabilities of women and girls. Rabbi Falk explicitly writes in *The Tznius Handbook: Educational Diagrams for Women and Girls* (a sequel to *Oz Vehadar Levusha*), that the use of diagrams is necessary:

> Experience has shown that even when explained clearly and precisely, whether in a *sefer* (book) or verbally at a *shiur* (lecture), the

requirements [of tznius] are often not properly understood... To many women the requirements of a Kosher neckline and hemline, loose-fitting skirt etc. are concepts from the past, and they find it difficult to understand what is required.[19]

Rabbi Falk here exhibits trouble differentiating a lack of comprehension on the part of women from temporary lapses in tznius or a general lack of willingness to fully comply with its strict rules. Rabbi Chaim Pinchas Scheinberg, too, in an introduction for a pamphlet derived from *The Tznius Handbook*, further underscores that diagrams are helpful because "due to household pressures and other commitments, many women neither have the stamina to read a long text nor to grasp guidelines by reading an instructive article."[20] The implication that women do not have the mental faculties to grasp the intricacies of tznius reduces the autonomy women exhibit in their outfit choices to a lack of capability to dress tzniusly without help from simplified guides and diagrams.

When one considers the origin of these diagrams, it is no wonder that the erasure of women's features is postulated as a necessary step for making these diagrams accessible. Rabbi Falk notes in the introduction to *The Tznius Handbook* that community leaders were consulted before the book's publication, and "their unanimous response was extremely positive and encouraging. They, however, stipulated the condition that the sketches must be kept as distant and as remote from real images as possible." In the forward to *The Tznius Handbook*, Rabbi Scheinberg additionally writes that because publishing diagrams is an unusual step, "great care is required to guarantee that no mishap occurs." Thus, "it is essential that neither the body shape nor facial features be seen on the diagrams."

But how does obscuring facial features protect women, the intended audience, or men, who are not meant to read this publication? Drawing on the work of philosopher Emmanuel Levinas, Shayna Abramson writes in an article about increasing restrictions in tznius

---

19. Falk, *The Tznius Handbook*, 3. Parentheses added.
20. Falk, *The Tznius Handbook*, 2.

and its ties to rape culture that "making the Jewish woman's face verboten not only contradicts hundreds of years of Jewish tradition, but also sends the message that Jewish men don't have a moral responsibility towards Jewish women."[21] Men's lack of moral responsibility is highlighted in the forward to the *Tznius Handbook* pamphlet (its subtitle, "educational diagrams for women and girls," denotes its intended audience), as Rabbi Scheinberg writes that "if in spite of this precaution [the gendered subtitle], a man browses through it's [sic] pages, it will almost certainly do no harm."[22] Besides exhibiting a double-standard on who must follow rules, because these illustrations are meant to be seen by women with only incidental male readership, erasing women's faces communicates that even this part of their body must be hidden so as not to possibly lead even transgressive men to sin.

This foreword underscores the lack of responsibility men are ultimately perceived as having over their gaze and actions. Tznius is currently framed as a woman's obligation, but according to textual support for tznius rules, the onus is often upon men not to look.[23] Rabbi Scheinberg, in his foreword, implies that the drawings' lack of body shapes and features ensures that this pamphlet is free of temptation, never mind that it may make it less interesting for women. This promotes the idea that the moral responsibility for a man's gaze and actions rests upon women and girls and the way they dress. To add insult to injury, Rabbi Falk, in his foreword to the first edition of *The Tznius Handbook*, writes that "ideally, even vague sketches of women should be avoided," implying that any semblance of a woman or girl is problematic, even in a book intended for women.[24]

---

21. Shayna Abramson, "Faceless: Do Extreme Tznius Codes Perpetuate Rape Culture?" The New York Jewish Week, *JOFA Blog*, August 16, 2017, http://jewishweek.timesofisrael.com/faceless/.
22. Falk, *The Tznius Handbook*, 2.
23. For several examples of this, see Dov Linzer, "Tzniut, Halakha and the Male Gaze: Lecture and Sources," *YC Torah Library*, August 10, 2016, https://library.yctorah.org/2016/08/tzniut-halakha-and-the-male-gaze-lecture-and-sources.
24. Falk, *The Tznius Handbook*, 1.

This is particularly troublesome as a substantial audience for tznius diagrams is developing girls as part of their tznius-learning process. By teaching adolescent girls that their bodies must be concealed from the male eye lest they lead the beholder to sin, the opportunity to form a healthy relationship with their maturing bodies free from societal pressures fades to the background. In this way, tznius seems to be taught at the cost of self-esteem, particularly positive body image. This is especially ironic as tznius is often framed as a way to *protect* women from secular culture's undressing and objectification of women.[25] Unfortunately, in its more reactionary forms, tznius becomes precisely that: a mode of objectifying its practitioners by breaking the body down into its composite parts in order to dress them "appropriately."

Indeed, positive benefits that may result from sheltering children in a religious community may be attenuated by an obsessive focus on tznius. Unhealthy relationships with their bodies puts many girls on the path to life-threatening issues, such as eating disorders, which are heavily linked to body image.[26] While studies have consistently proven that religious individuals have better mental and physical health, when it comes to disordered eating pathology (a group of behaviors displayed by someone who has or will develop an eating disorder) and body image dissatisfaction, Orthodox girls have no advantage – studies have shown them to be similar in this realm to secular or non-Jewish women and girls.[27] A cause of this may be tznius: psy-

---

25. Hartman, *Feminism Encounters Traditional Judaism*, 45–46.
26. "Feeding and Eating Disorders," in *Diagnostic and Statistical Manual of Mental Disorders, DSM Library* (American Psychiatric Association 2013), https://doi.org/10.1176/appi.books.9780890425596.dsm10.
27. Linda K. George, Christopher G. Ellison, and David B. Larson, "Explaining the Relationships Between Religious Involvement and Health," *Psychological Inquiry* 13.3 (2002), 190–200, https://doi.org/10.1207/S15327965PLI1303 _04; Harold G Koenig, "Research on Religion, Spirituality, and Mental Health: A Review," *The Canadian Journal of Psychiatry* 54.5 (2009), 283–91, https://doi.org/10.1177/070674370905400502; William R. Miller and Carl E. Thoresen, "Spirituality, Religion, and Health: An Emerging Research Field," *American Psychologist* 58.1 (2003), 24–35, https://doi.org/10.1037/0003-066X.58.1.24;

chologist Minna Loketch-Fischer found that modesty laws are a predictor of eating disorders among ultra-Orthodox women.[28] So while it has been theorized that religiosity contains protective factors that shield religious women and girls from eating disorder development, studies have not supported this claim. Furthermore, making women and girls feel guilty about their bodies via halachic pressure to cover them is likely to aggravate lurking psychological problems.[29] The pressure to conform to rigid modesty laws from a young age, combined with an expectation to be thin for the matchmaking process and other unique laws and social norms pertaining to Jewish women, may work against the protective variables that religiosity in Jewish Orthodox communities may offer, such as limited access to secular media and a community-oriented focus.

Thus, while they may be a useful pedagogical tool, tznius diagrams are likely doing more harm than good when it comes to the mental health of Orthodox adolescent girls. As Hartman so poignantly writes:

> Under the bright, surgical lamp of halakhic scrutiny of their bodies...and the inescapable spotlight of a gaze that is at turns domineering and fearful, but never less than severe, women are

---

Marjorie C. Feinson and Adi Meir, "Disordered Eating and Religious Observance: A Focus on Ultra-orthodox Jews in an Adult Community Study," *International Journal of Eating Disorders* 45.1 (2012), 101–9, https://doi.org/10.1002/eat.20895; Marjorie C. Feinson and Tzipi Hornik-Lurie, "Body Dissatisfaction and the Relevance of Religiosity: A Focus on Ultra-Orthodox Jews in a Community Study of Adult Women," *Clinical Social Work Journal* 44.1 (2016), 87–97, https://doi.org/10.1007/s10615-016-0574-5.

28. Minna Loketch-Fischer, *The Relationship Among Modesty, Self Objectivication, Body Shame and Eating Disorder Symptoms in Jewish Women* (Diss. Hofstra University 2016).

29. Julie Juola Exline and Ephraim Rose, "Religious and Spiritual Struggles," in *Handbook of the Psychology of Religion and Spirituality* (New York, NY: The Guilford Press 2005), 315–30; Nava R. Silton and Joshua Fogel, "Religiosity, Empathy, and Psychopathology among Young Adult Children of Rabbis," *Archive for the Psychology of Religion* 32.3 (September 2010), 277–91, https://journals.sagepub.com/doi/abs/10.1163/157361210X532040.

encouraged, both overtly and implicitly, to think of themselves not in terms of their ineffable spirit, of the whole that is greater than the sum of its parts, but of the parts themselves. This dismembering (in every sense of the word) is what has emerged, within contemporary Orthodox discourse, as a working definition of *tzniut*.[30]

Tznius diagrams, in their current form, reduce women to mere parts. This hyperphysicality runs counter to the values that religious teachers strive to teach their students about tznius. Thus, the popular tagline of tznius, *Kol Kevudah Bas Melech Penima* (all honor of the daughter of a king is within), seems to be at odds with the current practice of emphasizing so strongly what is without.

---

30. Hartman 54.

The *Shomer Negiah* Song: A Touchy Subject

Talia Weisberg

In the Orthodox Jewish community, *shemirat negiah* – the religious practice of not touching members of the opposite sex except for immediate family members – is part of everyday life. "The *Shomer Negiah* Song," a lighthearted take on the topic of interpersonal touch between girls and boys, is a popular ditty among girls in the left wing of the yeshivish community. The song both subverts and upholds communal norms, allowing girls to use humor as a way to create community around a shared in-group identifier and assert their belonging within Orthodoxy.

As "The *Shomer Negiah* Song" is a folksong, there is no definitive version. However, the lyrics are usually something like the following:

1. 'Cause I'm *shomer negiah*, so leave me alone
2. If you wanna get closer, then pick up the phone
3. Stay on your side of the line, and I'll stay on mine
4. 'Cause my body's exclusively mine

Some include a second verse:

5. That means no hugging or kissing, no touching at all
6. If you need something to lean on, there's always the wall
7. Stay on your side of the line, and I'll stay on mine
8. 'Cause my body's exclusively mine

Those who do not include the second verse often insert line 6 instead of line 2.

Another notable version changes line 2 to "If you (wanna) reach out and touch me, use Bell telephone," which is a clever take on Bell's "reach out and touch someone" jingle, which was launched in 1979 and stayed on the air throughout the 1980s.[1] Other versions of the second stanza finish the verse with "No touching is the rule / If you do I'll get kicked out of school" and "Because my parents will be home after nine." Another significant change is the usage of the word "beautifully" instead of "exclusively" in lines 4 and 8.

Context

"The *Shomer Negiah* Song" is thought to have originated in Camp Sternberg, a popular all-girls summer camp in Narrowsburg, NY. Sternberg is part of the SHMA network of camps that caters to the left-leaning, or "modern," wing of the yeshivish community. Its composer and her (or his) motives are unknown, although it was most likely a camper or group of campers who wrote it, as camp staff would have been almost certain to censor or otherwise quash such an edgy song. The exact date of composition is uncertain, but it parodies the chorus of the 1984 song *"B'Siyata D'Shmaya"* by the Miami Boys Choir,[2] a popular yeshivish singing ensemble, so it could not have been written earlier than the mid-1980s. It is also unclear whether it was composed, popularized, or just sung regularly at Sternberg; many also learned

---

1. "Remember that AT&T Jingle, 'Reach Out – Reach Out and Touch Someone? Hear It Again & Find Out more," *Click Americana: Vintage & Retro Memories*, n.d. https://clickamericana.com/eras/1970s/reach-out-reach-out-and-touch-someone-1979–1982.
2. Yerachmiel Begun, "B'Siyata D'shmaya," *Miami Boys Choir: B'Siyata D'Shmaya*, Yerachmiel Begun and the Miami Boys Choir, 1984. Some say that it's a parody of the "It's Min Hashomayim," from the 1992 album of the same name. The tune of both choruses are very similar and either could feasibly work. Line 3 of "B'Siyata D'Shmaya" and "It's Min Hashomayim" includes the word "'cause" in the same places, but it's possible that the song morphed to sound more like "It's Min Hashomayim" after it was released a few years later.

it while they attended programs through NCSY, a centrist, coeducational Modern Orthodox *kiruv* (religious outreach) organization that partners observant and non-observant youth to encourage the latter's religious growth. Although Sternberg and NCSY cater to notably different populations, it is possible that girls who attended Sternberg (or friends of those girls, or friends of those friends) volunteered at NCSY events and used "The *Shomer Negiah* Song" to encourage the (female) non-observant attendees to take on *shemirat negiah*.

Regardless of its point of origin, the song has spread beyond both Sternberg and NCSY, as women from a range of Orthodox institutional affiliations can wax nostalgic about singing it as teens. Although it is found in diverse corners of the Orthodox community on both the left and right, it is most popular in the modern yeshivish world, and is also popularly found in the adjacent right-wing Modern Orthodox community. Unless they have sisters or wives who taught it to them or were exposed to it while participating in a coeducational program, boys and men are largely ignorant of the song's existence. This is likely because it is generally only sung among women, as the religious dictate of *kol isha* prohibits men from hearing women sing. Additionally, mixed-gender spaces that would be conducive to singing lighthearted songs are relatively rare, if not entirely unheard of, in the communities where this song is most heard. Especially in light of the fact that it was popularized and most likely also composed at a single-sex girls' camp, it is clear that this song is not intended to actually warn away boys who might be tempted to touch a girl. Rather, it must exist for the sake of the girls themselves.

Arguably the main reason that girls sing the song is because it's funny and can make their peers laugh. Especially in settings like camp or a *shabbaton*, when school is out and everyone just wants to have a good time with their friends, singing something like "The *Shomer Negiah* Song" serves the same function as telling a joke. By the standards of even the most liberal sector of the yeshivish community, it is so edgy as to be basically off-color humor, but still just within the limits of acceptability. This is at least partially because the idea of touching a boy before marriage is fully foreign to the average yeshivish

The author with her classmates on the last day of high school in the lobby of the school building, interrupting dismissal procedures with an impromptu singing session (Manhattan High School for Girls, 2013). The Shomer Negiah song was sung in similar contexts across girls' institutions.

girl. Although "The *Shomer Negiah* Song" functionally advocates for the observance of *negiah*, the fact that it overtly acknowledges the possibility of violating it makes the song irreverently entertaining.

"The *Shomer Negiah* Song" is not only sung for humorous purposes, but also to create and reinforce a sense of community. It is validating for a group to raise their voices in song together and hear the sound of singing coming from every individual, for one girl to know the same words as every other girl in the room despite the fact that it's not a song heard on the radio or popularized by the mainstream media. This creates a bond beyond whatever actual meaning the lyrics hold. In this way, girls are able to connect with their peers, regardless of physical location. Song sung together is powerful and creates a strong bond of sisterhood, especially in an all-women's setting.

In addition, the song builds a sense of community around the shared value and observance of *shemirat negiah*, communicating a worldview in support of the practice. Considering the funny aspect of the song, it is clearly intended to be sung with others around to appreciate the humor. In this case, the listeners are not only there to laugh, but to give implicit approval of the practice of *negiah* in particular and observance of the halakhic system in general, to endorse the message that the singer is trying to send. For the individual singing the song, it is strengthening and affirming for other girls to sing along, but that much listener participation is usually not even necessary from the singer's perspective. The simple act of being there is enough to create a sense of shared community over *shemirat negiah*.

Subversive Elements

Although the song functionally legitimizes the practice of *negiah*, there is some more subversive content to the song. The line "Because my body's exclusively mine," which appears in both stanzas, clearly draws upon feminist discourse about women's right to control what happens to their own bodies. Although Bais Yaakov girls are not generally experts in feminist philosophy, the principles of "girl power" and women's right to bodily autonomy have become common enough in pop culture that they have trickled into Orthodoxy. It is likely that the composer unwittingly borrowed from this source, since the right-leaning Orthodox community is by and large apathetic or overtly hostile towards the modern feminist movement. In feminist parlance, this language is used to say that women should be the only ones to decide what happens to their bodies. For yeshivish girls, this sort of freedom is irrelevant, as all of their life choices are informed by the halakhic system and communal norms that are generally informed by halakhic mandates. Instead, "The *Shomer Negiah* Song" co-opts the idea of bodily autonomy and makes it relevant for a demographic that (at least, in theory) places the dictates of halakha above everything else. Nonetheless, there is irony in the fact that yeshivish girls who are singing the song are most likely unaware of the radical roots of what they are saying.

A more obviously controversial line is "If you wanna get closer, then pick up the phone." The idea of a teenage boy and girl speaking on the phone is, in a word, scandalous. In the yeshivish world, segregation of boys and girls begins basically at birth and never ceases in frequency or intensity. Although young women in the more modern subsections of the yeshivish community may have limited interactions with boys such as their brothers' friends or friends' brothers, the only officially sanctioned interactions that members of the opposite sex have with one another is once they start "*shidduch* dating" in their early twenties, when men and women can meet after being set up by a matchmaker and thoroughly vetted as suitably marriageable by each other's parents. "Stay on your side of the line, and I'll stay on mine" is an indication of the sex-segregated reality that yeshivish teens experience. Although many of the forms of sex segregation within Orthodoxy are not overtly required by halakha, contact between boys and girls is discouraged, especially in the teenage years, as marriage is still far off and casual dating is not accepted due to the likelihood of violating *negiah*. Because of this, a phone call between a boy and girl would be severely frowned upon, and would likely hurt both of their reputations.

Consequently, it makes sense that some versions of the song get rid of the mention of speaking on the phone, and replace the line with the much less iniquitous idea, "If you need something to lean on, there's always the wall." This contains feminist undertones in a similar vein to the line "Because my body's exclusively mine," since it is saying, in very bold and unapologetic terms, that the singer is not there for anybody else's benefit. Her body is her own to do as she pleases with, and if a boy wants "something to lean on," i.e., to touch a girl, he has to find someone else to do so with, because she is not willing to use her body for that purpose.

Although "Stay on your side of the line and I'll stay on mine / Because my body's exclusively mine" is a more popular way to end both stanzas of the song, there also exists a version that goes "No touching is the rule / If you do I'll get kicked out of school." It is important to note that the lyric indicates "If *you* do *I'll* get kicked out," reflecting a double standard for boys and girls. The girls singing this song are indicating that they understand that touching boys is "the rule" – i.e., it is halakhically forbidden – but that the punishment for violating *negiah* (or interacting with boys in general) extends beyond divine sanction in the form of getting blacklisted in the community and its institutions. Although boys who interact with girls may also be judged negatively and receive some communal backlash, girls suffer disproportionately for "bad" behavior; this largely reflects the situation in contemporary American society, where gossip centers on girls who engaged in sexual activity but not nearly as much, if at all, on the boy she did it with.

Another alternate ending of the song is "Stay on your side of the line, and I'll stay on mine / Because my parents will be home after nine." This particularly subversive version adds an element of honesty to the song that is absent in the others, as it acknowledges a mutual desire to violate *negiah* and "cross the line," even if both parties understand that the ensuing communal disapproval would not be worth the tradeoff. Assuming that the person singing is a girl who is attracted to boys, the rest of the song indicates that the boy is the one who wants to disregard *negiah*, as it begins with the command to "leave me alone" and continues on in this vein. In contrast, "Because my parents will be home after nine" recognizes that *negiah* is difficult for girls as well as boys and that people of all genders can feel sexual desire. As the yeshivish community actively suppresses the discussion of sexuality, it is not surprising that this is by far the least known ending to "The Shomer Negiah Song." Even an open-minded adult who could tolerate the rest of the song would be almost certain to censor this line for its notably immodest tone, and many girls would understand this in advance and self-censor by using a different version.

Normative Elements

Despite being intended for and primarily sung by girls, the song begins with the words "'Cause I'm *shomer negiah*," the word *shomer* being in the masculine (*shomeret* would be the correct feminine form). English-speaking Orthodox Jews do not generally gender or conjugate Hebrew or Yiddish words or phrases correctly when inserting them into an otherwise English sentence, so this could be dismissed as simply symptomatic of the Orthodox community's speech patterns. However, the fact that the masculine is used even when it comes to groups that are exclusively female is also indicative of how the Orthodox world still views "woman" as a marked category. It is telling that it uses the masculine form to express a commitment to adherence to halakha in particular. "The *Shomer Negiah* Song" functions as a way for girls to affirm their belonging in the yeshivish community despite being othered as female, upholding their adherence to communal norms and halakhic observance despite the fact that even the basics of yeshivish grammar places them on the outside.

In addition, "The *Shomer Negiah* Song" is normative because it is functionally an exhortation for girls to observe the halakha and abstain from touching boys until they marry one. Although the song certainly contains subversive elements when fully analyzed, the plain meaning of the lyrics clearly indicates that the purpose is to validate *negiah* as a social construct and strengthen girls' conviction to actually observe it. It may be humorous and irreverent, but it still upholds normative assumptions about heterosexual attraction, the gender binary, and the importance of halakhic observance in the individual's life.

Conclusion

The Miami Boys Choir likely did not expect one of their songs to turn into a decades-old parody about *shemirat negiah*, but the inventive minds of Orthodox girls created and perpetuated this amusing jingle. It is impossible to say for sure why the "The *Shomer Negiah* Song" has retained such popularity for over thirty years, but likely reasons include that it builds community among its singers; that it is provocative enough to be entertaining but not so sketchy as to be immediately censored; and that it has a familiar tune and repetitive, rhyming, easy-to-remember lyrics. Its references to female bodily autonomy, sex segregation, communal double standards, and sexuality (albeit in a veiled way) are all overt enough to make the song subversive in its yeshivish context, but the song's main purposes – as an in-group identifier, and to encourage the observance of *negiah* – add more normativity to the song. As a cultural artifact of Orthodox childhood and adolescence, "The *Shomer Negiah* Song" both shapes and reflects girls' self-perception in the yeshivish community, allowing them to experiment with its boundaries and find their place within them.

Part II
The Songs and Music of Orthodox Childhoods

Parody and Pathos: The Art of Country Yossi

Elli Fischer[1]

Yossi Toiv, who goes by the stage name of Country Yossi, has fashioned a remarkable career as a comic entertainer in the New York area's *frum* communities. His media empire includes a magazine, radio show, games, and other merchandise, in addition to royalties from perhaps the most recognizable Jewish tune in history: the "Kars 4 Kids" jingle, composed by Toiv and originally recorded as "Little Kinderlach."[2] This empire grew out of a series of albums that appeared in the 1980s, five albums of *Country Yossi and the Shteeble Hoppers* and four of *Kivi & Tuki*. Most of the *Shteeble Hoppers* recordings were reworkings of popular American songs of the 1950s, 60s and 70s, especially country music hits, that he supplied with new lyrics familiar to *frum* audiences. The *Kivi & Tuki* series is geared toward younger children and features two childlike, squeaky-voiced characters reminiscent of *Alvin and the Chipmunks*.

The lyrics supplied by Toiv, which playfully invert the lyrics of the imitated songs in both series, are often very humorous. Of course,

---

1. With thanks to Rabbis Daniel Goldstein, Uri Goldstein, Elli Schorr, Ariel Rackovsky, Daniel Yolkut, and the people of #FrumTwitter.
2. Yossi Toiv, "Little Kinderlach," *Country Yossi & The Shteeble-Hoppers Volume 1: Wanted!*, CY Productions, 1983.

there is a long tradition of American Jewish parody of popular tunes. Mickey Katz and His Kosher-Jammers were recording parodies like *"Haim afen Range"* in a mix of English and Yiddish even before Toiv's birth in 1949.[3] The year before the first Country Yossi album appeared, Martin Davidson released the first of over a dozen "Rechnitzer Rejects" albums, which the cover labels "musical parodies and paradoxes of modern day Jewish life."[4] Shlock Rock, the most prolific Jewish-themed parody band, got their start in 1986, soon after Country Yossi. Though undoubtedly comic, Toiv's lyrics often seem to be something other than parody. Their goal is not to satirize or make light of the themes contained in the songs he imitates or of modern Jewish life. Rather, in many cases he supplies a different narrative and linguistic context to capture the sentiments of the earlier works in a way that resonates with his *frum* audience.

Consider the relationship between "The Blind Man in the Bleachers"[5] and Toiv's "Deaf Man in the Shteeble."[6] Each song tells the story of a performer – in one case a high school football player, and in the other a synagogue cantor – whose disabled father insists on attending his son's every performance even though he does not have the physical tools to appreciate them. The stories reach their climax when, on one particularly meaningful occasion – the last game of the season and Yom Kippur Eve – the father is absent, and the son turns in the performance of his life. Afterward, the authority figure – head coach and rabbi, respectively – asks what inspired such a remarkable performance. The son responds that his father recently passed away, so: "It's the first time my father's seen me play / heard me pray."

---

3. Mickey Katz and His Kosher Jammers, *"Haim afen Range,"* Yiddish Square Dance, RCA Victor, 1947.
4. On Rechnitzer Rejects, see: Elliott Oring, "Rechnitzer Rejects: An Unorthodox Humor of Modern Orthodoxy," *Jokes and their Relations* (Lexington, KY: University of Kentucky Press, 1992), 68–82.
5. David Geddes, "The Last Game of the Season (A Blind Man in the Bleachers)," single, Big Tree Records, 1975.
6. Yossi Toiv, "Deaf Man in the Shteeble," *Country Yossi & The Shteeble-Hoppers Volume 4: Captured*, CY Productions, 1987.

Parody and Pathos: The Art of Country Yossi · 109

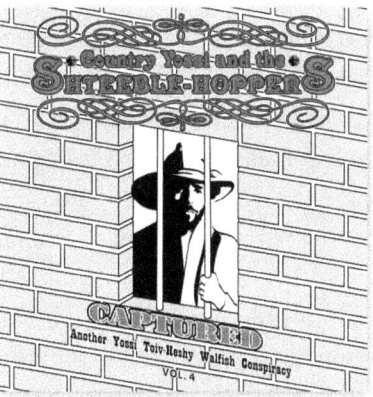
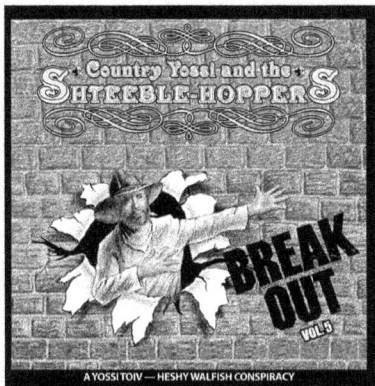

Country Yossi and the Shteeble-Hoppers, Volumes 1–6.

"Deaf Man in the Shteeble" is undoubtedly playful, and the listener who is familiar with "Blind Man in the Bleachers" cannot help but appreciate Toiv's clever imitations of the Geddes's lyrics: "And half the crowd can hear his coach yell, 'Where the hell you been?'" becomes, "And half the *shul* can hear the rabbi ask, 'How come so late?'" But it is also clear that this is not parody. Toiv is not poking fun at "Blind Man" but attempting to harness, replicate, and even heighten its sentimental effect for an audience that may not have familiarity with "Blind Man" but certainly understands the sense of awe, beauty, and tension that permeates the *shul* as the *chazzan* begins *Kol Nidrei* and the pride that a father must feel upon hearing his son offer a flawless rendition of its enchanting tune. I can personally attest that Toiv succeeds: "Deaf Man in the Shteeble" has indeed brought many people to tears.

With this in mind, we can take a closer look at songs from Country Yossi's earliest albums with an eye toward understanding the experiences that the lyricist is trying to evoke, through both his original lyrics and the lyrics of the imitated song. I will show that Toiv, in these lyrics, is describing the themes, characters, and landscapes that populate a world – his world – and, taken together, link him to a very particular set of experiences, bound by time and place. Ultimately, I will argue that Yossi Toiv, through his lyrics, successfully captures the voice and pathos of his generation.

The Men and Women, Parents and Children, of the Shteeble

FRUM JEWISH MEN

The first track on the first *Shteeble Hoppers* album is "'Cause I'm a Jew,"[7] which imitates Johnny Cash's "I Walk the Line."[8] In Cash's song, the key theme is fidelity: The singer – "I" – assures a significant other –

---

7. Yossi Toiv, "'Cause I'm a Jew," *Country Yossi & The Shteeble-Hoppers Volume 1: Wanted!*, CY Productions, 1983.
8. Johnny Cash, "I Walk the Line," *Johnny Cash with his Hot and Blue Guitar*, Sun Records, 1956.

"you" – that his love keeps him vigilant and makes it easy for him to stay out of trouble: "Because you're mine, I walk the line." Country Yossi's imitation introduces humor, but of a self-mocking sort. The entire song is a litany of things that Jews do that seem strange to outsiders:

> *Oh, once a year I twirl a chicken over my head,*
> *And it wouldn't be that bad if it were dead,*
> *And there's a time when I go outside and burn my bread,*
> *Cause I'm a Jew, I do that too.*

Though the refrain specifies, "Because the Torah tells me to, I do that, too," the litany is an amalgamation of Torah commandments ("I shake a *lulav*, which my neighbors think insane"), enactments of the early Rabbis ("I *daven Mincha* in the proper time"), established customs (the aforementioned chicken-twirling), and simple folkways ("I like to bury my *gefilte fish* in *chrein*"), without differentiating. Additionally, the "Jew" of the title is Ashkenazi, as evidenced by the Yiddish terminology and the particularly Ashkenazic customs and cuisine: one buries their *gefilte fish* in *chrein* because one is a Jew, notwithstanding the specific geographic location associated with *gefilte fish* and *chrein*, which Sephardic and Mizrahi Jews do not share.[9] Finally, the first line of the song, "I wear a *kippah* on this head of mine," and a line in the refrain, "I do the strangest things a man could ever do," indicate that the titular Jew is male.

The image that emerges from these lyrics is that the singer is reflexively observant. The details and origins of particular observances do not interest him, nor do the practices of unfamiliar and exotic Jewish groups (non-traditional Jews, non-Ashkenazim, and women) cause him to consider a broader understanding of what it means to be a Jew.

---

9. One of the best-known tracks on the same album, "The Cholent Song" (an imitation of: Dion, "Donna the Prima Donna," *Donna the Prima Donna*, Columbia Records, 1963) plays on a similar theme. The singer ate a traditional Jewish food on Shabbos and finds himself still paying a price a week later, as *cholent* is more of a fuel or weapon than a food. Country Yossi's lyrics also mention kugel (both potato and *lokshen*), latkes, Paskesz's (a brand of kosher candy), knishes – and pizza.

And yet, despite the self-mockery and patently narrow configuration of Jewishness implied by the song, it is a song about fidelity. This dimension of the song is reinforced through its relationship to the song it imitates, "I Walk the Line." The singer does all these things, despite the ridicule (with which he, on some level, identifies), because he is a Jew and the Torah tells him to.

CHILDREN: BOYS AND GIRLS

The song "Little Kinderlach," an original musical composition by Toiv, is likewise a litany, but rather than telling what a Jew does, it lists the things that will "make Moshiach come" if children will do them. This list differentiates "little boys" from "little girls." The former will bring the messiah if he "goes to *yeshiva*...learns Hashem's Torah...wears his *tallis katan* and kisses his *tzitzis* when he says the *Shema*...stays in *shul* and stands with his father to listen to the Torah." The latter "sings *Birchas Hamazon*, and says every word, with holy *kavana*... *davens* each morning, and gives her allowance away for *tzedaka*... goes every Shabbos to visit the sick and the lonely old people." "Little Kinderlach" does not list things as strange as those in "'Cause I'm a Jew," gives observance a higher purpose, relates to boys and girls in equal measure, and focuses on observances that apply to disparate Jewish communities. Still, it remains somewhat reflexive and unexamined.

The list for "little boys" consists primarily of extroverted, performative rituals. They dictate what he wears and demand his physical presence in communal institutions. The "little girls," on the other hand, will "make Moshiach come" through a mix of rituals like prayers and acts of kindness, giving charity and visiting the sick and lonely. Some of the ritual acts listed can be private: there is an expectation that she prays, but she need not stay in *shul*, and *Birkat Ha-mazon* is recited wherever one had a meal, regardless of institutional context. Moreover, non-performative dimensions of ritual – having "holy *kavana*" – are emphasized. The other ritual acts put the little girl in the role of caretaker of the community: she gives her allowance away to those who need it and takes care of the sick and elderly.

WOMEN

The role of women – particularly wives – is caricatured in "Peel One More Potato,"[10] an imitation of Shel Silverstein's "Put Another Log on the Fire."[11] In both the original and the imitation, the narrator instructs his wife to perform a series of menial and demeaning chores, "Then come and tell me why you're leavin' me." The chores assigned by Country Yossi's narrator ("Peel one more potato for the *kugel*; wash my *tzitzis* and hang them out to dry; dust my *shas* and bake some Shabbos *challahs*") are Jewish inversions of the chores assigned in the original ("Put another log on the fire; cook me up some bacon and some beans; go out to the car and change the tire"). The wife's many chores are contrasted with the husband's conviction that he treats her well. In both versions, the caricature works because it acknowledges and exaggerates prevailing disparities, in which the wife bears the brunt of the domestic burden and assists her husband's performance of ritual commandments ("wash my *tzitzis* ... dust my *shas* ..."). Neither song suggests what can be done to remedy the broken relationship. Should the husband wash his own *tzitzis*? Should he encourage his wife to wear *tzitzis* herself? More likely, he should merely temper expectations and do more around the house so that the burden is shared more equitably, without reassigning traditional roles.

"Peel One More Potato" is the closest that Country Yossi comes to acknowledging that there is something problematic about the way women are treated in the world he inhabits. Women are not frequently mentioned in Country Yossi songs, and when they are, they are invariably passive. In "A Boy Named Zlateh,"[12] the narrator's mother

---

10. Yossi Toiv, "Peel One More Potato," *Country Yossi & The Shteeble-Hoppers Volume 1: Wanted!*, CY Productions, 1983.
11. Tompall Glaser, "Put Another Log on the Fire (The Male Chauvinist National Anthem)," *Tompall (Sings the Songs of Shel Silverstein)*, Evil Eye Music Inc, 1975.
12. Yossi Toiv, "A Boy Named Zlateh," *Country Yossi & The Shteeble-Hoppers Volume 2: Strike Again*, CY Productions, 1984 (imitating: Johnny Cash, "A Boy Named Sue," *At San Quentin*, Columbia Records, 1969).

was abandoned by her husband, yet she keeps a photo of him. At the end of the song, the deadbeat father is credited with educating his son, and the angry son even begs his father's pardon for being angry at him. The mother's decades of single parenting barely register. In another instance, a woman in an original song is replaced by an inanimate object in Country Yossi's imitation: Tommy's girlfriend Becky, the victim of the Gatlin boys' assault in "Coward of the County,"[13] is transposed into a *shteeble*, which is being vandalized by "three *shkotzim*" in "Nebich of the Shteeble."[14] Likewise, both Tommy and his analogue, Moishy, are introduced as being fatherless: the narrator of the song is the dead father's brother who "looked after" Tommy/Moishy. We are never introduced to the mother. Finally, in a *Kivi & Tuki* number, "Who Did a Mitzva?"[15] Tuki claims that he did a mitzvah by kissing his Bubby. Country Yossi laughs at him and tells him that is not a mitzvah. Then the studious Kivi says that he kissed his *mezuzah*, which is celebrated as a mitzvah. In addition to being normatively problematic, in this equation the grandmother is contrasted unfavorably with an inanimate object. Both are objects, but Bubby is not even the object of a mitzvah.

RABBIS

Although the lyrics of some songs are implicitly didactic (as are most of the songs on the *Kivi & Tuki* albums), and they no doubt helped shape the attitudes of a generation of listeners, Country Yossi's lyrics never adopt the perspective of a recognized communal authority – a rabbi, teacher, or the like. The perspective is almost always that of a non-elite who received a Jewish education in the home, school, and yeshiva, is perfectly at home in Jewish culture, knows how to be a proper Jew, and is willing to share that knowledge. In fact, the

---

13. Kenny Rogers, "Coward of the County," *Kenny*, United Artists, 1979.
14. Yossi Toiv, "Nebich of the Shteeble," *Country Yossi & The Shteeble-Hoppers Volume 2: Strike Again*, CY Productions, 1984.
15. Yossi Toiv, "Who Did a Mitzva?" *Kivi & Tuki Volume 3: Boker Tov, Layla Tov*, CY Productions, 1987.

attitude toward rabbis expressed in Country Yossi's songs is somewhat ambivalent.

The natural place to start this discussion is with "The Rabbi,"[16] a song from the debut *Shteeble-Hoppers* album that imitates Kenny Rogers' "The Gambler."[17] The stories told in the original and in its imitation are similar. On a long ride, the narrator gets to talking with a fellow traveler, the titular gambler or rabbi, who, in exchange for a few sips of whiskey and a cigarette, dispenses a bit of sage advice that the narrator finds life-altering. Some features of the Country Yossi version simply alter the setting for a different culture. The advice dispensed by the rabbi is universal[18] and similar to that of the gambler. Both songs begin on "a warm summer evening," but instead of being "on a train bound for nowhere," Toiv's duo are "on a ride to Monticello," the Catskills village that becomes a center of activity for the myriad summer camps and bungalow colonies for New York's *frum* Jews each summer – the "country" of Country Yossi, to which I will return. As opposed to Rogers's gambler, Toiv's rabbi recites a traditional blessing before falling asleep and does not die during the course of the journey.

The most salient difference between the two songs is that in Toiv's version, the narrator speaks in English, while the rabbi speaks only in Yiddish. In "Moishe Shmeel,"[19] the rebbe calls the titular Moishe Shmeel a *"farshtupte kop"* (a "stuffed head," roughly "sh*t-for-brains"), and in "Then He Potched Me,"[20] the rebbe calls the narrator a *"toyg

---

16. Yossi Toiv, "The Rabbi," *Country Yossi & The Shteeble-Hoppers Volume 1: Wanted!*, CY Productions, 1983.
17. Kenny Rogers, "The Gambler," *The Gambler*, United Artists, 1978.
18. The rabbi's refrain, in a rough English translation, is: "One must know when to buy, know when to run; know when to shoot straight, and when to negotiate subtly; better not to speak when one need not, and not go where one should not; yeah, it's good to travel, but it's better to stay home."
19. Yossi Toiv, "Moshe Shmeel," *Country Yossi & The Shteeble-Hoppers Volume 2: Strike Again*, CY Productions, 1984. This is an imitation of: The Coasters, "Charlie Brown," single, Atco 6132, 1958.
20. Yossi Toiv, "Then He Potched Me," *Country Yossi & The Shteeble-Hoppers Volume 1: Wanted!*, CY Productions, 1983.

tze gornisht bum" ("good-for-nothing"). These three instances are among the only "speaking parts" that rabbis get in Country Yossi's early albums. Rabbis, both good and bad – even those whose lessons are universal – do not speak in the vernacular. In "Deaf Man in the Shteeble," the rabbi offers no consolation to his bereaved congregant and *chazzan* who shows up on *Kol Nidrei* night after the death of his father, but merely asks "How come so late?" in ungrammatical, Yiddish-inflected English.

In addition to verbal abuse, "Then He Potched Me" and "Moishe Shmeel" (who is "gonna get *petch* every day this year" according to the refrain) introduce another aspect of behavior ascribed to rabbis: physical abuse. "Then He Potched Me" is a particularly jarring inversion of the upbeat, romantic "Then He Kissed Me,"[21] in which the slap – the *potch* – replaces the kiss. "He quickly walked behind my chair; then he grabbed me by the ear; then he held me by the hair, and then he potched me."

FATHERS

It is not only rabbis who mete out physical and verbal abuse, speak only Yiddish, and occasionally offer sage advice: fathers do, too, in "Then He Potched Me," "Moishe Shmeel," and other songs.[22] However, as we have seen, fathers are more complicated. For instance, the titular "Deaf Man in the Shteeble" is there for his son, every time, even though he cannot hear him. Going to shul with one's father is a formative experience for young boys in "Little Kinderlach." These redeeming dimensions of fatherhood are generally not ascribed to rabbis. Among characters that populate Country Yossi's works, dads are complicated, while rabbis are usually distant at best, if not outright antagonistic.

---

21. The Crystals, "Then He Kissed Me," *Philles Records Presents Today's Hits*, Philles, 1963.
22. Parents speak only Yiddish in: Yossi Toiv, "Hello Mameh," *Country Yossi & The Shteeble-Hoppers Volume 4: Captured*, CY Productions, 1987. This imitates: Allan Sherman, "Hello Muddah, Hello Fadduh (A Letter from Camp)," *My Son, the Nut*, Warner Bros. Records, 1963. The father's advice plays a key role in "Nebich of the Shteeble" and "A Boy Named Zlateh;" see below.

NON-JEWS

The rest of the world outside the bounds of the *frum* community is barely mentioned in Country Yossi's songs. Non-Jews are usually portrayed as being hostile: Three *shkotzim* (lit. "insects," a pejorative term for hostile non-Jews) vandalize a *shul* ("Nebich of the Shteeble"); three *vilde ferd* (lit. "wild horses") jump "Big Bad Moish"[23] and wind up *"teef in d'rerd"* ("deep in the ground"); the narrator is jumped by "three hoodlums" and rescued by (a different) Big Bad Moish ("Along Came Moish"). In "Cholent," the narrator fantasizes about dropping a cholent bomb on "the Arabs."

Some non-Jews, like the neighbors in "'Cause I'm a Jew" or the titular "Shabbos Goy,"[24] are portrayed as benign, even helpful or useful. From the perspective of these non-Jews, however, the Jews are an odd bunch. The neighbors think the local practicing Jew insane, and the entire premise of "Shabbos Goy" is the narrator's difficulty inducing a random Black man to turn on the air conditioner without directly saying so. At one point, the confused erstwhile Shabbos Goy comments, "Man, these Jews is crazy!" Thus, even in the instances where non-Jews are portrayed in a somewhat positive light, their otherness is highlighted.

NON-FRUM JEWS

Non-*frum* Jews are even less frequently mentioned. An exception is the title character of "Shlomo,"[25] who is in the process of "returning." The song opens:

---

23. Yossi Toiv, "Big Bad Moish," *Country Yossi & The Shteeble-Hoppers Volume 1: Wanted!*, CY Productions, 1983. This imitates: Jimmy Dean, "Big Bad John," *Big Bad Jock and Other Fabulous Songs and Tales*, Columbia Records, 1961.
24. Yossi Toiv, "Shabbos Goy," *Country Yossi & The Shteeble-Hoppers Volume 6: Ride Again*, CY Productions, 2010 (an imitation of: The Shirelles, "Soldier Boy," *Baby It's You*, Scepter, 1962).
25. Yossi Toiv, "Shlomo," *Country Yossi & The Shteeble-Hoppers Volume 2: Strike Again*, CY Productions, 1984. This is an imitation of: Lorne Greene, "Ringo," single, RCA Victor, 1964.

Clutching the tefillin he never wore
His hair was long but his soul, it burned
He cried to Hashem, he said "I've returned"
I asked his name, he thought a while
Used to be Steven, he said with a smile
Now it's Shlomo.

These lyrics offer three markers of the unrepentant, improper (male) Jew: He has long hair and a non-Jewish name,[26] and he owns, but never wears, *tefillin*. However, he "returns" to God and begins a "new life." A non-*frum* Jew is thus characterized as someone who has been alienated from correct, *frum* Judaism and is a potential returnee. No other aspect of Jewish life outside of *frumkeit* is described.

"SHTEEBLE HOPPERS:"
THE PATHOS OF COUNTRY YOSSI'S MISFITS

A significant number of Country Yossi songs tell the stories of marginal figures in *frum* society, drifters and misfits who lurk in the periphery. They have funny names (by *frum* standards), are handicapped, are extremely shy, are not native to the culture, or have fallen through the cracks. In several cases, the misfit ends up becoming the unexpected hero, saving the day by performing some feat of courage, even at the cost of his own life. Some of Country Yossi's misfits, like the morbidly obese "Fetteh Shmeel" and the troublemaker "Moishe Shmeel," are almost purely comic, but most have a tragic element as well.

In each case, the "tragic misfit" trope originates in the imitated song, which is usually a country song. "Big Bad John" dies saving twenty miners from a collapsing coal pit, and "Big Bad Moish" carries twenty men to safety from a burning *shul*, but then dies trying to save a Torah scroll. The "Phantom of the Shteeble" and the driver of "Phantom 309" swerve to avoid hitting a group of children, crash, and die, but still occasionally pick up hitchhikers on dark and stormy nights, ferrying

---

26. Toiv's characters inevitably have Jewish names. Moishy (Moshe) and Shmeel (Shmuel) seem to be the most common.

them to the safety of a truck stop or *shteeble*. Whereas in "Running Bear,"[27] the "young Indian brave" drowns trying to cross the river to meet his lover, "Little White Dove," "Shalom Ber"[28] came to yeshiva from a foreign land and has trouble making friends. On an outing, he saves two children from drowning and then "whispered softly, 'Now we friends,' then he was pulled beneath the waters and was never seen again." Two of Country Yossi's more developed misfits are the title characters of "A Boy Named Zlateh" and "Nebich of the Shteeble," and I believe that they, more than any other characters, epitomize what Toiv is trying to say about his generation.

The premise of "Zlateh," like that of the "Boy Named Sue," is that a father abandons his wife and young son, but first gives the son a girl's name. The son grows up being ridiculed and thus becomes a social outcast ("I roamed from *shteeble* to *shteeble* to hide my shame"). He also learns to hold his own in a fight and swears revenge on his father. Ultimately, the son meets his father – Sue in Gatlinburg and Zlateh in Woodbourne in 1979 – and they fight. At the end of the fight, the father explains his behavior:

> *Son, this world is rough*
> *And if a man's gonna make it he's gotta be tough*
> *And I know I wouldn't be there to help you along*
> *So I gave you that name, and I said goodbye*
> *I knew you'd have to get tough or die*
> *And it's that name that helped to make you strong.*

In both songs, the father's central lesson is identical, and the son walks away with newfound respect for his father.

The "Nebich of the Shteeble," like the "Coward of the County," was orphaned from his father at the age of ten and tends to be retiring and non-confrontational. However, in some ways the stories of these two outcasts are mirror images. The Coward's father died in prison, the

---

27. Johnny Preston, "Running Bear," single, Mercury Records, 1959.
28. Yossi Toiv, "Shalom Ber," *Country Yossi & The Shteeble-Hoppers Volume 5: Break Out*, CY Productions, 1987.

Nebich's died "in Europe," in the Holocaust, as the lyrics imply: "Then he heard 6 million voices cryin' in the darkness; he recognized his Daddy's voice, high above them all." The fathers' final words to their sons thus contain the opposite lessons:

COWARD	NEBICH
Promise me, son,	Promise me, son,
not to do the things I've done	not to do the things I've done
Walk away from trouble if you can	I ran away from trouble my whole life through
Now it won't mean you're weak	Now I know I was wrong
If you turn the other cheek	Klal Yisroel must be strong
I hope you're old enough to understand	And son, these are my final words to you
Son, you don't have to fight to be a man.	Sometimes you gotta fight when you're a Jew.

The Coward's girlfriend is violated by the three "Gatlin boys" who were "takin' turns at Becky." The Nebich comes upon "three *shkotzim*" vandalizing the *shteeble* one morning. Both defy expectations by letting loose and beating up the vandals, but whereas for the Coward, "twenty years of crawling" were bottled up inside him, for the Nebich it was "two thousand years of silence." Here, the Nebich becomes an apotheosis of the exilic Jew, who remained silent in the face of every atrocity, but finally, after hearing six million voices rise up, and above all his father's final admonition, he stands and fights.

A key theme of both pairs of songs is manliness, specifically whether being a man demands toughness and the ability and willingness to fight. "Nebich" goes a bit further: The father taught, and the son eventually realized, that "sometimes you gotta fight" to be not just a man, but a Jew.

The "Country" of Country Yossi

There is a certain self-deprecating humor, as well as something very revealing, in Yossi Toiv's self-styling as "Country" Yossi. The moniker is ostensibly a nod to the country music that many of his songs imitate and the gritty, rough-and-tumble, tragicomic world that they portray, and which Toiv attempts to translate into a more familiar landscape. In the parlance of *frum* Brooklyn, however, the "country" refers to an area along State Route 17 in Sullivan County, New York that is thick with *frum* summer camps, resorts, and bungalow colonies. Toiv's songs refer to several summertime "country" hubs of activity: Monticello,[29] Woodbourne ("Along Came Moish,"[30] "A Boy Named Zlateh"), and South Fallsburg.[31] Several others[32] ("Fetteh Shmeel;" "Hello Mameh") are set in the camps and bungalows of the "country."

The "country" is set in opposition to "home" – Boro Park, the Brooklyn neighborhood famed for its densely *frum* population and culture. (Toiv himself emphasizes the variety of Ḥasidic courts in the neighborhood in "Boro Park."[33]) In "I Wanna Go Home," the narrator

---

29. "The Rabbi;" Yossi Toiv, "I Wanna Go Home," *Country Yossi & The Shteeble-Hoppers Volume 5: Break Out*, CY Productions, 1987 (an imitation of: Bobby Bare, "Detroit City," *Detroit City and Other Hits*, RCA Victor, 1963); Yossi Toiv, "Phantom of the Shteeble," *Country Yossi & The Shteeble-Hoppers Volume 4: Captured*, CY Productions, 1987 (an imitation of: Red Sovine, "Phantom 309," single, Starday Records, 1967).
30. Yossi Toiv, "Along Came Moish," *Country Yossi & The Shteeble-Hoppers Volume 3: Still On the Loose*, CY Productions, 1985 (an imitation of: The Coasters, "Along Came Jones," single, Atco, 1959).
31. Yossi Toiv, "The Big K'nocker," *Country Yossi & The Shteeble-Hoppers Volume 5: Break Out*, CY Productions, 1987 (an imitation of: The Big Bopper, "Chantilly Lace," *Chantilly Lace*, Mercury Records, 1958).
32. "Hello Mameh;" Yossi Toiv, "The Ballad of Fetteh Shmeel," *Country Yossi & The Shteeble-Hoppers Volume 5: Break Out*, CY Productions, 1987 (an imitation of: Johnny Horton, "The Battle of New Orleans," single, Columbia Records, 1959).
33. Yossi Toiv, "Boro Park," *Country Yossi & The Shteeble-Hoppers Volume 6: Ride Again*, CY Productions, 2010 (an imitation of: The Beach Boys, "Kokomo," *Still Cruisin'*, Elektra, 1988).

complains about hot, mosquito-infested Monticello and yearns for the amenities and climate-controlled environment of "home." Though the location of "home" is not mentioned explicitly, the ultimate lyric of the song – "I'm gonna sneak outside and get in my car and ride down old Route 17 and back to good old 13th Avenue" – leaves no doubt: 13th Avenue is Boro Park's main thoroughfare. Boro Park provides the setting for other songs as well,[34] and even when the action happens elsewhere, it remains in Brooklyn.[35]

Much of the action in Country Yossi's songs take place in *shuls* and *shtiblekh*, the synagogues and prayer houses where *davening* and learning take place, and which are central to the life of a *frum* man. This is true of "Shlomo," "Big Bad Moish," and "Bubba Basra."[36] "Nebich of the Shteeble," "Deaf Man in the Shteeble," "Phantom of the Shteeble," "The Shteeble Hop,"[37] and other songs have "Shteeble" in their titles, and, of course, Country Yossi is accompanied by the "Shteeble Hoppers." The *shul* or *"shteeble"* refers not only to the physical institution, but also to the community of men who congregate there. In "Nebich of the Shteeble," for example, the titular prayer house signifies both the building and the community centered there.

The only other place that recurs as a landscape of Country Yossi's songs is Eretz Yisrael – the land of Israel – and Jerusalem ("Yerusholayim") specifically. Though there is some awareness that Israel is a real place with real geopolitical conflicts ("Cholent," "Shlomo"), it is

---

34. "Along Came Moish;" "Big Bad Moish;" "In the Year TSHA"G" (Yossi Toiv, *Country Yossi & The Shteeble-Hoppers Volume 1: Wanted!*, CY Productions, 1983; an imitation of: Zager and Evans, "In the Year 2525 (Exordium & Terminus)," *2525 (Exordium & Terminus)*, RCA, 1969.
35. "Shabbos Goy" is set along King's Highway, a major Brooklyn thoroughfare that goes through several heavily Jewish neighborhoods, but not Boro Park.
36. Yossi Toiv, "Bubba Basra," *Country Yossi & The Shteeble-Hoppers Volume 4: Captured*, CY Productions, 1987 (an imitation of: Eydie Gormé, "Blame it on the Bossa Nova," *Blame it on the Bossa Nova*, Columbia Records, 1963).
37. Yossi Toiv, "The Shteeble Hop," *Country Yossi & The Shteeble-Hoppers Volume 2: Strike Again*, CY Productions, 1984 (an imitation of: Bobby "Boris" Pickett & The Crypt Kicker, "Monster Mash," *The Original Monster Mash*, Garpax, 1962).

mainly portrayed as an imaginary, aspirational place, which all good Jews have in their hearts ("Oh My Yerusholayim")[38] and occasionally visit ("Peel One More Potato"), where children sing and where all Jews will go in a future messianic era, where they will sing and dance together with resurrected heroes of the Jewish past ("When Moshiach Comes").[39] Though there is no overt Zionism, there is a strong sense that Eretz Yisrael and Jerusalem are exclusively Jewish places: "No one can take Yerusholayim away."

Thus, Country Yossi's "world" consists of three centers. Home is Boro Park, or Brooklyn more generally, with its myriad schools and synagogues. The "country," rural areas where summers are spent, is along State Route 17. And the imagined future will play out in a perfectly rosy Jerusalem.

Country Yossi, the Post-Holocaust Generation, and the Post-Post-Holocaust Generation

In *Judaism Straight Up*,[40] Moshe Koppel describes, idealizes, and aspires to the Judaism that he encountered in his youth among Holocaust survivors. He describes their reflexive, non-elitist, intuitive *frumkeit*, their fierce tribal loyalty, and their impatience with overly sophisticated ideologies, and he contrasts it with the values he encounters in universities and other centers of cosmopolitan culture. Country Yossi represents the photographic negative of the relatively seamless Judaism that Koppel describes. Country Yossi, while not the child of Holocaust survivors, belongs to the generation born in

---

38. Yossi Toiv, "Oh My Yerusholayim," *Country Yossi & The Shteeble-Hoppers Volume 2: Strike Again*, CY Productions, 1984 (imitating: George Baker, "Una Paloma Blanca," single, Warner Bros., 1975).
39. Yossi Toiv, "When Moshiach Comes," *Country Yossi & The Shteeble-Hoppers Volume 4: Captured*, CY Productions, 1987 (imitating: Willie Nelson, "On the Road Again," *Honeysuckle Rose*, Columbia Records, 1980).
40. Moshe Koppel, *Judaism Straight Up: Why Real Religion Endures* (Jerusalem: Koren, 2020). See my review, "The Torah of the Kishkes," *The Lehrhaus*, December 4, 2020, https://www.thelehrhaus.com/culture/the-torah-of-the-kishkes/.

the USA to immigrant parents in the Holocaust's immediate aftermath, conversant in Yiddish, and, to borrow Koppel's term, able to speak "Judaism as a first language." My father is of this same generation, and the world in which he was raised shares some of the key features of the world described by Toiv – the all-pervasive shadow of the destruction of European Jewry, the culture and communication gap between the generation of survivors and their children, and the internalized expectation to remain loyal to the faith for which one's family lived and died.

Koppel emphasizes the positive aspects of the Judaism he absorbed from these survivors, whereas Toiv explores the generation gaps and the characters lurking in the shadows. He highlights the incongruities produced by the attempt to transplant and translate a destroyed Jewish culture in America. Some of these songs are like scar tissue that forms over wounds inflicted, often unwittingly, by a traumatized older generation that never learned the new language. But all of his songs are an attempt to bridge this generational divide, to create a language that includes both of his cultures, and to use country ballads to express Jewishly-inflected tragedy. This is, after all, the inevitable fate of a "Shteeble Hopper," who is at home everywhere – and nowhere.

When I listened to Country Yossi as a child of about ten, I found it funny even though I did not understand its Yiddish, was not familiar with the imitated songs, and missed many of the cultural references. Still, I was part of Country Yossi's core demographic, and I remember the lyrics of many of his songs by heart. Over the years, as I grasped more and more of the meaning of his songs, I found that they helped me understand my father and the peculiar challenges faced by his generation.

And that is the whole point. The songs of Country Yossi are a sort of apologia for the idiosyncrasies, hybridities, and neuroses of the children of survivors. They represent an effort to convey a set of experiences that will simply help his generation's children – the grandchildren of survivors – understand his world.

Passing on the *Journey*

Hannah Lebovits

My father could never do the drive from our home in Pittsburgh, PA, to his brother's in Brooklyn, NY, in fewer than six hours. Sure, there were a number of times we might have made it in five-fifty, if he hadn't been pulled over for speeding. But those were the six-twenty times we never spoke of again. No, it was six hours, and it wouldn't be a minute less.

The media choices in my father's silver Pontiac Montana were either the angry sounds of conservative talk radio or contemporary Jewish music. I vastly preferred the latter to the former. But living in a dense city, most of our drives were only a few minutes in length. Even a trip to the suburban mall was less than a twenty minute drive. The long periods of cross-state driving punctured by magically swift pit stops were special in that way.

Though we were seven children, I can't remember more than five of us driving together at once. Not because we couldn't: we had an eight-seater van, after all. Simply because of our years between us. By the time my little sister was traveling, the older boys were in yeshiva close to Brooklyn and wouldn't drive with us from Western Pennsylvania. And we hardly ever met them in New York either. They couldn't simply leave and come visit. They had to be in yeshiva. To be learning. If it wasn't an off Shabbos, a weekend break, they would be sitting in a classroom on Sunday morning while we drove across the state to purchase food, buy Shabbos clothes, visit family, or attend a simcha. No, instead of nine, it would only be seven Lebovitses in the car – three girls, two boys, and two parents. And one highly-coveted book of CDs.

They who held the half-broken bound case with countless sleeves of Jewish music CD-roms had the power. That sibling decided the entire trip vibe. Would it be a soulful Mordechai Ben David experience or a hip DEDI one, or would the sweet voice of Avraham Fried accompany us through the Pennsylvania hills? The truth is, though I was invested in and recognized the strength of the book, I didn't much care for most of its contents. Not because they weren't enjoyable, but because they were unrelatable. Though I grew up in a home where we cherished the halls of the yeshiva, as a child I was less frequently surrounded by and entrenched in the linguistic mechanics of Hebrew and Yiddish, making the music somewhat foreign to my younger self. In that respect, one set of CDs stood apart. The simple melodies, the self-contained stories, and the English words made Abie Rotenberg's *Journeys* series my top pick.

Despite referring to him colloquially by his nickname, I've never met Abie. But if it's possible to know someone through their work, as I believe it is, Abie and I are good friends. He began his work an entire generation before I was born, joining the growing 1970s movement to provide Jewish folk music beyond cantorial songs or Hasidic *niggunim*. Abie's massively popular and broadly consumed *D'veykus* albums (produced in 1973, 1975, 1982, 1990, 1995, 2001), *Journeys* volumes (1985, 1990, 1993, 2003) and the *Marvelous Midos Machine* series (1986, 1987, 1988, 2011) both satisfied and further propelled a growing hunger for kosher media consumption within the budding yeshivish community. From living room record turntables to car CD players and then personal MP3 devices, Abie's music moved from inside the home to wherever an Orthodox Jew might go.

There's a signature style to his work, one I noticed even as a child: folk elements – acoustic instruments and basic chord progressions – along with melodic lyrics and smart but concise word choices. Abie doesn't talk down to the musical consumer, but his work is also entirely accessible to a novice. His English lyrics, in both the *Journeys* and *Marvelous Midos Machine* productions, tell a story or teach a

Passing on the Journey · 127

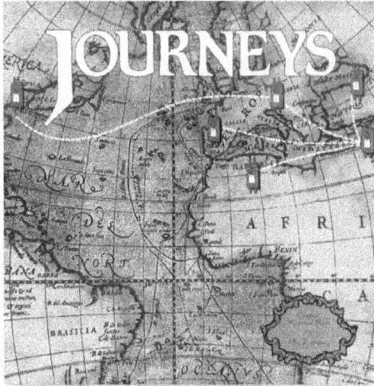

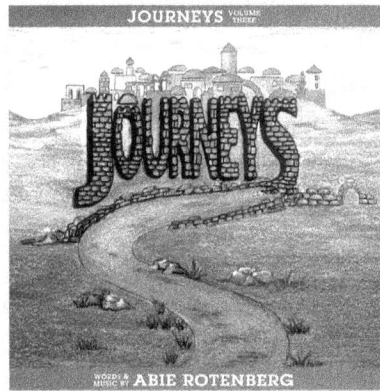

Abie Rotenberg's *Journeys*, Volumes 1–4.

lesson, often through the lens of historical Jewish events (covered with varying levels of accuracy) as well as modern-day practices and personal dilemmas.

Abie's songs joined me and my family on our multi-yearly trips to New York City. As an out-of-town family, our community schools, shuls, kosher stores, and *mikvaos* satisfied our regular daily and weekly Jewish needs, but we couldn't entirely escape the Jewish mecca of the tri-state area. My brothers, who attended a yeshiva much closer to New York, often brought home special candies and new musical items our Judaica store didn't yet carry. But a cousin's wedding, the need for a new suit, or an upcoming *yom tov* would require a full family trip. And hours with Abie, if I had any say in the matter.

The *Journeys* CDs took on an unironic, geographic meaning to me – they emerged during a physical shift from one place to another. But they were also representative of a sociological expedition. Abie's songs grew to represent my journey from a provincial Jewish life to a larger, more complex Jewish community. My home community had all of the core amenities of the frum world I was entering, but it lacked the *taam*, the intangible and sometimes immeasurable tastes that made it right. What was right in my mind, what world was I yearning to be a part of? The one Abie sang to me about.

As a child, I assumed that the Orthodox world that crossed the streets of Flatbush and Boro Park was a cohesive community full of Jews and the Jewish experiences that Abie described. I was certain that every yeshiva student was waiting to be excited by a kind and fun *rebbi* and that countless *rebbeim* were waiting for that perfect life-changing moment to show their true nature ("The Ninth Man," *Journeys 2*). And, of course, it was obvious to me that every Orthodox Jew in New York had a natural desire to be embraced by the spiritual holiness and warmth of Jerusalem (*"Yerushalayim," Journeys 3*). Even the songs we were meant to understand as comedy or parody ("Wedding Song," *Journeys 2*; "Pesach Blues," *Journeys 3*) were like an inside joke between me and these Jews in Brooklyn.

I couldn't be fully embedded in their world, in a Judaism that seemed to be more true and more pure than my own. With so few yeshivish families, as a child, I never considered the right-wing people I knew in Pittsburgh to be a socio-cultural community. They were the Rosenbergs, the Eisens, the Nadoffs. Real people who ate the same foods I did, who sent their children to yeshivas in other cities where my brothers were, and who owned enough *seforim* to fill several bookcases like the ones in my own den. But while they spoke with the mixture of Yiddish and Hebrew Abie described in *"Yeshivishe Reid"* (*Journeys 3*), they didn't appear to me as a unified group. I knew them too well and understood their idiosyncrasies too intimately. I could never consider them with the admiration and longing I had for the nameless families walking down Avenue J as I munched on pizza in the correct *tzniusdig* way that would suit a young woman from the world Abie described. I was familiar with all of the elements – the organizational settings, the mechanics of the story, the sense of Jewish identity – and I saw some of myself and the yeshivish life of his songs.

So naturally, as I grew older, I chose to identify more closely with the yeshivish world, Abie's world, as my older brothers had done years earlier. I shunned non-Jewish music entirely, even when my peers consumed that music and its talk of the foreign desires for sexual relationships and closeness with the opposite gender. My own personal development as a musician happened at this time, as well, with Abie right along with me. I sang "Dreams Come True" and "The Man from Vilna" (*Journeys 4*) countless times while learning which specific guitar chords and piano keys best matched the notes. Along with my electronic keyboard, I discovered the complexity of Yaakov Shwekey's "Mama Rochel" (*Journeys 4*). And I would play the earlier songs, now on MP3 rather than CD, in my ears while I studied musical theory.

And Abie was with me when I got on a plane to leave for Israel to attend Beth Jacob Jerusalem Seminary – the Harvard of extended Jewish women's education, and ostensibly considered, though by those who might say it to other women but never in earshot of men, to be the female counterpart to the historic Brisk yeshiva system. My guitar came with me, as well. We both settled into an El Al flight, one of us arguably more comfortable than the other. And we both arrived in Ben Gurion a bit more worn than when we left. The guitar had been tossed around in the luggage compartment while I experienced a different kind of depreciation.

My interactions with the in-town Bais Yaakov-built and BJJ-bound girls on my flight, a social group that I hadn't until then noticed were eerily missing from Abie's descriptions, were not kind and lighthearted. They didn't seem to have that simplistic clarity about Judaism and its inherent light that I thought they most certainly would. They didn't model themselves on Rabbi Akiva or the lessons of the Rabbi of Lublin (*Journeys 1* and *2*) and they certainly didn't seem like they were searching, like souls entering the physical world ("Neshomele," *Journeys 2*) or someone looking for their roots (*Journeys 1* and *4*). They were just ordinary girls. No different, in fact, than the ones I had left in

Pittsburgh. Though they were externally more observant and stricter in their adherence to certain cultural norms, they were not the image Abie had painted for me.

I heard them sing his songs and grimaced. Never on Shabbos, because God forbid English music should make an appearance at a holy Sabbath meal or singing session, but I heard them occasionally. When a girl forgot herself and sang in the hallway. At a try-out for the Erev Shira, the yearly production. His songs emerged here and there. And it hurt. It pained me to hear his finely constructed world tossed around by girls who seemed foreign to it. Girls who emerged from the New York and New Jersey area but who seemed to have somehow entirely missed out on the frum world I knew to be hidden there. *They were the exception*, I told myself. And I repeatedly did so, for years. Until I simply could not lie any longer.

My childhood with regular visits to New York shifted into an adulthood with regular visits to Pittsburgh. In accordance with the advice from my mentors, I moved back from Israel to Brooklyn, to be entrenched in that world from which so many girls I didn't care for had come. And while I fell into the patterns I was expected to follow, teaching during the day and attending a frum, female-only college at night, I could not find Abie's stories anywhere. Not in my apartment in Flatbush, not at the suppers with my cousins in Boro Park, not even while sitting with my siblings in Lakewood, home to the famous yeshiva where I was certain a Rosh Yeshiva had once proudly collected baseball cards ("Joe Dimaggio's Card," *Journeys 3*). Abie was there, in my ears, but the imagery he painted never materialized in front of me. While *Journeys* remained in my top list of "Frequently Played Songs," I came to believe that the moments of learning and growth his songs presented were infrequent if not entirely nonexistent phenomena in the world around me.

It had been some time since I believed that life was full of interactions between atheists and chassidim in which some universal truth was exposed ("Atheist Convention," *Journeys 3*) or that someone who returned to Judaism might do so because of a hidden message in a license plate ("Country Boy," *Journeys 4*). But I thought that those songs were seen by other mature Jews through the same framing I applied – a focus on the value of an acceptance of and constant interaction with people who might not be like you – but who could be, some day. Until finally on the MegaBus rides back to my hometown, for holidays and happy gatherings, I had to admit that Abie's world does not exist. I was returning, almost too frequently, to my smaller and more nuanced Jewish community specifically so that I could retain idyllic ideas about another one, and I had to finally admit the truth. There are Jewish experiences that align with the ones he shares, but the universe that I believed he was showing me, the community I felt I had a natural affinity towards – that isn't real. His songs are imagined, impossible examples that oversimplify incredibly dynamic socio-cultural phenomena. They are children's stories, the images of life we tell our young people, and even ourselves, about a world we know will never come to be. Because we so badly want it to be true.

So I stopped listening. I traveled to dates with my husband without Abie. We moved across the country while pregnant with our daughter and the *Journeys* songs were nowhere to be found. My new iPhone couldn't support my old MP3s and I figured it was fine, the end of an era.

But then, my daughter grew up. And she started asking for more English music, words she could sing while she bathed or burst into song in the hallways – music she could relate to. So, Abie returned, on occasion, courtesy of Apple Music and my desire to avoid KidzBop at all costs. And soon, the random occurrences become more frequent and he traveled with us to a reservoir in Deep East Texas and began joining my kids as we shuffled them from the city to the suburbs for school and shopping. Because, though his world never materialized for me, maybe for someone else it can. Perhaps, with time, I've come to think of him like a date who you might recommend to a friend. *He's not for me, but maybe he'd be great for you,* we tell our single peers when we realize the failed potential of a relationship. And like all not-so-subtle exes in the information age, I still keep tabs on Abie – I can hear him while my kids listen – but it's at a distance. He's with them on their *Journey* now.

The Music of
the Marvelous Midos Machine

Lonna Gordon

As a group that eschews television and movies, yeshivish Orthodox Judaism relies more heavily on the audio medium for childhood entertainment. Story and song albums directed at entertaining and educating children proliferate. Some are primarily storytelling, such as Shmuel Kunda's stories of adventure and danger in Jewish history or Rabbi Juravel's narratives of the *parsha* [weekly Torah portion]. In these productions, the narrative is the primary medium. If any songs are included, they are for amusement only and secondary to the narrative component. Other albums lean the other way. The songs are the primary focus in *613 Torah Avenue* and *Uncle Moishy* albums, and the narrative functions only to introduce and contrive a reason for singing the songs. Any resemblance to a plot is strictly accidental.

Between these two extremes, the *Marvelous Midos Machine* series stakes a middle ground. Across three separate albums released between 1986 and 1988,[1] it provides a dual-threaded plot about rabbi-scientist Dr. Midos who uses his knowledge of science to aid his mission of

---

1. Abie Rotenberg and Moshe Yess, *Marvelous Midos Machine, Episode 1: Up and Away* (1986), *Marvelous Midos Machine Episode 2: Shnooky to the Rescue* (1987), and *Marvelous Midos Machine, Episode 3: Does anyone Have the Time?* (1988). A fourth album, *Marvelous Midos Machine Episode 4: Shnooky's Bar Mitzvah*, was released two decades later in 2011.

134 · The Songs and Music of Orthodox Childhoods

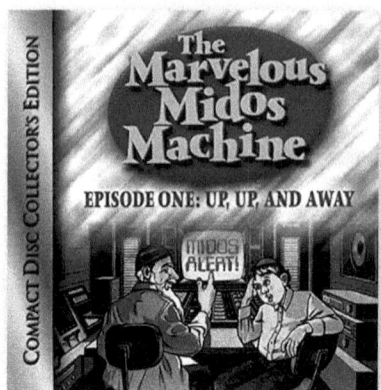

The Marvelous Midos Machine CDs, Volumes 1–4.

teaching Jewish children to behave properly. The first album opens with Dr. Midos launching his neighbor Dizzy into space with a satellite. The satellite is used to beam songs about good behavior at children whose conduct is lacking. On the ground, Dr. Midos has to deal with another neighbor, Shnooky, whose good and helpful intentions keep ruining and diverting Dr. Midos's plans. In space, he has to battle Dr. Doomstein, who intends to foil the attempts to improve children's behaviors, in a suggestion of the battle between good and evil forces controlling children's emotions and behavior.

The primary action surrounding the pseudo-scientific contraptions is routinely interrupted by "Midos Alerts," in which the machines pick up signs of negative behavior and which require Dr. Midos and his assistants to beam edifying songs at the misbehaving children. The melodies and the messages intertwine in an entertaining and meaningful way, so that a song about alacrity, for example, is set to a march which itself signifies alacrity. The catchiness, cleverness, and applicability of the songs have made some into community classics, and many children learn the songs in school or summer camp, even if they are never exposed to the stories or the albums themselves. Although the original audience for the *Marvelous Midos Machine* were children born in the 80s and 90s, the story was (ironically) remade into a YouTube puppet performance[2] for more recent generations as part of the Oorah organization's fundraising campaigns, proving the enduring appeal of the production. Following are some snippets of the more popular songs from the series, along with some thoughts on their appeal and their effects on children (and teens and adults).

Zrizus (Alacrity):

> The Torah says you shouldn't shirk!
> Roll up your sleeves and get to work!
> Don't put off till tomorrow something you can do today!
> …So be on time!
> Instead of late!
> *Zerizim* never hesitate!
> Don't put off till tomorrow!
> Don't put off for an hour!
> Just do it right away!

The energetic tune of the song about alacrity is a brisk march, urging the listener to stop slacking and get moving. Lively, demanding, and full of exclamations, the short lines practically jump from the mouth of the singer.

---

2. Oorah, *Shmorg 8: Marvelous Midos Machine*. Available in separate video on YouTube in on Oorah's channel or in full at this link: https://www.youtube.com/watch?v=wuh-gl498-c.

I'm a Hippopotamus:

> I'm a hippopotamus
> From my top to my bottomus,
> And I know I'm very lazy and slow.
> Though there may not be much I like to do
> Except to sleep the whole day through
> All the hippopotami have hippopata feelings too!

The hippopotamus song is sung by a hippo in a zoo. (Any zoological statements in this song should not be taken as fact.) The hippo acknowledges its shortcomings – it is lazy and slow – but points out that it still has feelings and should be treated kindly. While the song imparts lessons about accepting others, it is the second-most popular song (a result obtained by informal polling) because of its fun tune and general silliness. The singer on the album uses voice effects similar to the reindeer Sven's voice in Disney's *Frozen*, modulating his voice in a manner that is fun to mimic. The first two lines are followed by sound effects ("hoo-hoo-hoo") which singers often accompany with hand and body motions indicating large body size and difficulty moving. While these sound effects and motions accentuate the hippo's non-conforming factors, the lesson of the song is emphasized by the intonation of "feelings," often accompanied by body language indicating the pain felt when one is verbally bullied.

Ahavas Yisroel (Love for Fellow Jews):

> I am an ancient wall of stone atop a hill so high.
> And if you listen with your heart, you just may hear my cries.
> Where has the *Bais Hamikdash* gone, I stand here all alone?
> How long am I to wait for all my children to come home?

The minor-key tune of "Ahavas Yisroel" is impossible to sing without a mournful, furrowed brow. In this song, a personified Western Wall endlessly bereaved at the loss of the Temple in Jerusalem entreats all Jews to love their fellows and be kind to each other. The beautifully despondent song combines pathos ("listen with your heart" to "hear my cries") with subtle Jewish guilt (How long must the wall wait for

Jews to just get along already?). This winning combination made it an instantaneous Tisha B'Av classic, sung a capella in summer camp performances by children and teens alike.

Who Spilled the Milk:

> Who spilled the milk on the kitchen floor?
> Not me! Not me!
> Who took a pen and wrote on the wall?
> No, it was not me.
> Who let in the neighbor's cat?
> Not me! It wasn't me!
> And who sat on my Shabbos hat?
> No, it was not me.

The song about honesty takes the form of a question-and-response children's song, akin to "Who Stole the Cookie from the Cookie Jar," but more melodious. The adult asks who has committed an amusing offense like "splashed ketchup on the baby's head" and the children emphatically (and presumably dishonestly) deny it. Then the chorus exhorts the children to come clean to their parents, because God already knows the truth:

> *Midvar sheker tirchak*, never tell a lie.
> *Hashem* knows just what happened, there's no reason to deny.
> Honesty means *emes*, make sure all your words are true.
> So Tatty, Mommy, and *Hashem* will be so proud of you.

Every child knows this argument is specious at best, but the song is still fun to sing and is the runaway favorite song in the collection.

Anger Song:

> Does your blood begin to boil when things don't go your way?
> Do you get all hysterical and start to rant and rave?
> Your face is changing colors –
> You're ready to attack –
> Like a big volcano that's gonna blow its staaaaaack!

The anger song is short and sweet. The first part builds to a crescendo while describing a growing rage, and then immediately drops to a soothing second half that urges the listener to just have self-control and not allow the anger to win. Although the recommended anger-management techniques are suspect, the song does drive home the ugly explosivity of anger. The song allows the child to sing along and revel in the expression of someone else's anger, providing a fun outlet for their own pent-up feelings even while they condemn the actions they sing about.

Conclusion:

When I bring up the *Marvelous Midos Machine* in conversation, people's faces light up and their enthusiasm is palpable, even through text-based communication. "That's my childhood!" "I LOVE those songs!" It's clear that the *Marvelous Midos Machine* holds a special place in the canon of Orthodox Jewish story tapes. I believe it's because both the story and the songs speak to children in a way that makes them feel understood – and makes them feel.

The fact that the tapes have a complex story line illustrates an intent to amuse children, not just lecture them (or sing morality songs at them, as the case might be). The story itself is sympathetic to the children who receive the attention of the Midos Machine; they aren't seen as malicious, and the desires that drive them to misbehave are not caricatured or maligned. Rather, the tape explains, they need to strive to do better because they are Jewish children. Finally, the songs themselves speak on a visceral level through the music, making them poignant and memorable. I don't think I'm the only person who sang *Marvelous Midos Machine* songs to herself as a reminder of how to behave well.

Another common response I received related to a desire to share the *Marvelous Midos Machine* with their children. People want to share their most magical childhood experiences with their progeny. The *Marvelous Midos Machine* falls in that category. They may turn on Uncle Moishy to entertain their kids, but they put on the *Marvelous Midos Machine* to share the joy and meaning it provided them.

An Old Kind of Song

Miriam Moster

> When anyone says that mankind must regard "The newest song which the singers have," they will be afraid that he may be praising, not new songs, but a new kind of song; and this ought not to be praised, or conceived to be the meaning of the poet; for any musical innovation is full of danger to the whole State, and ought to be prohibited.
>
> – Plato

Starting a family has meant re-imagining my Haredi childhood to align with my twenty-first century, post-Haredi sensibilities. As a mother, I want to raise my children in the tradition in which my personal narrative is rooted, but I also feel responsible to shield them from the facets of that childhood that drove me to leave the Haredi community in the first place. And so I pass on to my children a potpourri of selected Haredi traditions, stories, rituals, and tunes that we interrogate and challenge together.

The weekly *parsha* has morphed into a kind of child-friendly Bible criticism as I offer to my son historical context that was lacking in my own childhood. My recounting of the story of Chanukah does not end with the reclamation of the *Bais HaMikdash*, but with the Maccabees' later abuse of power. As we reenact the children learning Torah in hideout caves, and then playing dreidel to hide their banned studies when the Greeks arrived, I am sure to add that the game of dreidel is a modern invention, and that many of the traditional stories are as fictitious as many of the other books my son loves to read. We talk about the distinctions between fantasy, myth, and legend in the literature he reads and in the literature of the Haredi tradition. But the greatest challenge I continue to grapple with is how to share the music of my youth. A story, I can retell and reimagine. It lends itself to interpretation. But music tends to speak for itself.

As far back as ancient Greece, philosophers like Plato and Socrates and Aristotle mused about the power of music as a socializing force. Aristotle writes, "If one listens to the wrong kind of music, he will become the wrong kind of person."[1] In *The Republic*, Plato writes: "And what shall be their education? Can we find a better than the traditional sort? – and this has two divisions, gymnastic for the body, and music for the soul."[2] Plato goes on to voice concern over new music – "a new kind of song" – and the danger this signals: "when modes of music change, the fundamental laws of the State always change with them."[3] Writing more recently about Orthodox beliefs about music, based on interviews with Orthodox rabbis and a review of online discussions, Rebecca Cypress notes a similar concern over the influence that secular, non-Haredi music can have on a Haredi listener.[4] But what of the opposite? What about the influence Haredi music can have on a non-Haredi listener?

To be fair, Haredi music is not exactly sui generis or purely traditional, but rather is changing and modernizing, too, mimicking pop trends in secular music and often borrowing their tunes.[5] As with

---

1. Quoted in Donald Jay Grout, *A History of Western Music* (New York: W.W. Norton and Company, 1960), 9.
2. Plato, *The Republic*, Book II. The Gutenberg Project. https://www.gutenberg.org/files/1497/1497-h/1497-h.htm
3. ibid., Book IV.
4. Rebecca Cypress. "The Community as Ethnographer: Views of Classical Music in the English-Speaking Orthodox Jewish Community." *International Review of the Aesthetics and Sociology of Music* 41 (2010): 117–139.
5. See Mark Kligman, "Contemporary Jewish Music in America," *The American*

Haredi literature,[6] Haredi music is a "space of transaction, where cultural materials [both Haredi and non-Haredi] are transformed, mediated and sold."[7] Writing about *kiruv*, the work of proselytizing the Haredi lifestyle to secular Jews, Matt Williams demonstrates that *kiruv* is a space for exchange in both directions.[8] The outreach work seeks to invite secular Jews to embrace a Haredi lifestyle, but it also creates a space for Haredim to interact with and adapt to secular culture.[9] That interaction, and the figure of the *baal teshuva* himself – newly Haredi but still retaining the life experiences and education of a secular upbringing – allows for the infiltration of some outside ideas into the Haredi world. Gordon Dale argues that Orthodox Jewish music, specifically, negotiates boundaries with the secular world in a manner similar to that articulated by Williams.[10] What role does Chanukah music play in this exchange? And how do they function to negotiate boundaries with the secular world?

One of our Chanukah traditions is a nightly family dance party following the lighting of the menorah. I turn up the volume to the Miami Boys Choir's (MBC) Chanukah tunes I grew up with back in the nineties and early aughts, along with some newer songs from the Yeshiva Boys Choir (YBC). The English-language songs on their albums include "Light up the Nights" (MBC),[11] "Those Were the

---

Jewish Year Book 101 (2001), 88–141; Gordon. A. Dale, *Music in Haredi Jewish Life: Liquid Modernity and the Negotiation of Boundaries in Greater New York* (Diss. City University of New York 2017).

6. See Yoel Finkelman, *Strictly Kosher Reading: Popular Literature and the Condition of Contemporary Orthodoxy* (Academic Studies Press 2011); Dainy Bernstein, *Reading the World: American Haredi Children's Literature, 1980–2000* (Diss. City University of New York 2021).

7. Wood, Abigail. "Pop, Piety and Modernity: The Changing Spaces of Orthodox Culture," *The Routledge Handbook of Contemporary Jewish Cultures*, eds. Roth, L. and Valman, N. (London: Routledge, 2014).

8. Matt Williams, untitled manuscript.

9. Williams, personal communication.

10. Dale, 166–207.

11. Yerachmiel Begun, "Light up the Nights," *Chanukah: Light up the Nights*, Yerachmiel Begun and the Miami Boys Choir, 1997.

Light Up the Nights, The Miami Boys Choir; *Chanukah*, The Yeshiva Boys Choir.

Nights of Chanukah" (YBC),[12] and "Daddy Come Home" (YBC).[13] Listening to the lyrics more critically as an adult, I noticed something was different about the Yeshiva Boys Choir's English tunes compared to those of other Haredi singers. Their message seemed incongruent with typical Haredi talking points and lyrics. The diction was not entirely Haredi and neither were the narratives.

In "Daddy Come Home," a child yearns for his father, away in the military, to come home to light the menorah. However, in contrast to what the lyrics might suggest, it is practically unheard of for a Haredi child to have a father in the military. In fact, there have been documented cases of Haredim abusing Israeli soldiers and violently protesting conscription. Who is the audience for this song, then? And who is the narrator?

A thread on I'm a Mother (imamother.com), a forum for married Orthodox women,[14] found others equally confused. The comments in the thread were mixed: some women were moved by the child's singing while others were perplexed, pointing to contradictions in

---

12. EG Productions, "Those Were the Nights," *YBC 5: Chanukah*, 2010.
13. EG Productions, "Daddy Come Home," *YBC 5: Chanukah*, 2010.
14. In order to receive logon credentials for the site, individuals must answer a series of questions on halakhot unique to married women.

the language that made the narrative arc of the lyrics hard to follow.[15] The father is described as in the corps "fighting a war / somewhere far away," seemingly fighting for the U.S. Army. But in other ways the song seems to be about a Jewish father in the Israeli army: the lyrics say he will come home for Chanukah, and the music video features a soldier wearing the uniform of the IDF. Who is this father? Is he Haredi? What country is he fighting for? And why would a Haredi songwriter write about a father in the military, whether U.S. or Israeli? On the other hand, the song is not glorifying the soldier. Rather, it is about a child yearning for the father to be home and not engaged in war. Even so, it is not anti-war or anti-military participation either – which would be more in line with the Haredi stance – but rather about the fear of losing a father.

In his dissertation on the way Haredi music negotiates boundaries with the outside world while simultaneously reinforcing social bonds within the Haredi community, Dale includes a chapter on Haredi children's choirs as sites of cultural continuity that stage a secure Haredi future.[16] In that chapter, he analyzes "Daddy Come Home," among other songs. He writes that he interviewed Gerstner, the songwriter, who shared that initially the song was going to be about a father in the U.S. Army: "the song was written with the American military in mind, but when conflict between Israel and Lebanon erupted, [Gerstner] decided to depict an Israeli soldier in the music video 'for *chizuk*' [moral support]."[17] The interchangeability of the two identities and experiences – American vs. Israeli soldier – betrays a Haredi worldview that does not understand what it means to serve in the army, why someone would serve, or the difference between serving in one nationality's army as opposed to another. Gerstner's foreignness to the experience and incomplete revisions when he decided to change

---

15. Sleepwalking, "Daddy Come Home...YBC Speechless!!" *Imamother*, November 27, 2012, https://www.imamother.com/forum/viewtopic.php?t=200361.
16. Dale, 166–207.
17. ibid., 192.

the song to be about an Israeli father in the military – and the seeming lack of an editing process that would invite people with the lived experiences he tries to communicate – are evident to the attentive listener. And that confusion is communicated in the lyrics. At the same time, the song is heartfelt and moving, despite the inconsistencies.

What is clear, as Dale notes, is the Haredi messaging on the power of prayer, and the way this reinforces the Haredi worldview: "The effectiveness of the prayers, as seen in the father's safe return from war, validates Haredi beliefs, and thus the accompanying lifestyle."[18] Interestingly, however, the word choice throughout the song as the child pleads for his father to return, is the English "pray": "For him I pray;" "I need to pray." This stands in contrast to the way Haredim speak, mixing Hebrew and Yiddish terms into their dialogue, specifically when referencing religious practices. A Haredi individual does not "pray;" the Haredi "*davens*" or says a "*tefilla*." Dale likewise notes the multilingual character of Haredi music in his analysis of Abie Rotenberg's "Lulei Sorascha."[19] Contrast this, for instance, to the Miami Boys Choir's "We Need You," another song on the importance of prayer. "We Need You" is clearly aimed at a Haredi audience, sprinkled with insider jargon. Take the chorus:

> We need you,
> We need your *tefilla*
> Each and every *Yid* can bring the *geulah*
> Don't talk! Shh! Just daven,
> So your *tefillos* can reach *Hashem*.[20]

Here, prayer is *tefilla*, the Jew is a Yid, redemption is the *geulah*, and God is *Hashem*. This is how Haredim speak, and it is also typically how they sing, even when singing English language songs. This is true for other popular Haredi singers and songwriters as well. Dovid Gabay's

---

18. ibid., 193.
19. ibid., 172.
20. Yerachmiel Begun, "We Need You," *Shabbos Yerushalayim*, Yerachmiel Begun and the Miami Boys Choir, 1989.

song on the power of prayer uses "daven" for pray: "Daven for me and I'll daven for you."[21] Other Haredi singers similarly pepper their English language songs with Hebrew and Yiddish jargon.

Yet several English-language Chanukah songs by Haredi songwriters substitute English words for prayer. In the Miami Boys Choir's English-language Chanukah song "Light up the Nights" (lyrics by Yerachmiel Begun), the English "pray" is used as well:

> Their prayers were answered each day
> Their minds fixed on their destination
> With victory they made their way
> No longer deprived
> At last they arrived
> A miracle lasting for all generations.[22]

The wording in other parts of the song is also strikingly similar to wording in "Daddy Come Home." In Yerachmiel Begun's song, the chorus contains: "Light up the nights/the candles burning bright." Gerstner's chorus is similar: "Eight candles burning bright/And they're lighting up the night." Light is a theme of the Chanukah holiday, the menorah is lit at night, and "bright" fits thematically and rhymes with light and night. Perhaps the common language is simply because they are drawing on the same holiday traditions and themes. Alternatively, Gerstner might have knowingly or unknowingly been drawing inspiration from Begun's lyrics, both with the English "pray" and his similar lines.

More importantly, Gerstner's use of English-language terms that would be accessible to a non-Haredi listener, as well as a narrative about a soldier which would be foreign to the Haredi listener, align with his interest in outreach. In an interview with Yosef Shidler of TheCoolJew.com, Gerstner shares that his Chanukah album was released by Universal, a non-Jewish record label (after a limited release

---

21. Dovid Gabay, "The Letter," *Omar Dovid*, 2008.
22. Yerachmiel Begun, "Light up the Nights," *Chanuka: Light up the Nights*, Yerachmiel Begun and the Miami Boys Choir, 1997.

to Haredi stores in time for Chanukah).[23] Gerstner explains: "They [Universal] said, do you have any idea of how many millions of unaffiliated – they're telling me – Goyim! – not even like – how many millions of unaffiliated Jews that we're going to be able to reach now? Now they're talking about reaching for their pockets, but I'm hearing that, I'm like 'wow, that's amazing…'" Gerstner saw his music as a vehicle for *kiruv*, outreach, to draw unaffiliated Jews closer to Haredi Judaism, and the diction seems to be aimed at this non-Haredi audience. The narrative about the soldier, with all its inconsistencies, is subordinated to the message about the power of prayer, meant to inspire the non-Haredi listener and draw this listener closer to a Haredi lifestyle.

As a mother who identifies as post-Haredi, raising my children in a post-Haredi lifestyle, I wonder what effect this kind of music has on my children. Is it vicariously nostalgic? A taste of their family history? Or will music like this have the effect Gerstner is hoping for, of bringing less Haredi Jews closer to a Haredi lifestyle?

A second English-language song on the same album as "Daddy Come Home" is "Those Were the Nights of Chanukah."[24] In his interview with Yosef Shidler, Gerstner explains that the song was added on at the request of Universal for a more upbeat English-language song for the album. A song whose narrator reminisces about the joyful family Chanukah parties of his youth fills that purpose. This song too is about a non-Haredi family. There are many indicators of this: The names of the family members are English, rather than the Biblical Hebrew or Yiddish names of most Haredim. One uncle is "Jake;" the aunt is "Bertha." The grandmother in this song is unable to make traditional Chanukah foods properly – in contrast to the ideal Haredi *balebusta* who prepares these traditional foods annually and to perfection.

Another indicator that the song is about a non-Haredi family is the candle menorah – "multi-colored candles burning." The Miami Boys Choir's English-language Chanukah song, "Light up the Nights,"

---

23. Shiezoli, "Eli Gerstner CBS, FOX, Universal & YBC Live 4 Part 2 (of 3)," YouTube Video, 10:37, December 22, 2011, https://www.youtube.com/watch?v=IoOdoGFdOh4.
24. EG Productions, "Those Were the Nights," *YBC 5: Chanukah*, 2010.

similarly references a candle menorah ("Light up the night/the candles burning bright") as does Eli Nathan's "Colored Candles" on his album entitled *Destiny*.[25] Nathan's songs on his *Destiny* albums were nearly all English-language (in contrast to Yeshiva Boys Choir, Miami Boys Choir, and other Haredi albums where the majority of songs are Hebrew-language with at most one or two English-language songs per album), and they were consumed by moderate and fringe Haredim and those outside of Haredism. "Colored Candles" is about an assimilated Jew whose memory of the Chanukah candles draws him back to his Jewish faith. The narrator remembers his father, who had lit "colored candles on the windowsill." When the narrator's son comes home from school asking his father for a Christmas tree like his classmates have, the father is awakened to his Jewish heritage and instead lights a menorah that year with his son. Over the next few nights of Chanukah, the narrator's "Christian" neighbors reveal that they, too, are actually assimilated Jews, and are inspired to light Chanukah candles, too:

> Yes, they had one memory
> Yes, their fathers they did see
> Lighting colored candles on the windowsill
> Eight days a year they'd light
> Another candle every night
> It lingered in their memory still.

In contrast to the candle menorahs that these assimilated Jews light, however, Haredim use oil menorahs. In fact, the oil menorah is a kind of rite of passage in Haredi homes. Fathers and older children light oil menorahs, while young children light colored candle menorahs for safety reasons. In Haredi Chanukah music, the colored candle trope seems to serve as an identifier for non-Haredim.

Additionally, in some ways, the image of the colored candle menorah associated with the non-Haredi infantilizes the non-Haredi, whom the Haredi might view as a *tinok she-nishba*, an abducted infant, so to

---

25. Eli Nathan, "Colored Candles," *Destiny 1*, 1985.

speak. This phrase is used by Haredim in reference to the assimilated Jew who grew up with no knowledge of Haredi culture or halakha. (It is used in Jewish law to distinguish the reprehensibility of a sin committed by one knowledgeable in halakha, who should know better, from one committed by a non-Orthodox Jew who commits it unknowingly, as he was not raised to know that he is even sinning.) The assimilated Jew is analogous to one kidnapped in infancy with no knowledge of his heritage and hence has the halakhic status of a *tinok she-nishba*. And the imagery of the colored candle menorah lit by the non-Haredi Jew reinforces – albeit subconsciously – the Haredi perception of the non-Haredi as less educated and more childlike (lighting a child's candle menorah) in comparison to the Haredi.

At the same time as it reinforces these notions for Haredi listeners, the colored candles in Gerstner's "Those Were the Nights of Chanukah" and Nathan's "Colored Candles" can also serve as a *kiruv* mechanism to make the song relatable to the non-Haredi who typically lights a candle menorah. The colored candle trope might be a marker that the song is intended to also reach a non-Haredi audience.

While Gerstner's "Those Were the Nights of Chanukah" does not outright denigrate the non-Haredi, it does make a kind of mockery of the non-Haredi Chanukah. For the Haredi listener, the song offers an amusing tale of the non-Haredi struggling to get the traditions right. And this song, too, raises questions. Is the narrator nostalgic for the family gatherings of the Chanukahs of his youth? Or is he nostalgic for the holiday, now that he is grown and his practice has perhaps lapsed? Has he drifted from the tradition and now Chanukah calls him back?

It is not insignificant that Haredi Chanukah songs speak to these themes of assimilation and outreach, and that Haredi Chanukah music in particular reaches outward toward assimilated Jews and tries to bring them into the Haredi fold. For the Haredi, Chanukah represents the fight against assimilation.[26] The olive oil with which the Haredi lights his oil menorah is said to represent Jewish separatism. I cannot

---

26. See MBC's "Stand Up" and "One by One" for examples of the ideology of fighting against assimilation, albeit not in the context of Chanukah.

count the number of times I heard the following Dvar Torah growing up: that just as olive oil refuses to mix with other liquids, the Jewish people must cling to their religion and resist the forces of assimilation. The Chanukah story as told to Haredi children frames the Maccabean war as one against assimilation, a fight to preserve the Jewish soul.

And so the question remains: as a mother, what do I do with Haredi music, and specifically Haredi Chanukah music designed to draw non-Haredim like my children toward Haredi life? Do I offer them to my children as tunes of my *"alter heim"*? Abigail Wood writes that "more important than musical features in defining this genre [Haredi music], however, is the overt self-identification of this body of musical material with Jewish Orthodoxy... Religious values are subtly cued..."[27] The tunes deliver Haredi messages and Haredi interpretations of texts, and they are sung, for the most part, by male Haredi singers. They stand to some degree in opposition to an egalitarian, progressive worldview. In his analysis of Haredi music, Dale writes:

> Music helps to summon people into various relationships with their social categories. While niggunim summon people to the imagined core of the Haredi community, Haredi popular music and the music of the Haredi periphery call people into complex and diverse relationships with the imagined Haredi ideal, depending on both the music's features and one's own perspectives. This form of summoning reinforces ties between individuals and others in their communities through the musical articulation of group identification. These identity politics are negotiated within a context of dense social ties that are reinforced as one is summoned into Haredi life, or its outskirts, through music-listening choices.[28]

As I play the familiar Haredi tunes for my children, I wonder about what I am inculcating in them. Is it just a song? Plato feared new music would bring destabilizing change. As I seek change, does the music hold us back?

---

27. Wood, 286.
28. Dale, 251.

Pesach with Rebbe Alter

Miriam Bernstein

The last time I listened to *Pesach with Rebbe Alter* was the Pesach I was in fourth grade, at nine years old. I remember turning it on and everyone in the house groaning at the thought of hearing the same songs again. The songs stay in your head for days after listening to them, the repetitive melodies playing on, and my parents and older siblings were past the age of enjoying the cheerful smiling voice of Rebbe Alter singing about Pesach. But my family allowed me to turn the tape on because to me – the youngest child – Pesach cleaning could not happen without Rebbe Alter's songs playing in the background. The songs were an integral part of the cleaning process. Once the tape was playing, the cleaning supplies could come out and the cleaning marathon could begin. Without the songs, the feel of Pesach in the air didn't exist, and the excitement that came with all the special items for Pesach wasn't there. Turning the Rebbe Alter tape on signified the start of the holiday and the holiday atmosphere.

The tape's cover is clearly imprinted in my mind. On a deep purple background reminiscent of the color of sweet sticky grape juice, a golden glow surrounds the cup of Eliyahu, the seder plate, and matzos – the fundamental aspects of the seder. Even a child who is too young to read the large title on the cover will recognize these objects which will be used at their own tables in a few weeks. Once the tape is slipped out of its case and into the cassette player, the child will listen to Rebbe Alter singing about the preparations for the seder night. Through

Pesach with Rebbe Alter

his songs, he teaches the listeners what to expect from the adults around them leading up to and at the seder, as well as which rituals the children would be expected to take part in themselves. The songs function as an educational tool, teaching the children how and when to interact with the adults around them both during the seder and throughout the rest of the year. The interactions of the adult Rebbe Alter and the children responding on the tape provide a template for the listeners in their own lives.

A typical method of learning in ultra-Orthodox schools is through repetition and memorization, where the teacher will prompt the students to repeat verses he had said. Many times these verses are Biblical verses or sayings from *gedolim* which are deemed essential for students to know. The songs on the tape imitate this method of teaching, using the style the children are familiar with to introduce new concepts to them. Track 3, the song *"Ma Nishtana,"* uses this method in teaching the children the words to say on the night of the seder. The song begins with the children singing the first question in Hebrew, as it is in the Haggadah, and Rebbe Alter singing the same question in the Yiddish translation. The order is then switched, with Rebbe Alter singing the second question in Hebrew and the children singing the same question in Yiddish. The Yiddish translation of the questions is not found in the Haggadah, but it is commonly taught in ultra-Orthodox schools. Children are expected to recite the Yiddish translation along with the original Hebrew at the seder. The teaching method of repetition and memorization is used in this song to teach the children what they are expected to recite at the seder, even though it does not show up in the Haggadah. The song acclimatizes the children to the proper way of learning and the responses expected of them from their teachers.

Although this is the standard teaching method, it adapts to match what is being taught. The children do not always repeat everything Rebbe Alter sings on the tape, as not all of it is important for them to memorize and internalize. On Tracks 4 and 5, "*Avodim Hayinu*" and "*V'hi Sheomdo*," the children do not repeat all the verses that Rebbe Alter sings. These two songs draw their lyrics from verses in the Haggadah which describe how God saved past generations. "*Avodim Hayinu*" discusses how Jews were slaves to Pharaoh in Egypt, and "*V'hi Sheomdo*" discusses how nations have tried to destroy the Jewish people in every generation. The outcomes in both of these songs share the same message, that God saved the Jewish people from destruction at every turn. On these tracks, Rebbe Alter begins singing the verses, as he does on "*Ma Nishtana*." However, the children do not repeat all the verses he sings. Instead, they sing only the verses which discuss how God saved the Jewish people. These are the verses that are essential for the children to know. The children are not singing about the many enemies who are trying to destroy the Jewish people, as Rebbe Alter had. The tape reminds the children that their primary concern should be that God is the one who consistently saved them in the past, and therefore will do so in the present as well.

There are some verses that do not need to be taught through the traditional repetition method because children should already know these verses. The second half of Track 8 focuses on the verse "*Leshono Habah*," which is only four words and yet takes up over a minute-and-a-half of the song's runtime. The passage is an expression of hope that next year the seder will be conducted in Jerusalem with a rebuilt Temple. The track does not follow the formula used by earlier tracks with Rebbe Alter beginning the song and the children joining in later. For "*Leshono Habah*," the children immediately join in singing with Rebbe Alter. There is no need for Rebbe Alter to teach them the verse before they can join him, as this verse is such an integral part of the ultra-Orthodox community that the children are expected to already know it. Children in the community have this verse memorized from a very young age and so it does not need to be taught to them here, as the other verses in the Haggadah are taught to them.

Two tracks on the album do not engage in back-and-forth repetitive learning between Rebbe Alter and the children at all. Track 7, "The Afikomen Song," is sung primarily by the children. In this song, they are not repeating what Rebbe Alter has said, but instead he is responding to what the children are saying. Rebbe Alter only sings in the role of the father, who is given a small role compared to the children's part in this song, indicating that the children are leading this part of the seder.

> *Children*:
> I took it, I snatched it
> I *chapped* the afikomen
> From under the pillow
> That was on Tatty's chair.
>
> *Rebbe Alter as father*:
> My dear *kinderlach*, I've looked high and low
> And I must say it's getting very late
> Please return to the me the afikomen now
> And I'll buy you something really great.

In most interactions, the children are supposed to respond when the adult initiates a conversation. Here, on the other hand, the children are supposed to initiate and the adult responds to them. The song reminds the children that there are situations where they are expected to take the lead, although their leadership stays within the confines of adult expectations.

> *Children*:
> I took it, I snatched it
> I *chapped* the afikomen
> From under the pillow
> That was on Tatty's chair.

Rebbe Alter as father:
My dear *kinderlach*, I've looked high and low
And I must say it's getting very late
Please return to the me the afikomen now
And I'll buy you something really great.

Track 10, "Closing Medley," is another song on the tape which does not consistently use the repetitive method of teaching children. The first song on the track is about the counting of the Omer, which begins the second night of Pesach and ends with Shavuos. The first lyrics of the song are the verses to be recited every night over the coming weeks when they count the Omer. The children immediately join Rebbe Alter singing these verses, as they had on the track "*Leshono Habah*," because once again these are important verses which they are expected to know and recite every night. The song then transitions to lyrics in English, in which Rebbe Alter explains what they are doing, for how long, and what they are counting towards. Rebbe Alter sings:

> We're counting, we're counting the days,
> *Hayom yom echad*, we're on way,
> From Pesach until Shavuos time,
> Seven weeks times seven's forty-nine.
> Day after day, the weeks are going by,
> We count towards the day that we stood at Har Sinai,
> The day that we love, of *Chag* haShavuos,
> When Hashem gave us the *Aseres Hadibros* / Torah and mitzvos![1]

The children do not sing along with Rebbe Alter on these lyrics because it is purely a lesson to be taught. There is no need for the children to memorize these words. Once Rebbe Alter starts singing the Hebrew verses again, the children sing along, because those verses are necessary for the children to have memorized. This pattern indicates that there is no need for children to memorize the lessons they are

---

1. The last line changes from the first instance of the refrain to the second.

taught about the reasons for what they are doing, but it is necessary for children to memorize the right words to recite in each situation.

The songs on this tape teach children an important lesson about their place in society and how they should respond to the adults around them. Through the interactions of Rebbe Alter and the children on the tracks, children are exposed to the proper way of interacting with adults in a variety of scenarios. They are taught when and how to respond, when they should listen, and when they should initiate. The tape does not merely provide entertainment for children, but instead its primary purpose is to be an educational tool teaching children how to behave.

Lubavitch Summer Camp Songs

Schneur Zalman Newfield

The songs sung at American and Canadian Lubavitch boys' camps during communal sing-alongs had English lyrics composed in sleepaway camps and were primarily intended to be sung there. These songs were not merely created to promote camaraderie and camp spirit but were also intended to educate and instill the proper Hasidic values and commitments in the next generation of devout Lubavitchers.

As a camper and later a staff member in several Lubavitch summer camps in the 1990s and early 2000s, I remember that photocopies with lyrics would sometimes be passed around for those unfamiliar with the songs, and I once saw several staff members huddled around a thick booklet of camp songs, discussing their favorite entries. But for the most part, the songs and their backstories were part of the *torah sheba'al peh*, the oral tradition of camp, passed down from counselors and staff to the next generation of campers during late night sing-alongs. As the lyrics of one popular song put it, campers were "small and immature trees" whose proper cultivation was crucial since "these young years will set the way/the fate of its life does lie here."

As campers we didn't know who authored these songs. It was as if these composer-less songs simply materialized, a natural and pure expression of what we all felt in our hearts. Most of these songs were originally composed for Color War, and after a brief life on stage many simply disappeared. But dozens of them, the most evocative

The author at a Lubavitch summer camp, photographed
with his counselors and fellow campers, 1991

and eloquent ones, have joined the canon and continue to be used even decades after they were first composed. There are Lubavitch boys' summer camps in various rural locations, including Parksville, New York; Kalkaska, Michigan; and La Minerve, Quebec, Canada. In addition to songs that are specific to each camp, they all use some of the same songs, regardless of where they were composed. This contributes to the sense of a shared Lubavitch community and identity across these geographical areas.

Some songs consist of playful tunes with catchy lyrics, such as the following ditty:

> Shake it up *Zaidy* [Grandpa]! Shake it up *Zaidy*!
> You look so cool when you daven [pray] in shul [synagogue]!
> You look so hip when in the *mikvah* [ritual bath] you dip!
> You look so weird when you shave your beard!

But for the most part, these songs were somber affairs, imbued with anguish and longing. The title of one song, "A Tear Runs Down from His Cheek," aptly captures the emotional mood in which many of these songs were sung. These songs highlight numerous topics, but three focal points are *mesiras nefesh* (self-sacrifice), *shlichus* (a commitment to Jewish outreach work), and *hiskashrus* (devotion) to the Lubavitcher Rebbe, Rabbi Menachem Mendel Schneerson, the spiritual leader of the community.

One of the most poignant examples of the theme of *mesiras nefesh* is a haunting melody titled "Awaiting His Turn" about a Jew during the Spanish Inquisition. He faces the terrible choice of remaining alive as a "goy" or dying as a Jew in an auto-da-fé:

> Just because I was born as a Jew
> Does it mean I must die as one too?
> What is there to gain for the suffering and pain?
> Better as a goy to remain.

After an internal struggle where his reason "was making him blind," his "Jewish spark" emerges, and in an emotional eruption he chooses to die as a Jew:

> With this burst of emotion he lunges towards the flame
> As he cries *Shma Yisroel*! [Hear O Israel!], ash he became
> But with *libi eir* [an awakened heart], his soul was saved
> A Jew he forever remained!

While not all the songs were quite as macabre, they did contain tremendous pathos. For example, one describes a camper from a non-Orthodox home who struggles to maintain his new religious observances in the face of his friends' ridicule. The camper, Yossi, writes to his Lubavitch counselor complaining about his uninformed and less religious Jewish friends, who presumably attend non-Orthodox synagogues, but are not truly committed to their faith:

> But so many are lost in a world of confusion
> Their faith isn't real, it's just an illusion

> I cry for them all, I pity them so
> For the beautiful things they don't know.

Yossi's counselor, Dovid, responds, "Don't cry for them all, but teach them to do/The beautiful laws of the Jew." For us Lubavitch campers the message was clear. It was our mission to educate those who were not Orthodox and to help them embrace the beauty of our way of life.

Although the songs covered many themes, by far the central one was the Rebbe, our love for him, our dedication to his teachings, his continued presence in our lives even after his passing in 1994, and his eventual return through the messianic redemption. One song, titled "Despondently Crying," summed up the ethos of Lubavitch and its attitude toward its absent leader:

> Oy, Rebbe! Although we feel so alone
> Connected to you we must be
> For a *chosid* [a follower of Hasidism]
> I am, I will carry out your plan
> Your return inspiring me.

In the wooded forests of camp, far removed from our family and familiar streets and stores, our sense of what was possible expanded. A young boy from Brooklyn could be transported by a song and imagine himself as a martyr in the Spanish Inquisition. He could be motivated by a song to renew his commitment to piety and to the Lubavitch way of life.

Singing Our Sadness at Sleepaway Camp

Jessica Russak-Hoffman

Daniel hands out our song sheets. Other than morning *shiur*, music is my favorite part of the tightly scheduled day at Machaneh Morasha. As a Modern Orthodox Seattle girl three thousand miles from home for eight weeks, surrounded by mostly New Yorkers who go to yeshiva day schools with choirs, I know I'm out of my league. I am perfectly aware that I'm tone deaf, even at eleven years old, as it's my third year at camp and I've never had a solo. Still, lined up on wooden benches facing a low stage with a single piano, reading the lyrics, I am eager to learn the notes.

Immediately I know this song isn't for Color War or for the all-camp *Shiriah*. This one is in English and includes the word "blood," so it's probably another Holocaust song and we're learning to sing it just for fun. As usual, Daniel brings up his superstars, girls from Brooklyn who he knows from the school year, and they demonstrate each line in their signature high-pitched voices. "Up heeeeere," he sings, hitting a higher note and holding up a hand until the girls meet his pitch.

When it's our turn – and this is the part I've been waiting for – we look down at our song sheets and sing along. *Yisroel, Yisroel, where have you been all these years, I've been awaiting your return, come on home, let me dry off your tears.*[1] I love a sad song. Intergenerational trauma

---

1. Dov Levine, *"Yisroel,"* composed by Chumi Berry, *Kumzitz Classics*, Suki and Ding Productions, 1992.

and Jewish guilt, I welcome thee into my impressionable young soul. Daniel stops us. "Again, but a little higher."

You mean more nasal, I think a little bitterly, already relatively salty for a fifth grader. *I recall as a young bride, how you were faithful and true. But since then you've wandered to strangers, who tried to make a traitor of you.* All right, so this song is about betraying Hashem. Last week we learned a song from the perspective of a dead Zeide who survived the Holocaust and mournfully asks what will become of all the memories.[2] We've had songs in which we declared "it could have been me," and songs about going to heaven and meeting the six million souls murdered in the Holocaust, including our Bubbe and Zeide who said we must return to the world to tell their story. My own grandparents were in America during the war, but that doesn't take away from how deeply and passionately I sing along.

This new song is about devotion to Hashem, so it's a welcome change of pace. Instead of guilt, I can feel how much Hashem needs me to look away from the secular world around me and commit myself to Him. After music we have basketball and tonight is 1970s Disco Night, both of which I am not looking forward to, so devotional lyrics, please fuel me up for the rest of the day! Here comes the chorus, and the high notes are above what I can do but that doesn't mean I'm not going to give it my all. *Don't you be fooled by their lies. Their only aim is to lure you away from me.* It's really beautiful. *Won't you believe that it's true, I'm the only one for you.*

Not only do I not sing like the others, I also don't look or dress like them. This place has been my first exposure to the yeshivish version of Modern Orthodoxy, and we come from lots of backgrounds, so there's girls in skirts and girls in knee-length shorts, girls who *shukel* when they daven and girls who have secret boyfriends on the boys' campus. They've got blow-dryers and contact lenses and Umbra gear, and I've got a JewFro and glasses and a stack of tie-dye t-shirts. When I want to disappear in my crowded bunk, I put a Pearl Jam CD into my no-skip player and read a book. Music is how I escape, any kind

---

2. Abie Rotenberg, "Memories," *Journeys II*, M&M Enterprises, 1989.

of music, but especially dark and sad. Give me an angry girl band or a depressing grunge track and I feel much more relaxed. So when I'm sitting on the wooden benches and Daniel hands out a song sheet like this one, I'm perfectly at ease. Right where I belong. This song is really in my emotional wheelhouse.

We sing: *How long, till when, will you endure all their scorn. Though you've been beaten by wind and rain, you still are a rose among thorns. Battered crown, tattered gown, your garments are covered with mud. Still you continue to wander* – and here is where it starts to get really good – *though the earth has been soaked with your blood.*

Music isn't supposed to be competitive here at camp, but to some girls, it really is. They want solos and duets and to be picked for the camp musical. I usually end up painting the set. Once I got a brief speaking part in the camp production of *Kindertransport*, and even got to sing in the chorus of *Oliver*. Most of the time, though, it's these sit-downs on the wooden benches with the printed song lyrics that recharge me. Music is energizing. It gives me a spiritual boost that carries me through. They can compete for the solos; I'll stick to the group harmonies and belting out the chorus. These lyrics speak to me, to my love of learning and Torah. I selfishly internalize them while hoping I can judge the girls around me who care more about basketball and looking cute for co-ed activities. Except they seem to be enjoying themselves, too. They also seem to be passionate and to have deep *kavanah* when they sing. Perhaps this is the one place, on these wooden benches, where we can all be the same.

What are you hoping to find, I sing. *Haven't I given you all you could wish for? Come back and we'll start anew. I'll be here waiting for you.* By this point I've really worked myself up, feeling every word. We all have. *Oh, to behold your countenance, let the sound of your voice fill my palace, only then, my dear one, will you experience true happiness.* Hashem hears my voice, I think. I am here, on this wooden bench in this wooden theater in the woods of Pennsylvania, with true *emunah*. Music gives me faith. I have forgotten about the mud and the blood and the betrayals. The voices around me are just as devoted to the lyrics and notes, and we sound beautiful. When I take home a camp cassette and play it back in my Seattle bedroom, my first thought is: this is a faulty recording, we sounded *much* better in person.

The best part of this song is the final chorus. The moment we all *shukel*, arms around each other's shoulders, and Daniel has lost control of the pacing and notes. He pulls out two of his favorite singers and brings them up to the stage. "This part will be a duet," he says, and I'm disappointed. I really wanted to belt it out, not just sing the background harmonies. When the soloists are done, we beg him for a chance to sing it, too, and he says yes.

Tell me it's only a dreeeeam. He waves his hand back and forth like we're a choir, but I have no idea what those hand motions mean.

Tell me your heart and your soul are still here with me.
Wake up and we'll be togeeeeether.

Yisrael vekudsha brich hu. Our voices grow louder and we repeat the chorus again. Daniel continues his hand motions, pointing at his throat and his head, as if somehow I'll understand if he means go higher or sing from my nose. I can't do either of those things. The song slows down as we approach the final lyric. *Chad hu.*

Daniel claps his hands together. "Again."

Part III
Orthodox Childhoods: Personal Essays

"This is the Greatest Show": Bais Yaakov Production and My Orthodox Girlhood

Leslie Ginsparg Klein

When I entered a Bais Yaakov high school in the fall of 1990, everything was new to me. I had attended a co-ed Modern Orthodox elementary school, and the differences abounded. I now attended a single-sex high school with a uniform, many rules dictating behavior out of school (no wearing pants, no dating), and a strong emphasis on theatrical performance. I was most excited about the last one. I had always been a drama kid and was quite excited at the thought of performing on a massive stage in front of hundreds of women. Because of the traditional Jewish laws of modesty, boys and men did not attend Bais Yaakov productions, as they had in my Modern Orthodox elementary school, but I didn't care. The Bais Yaakov production stage beckoned.

In my forthcoming book on the history of Bais Yaakov in America, I discuss how production became a key component in the girl culture created by female students and teachers within Bais Yaakov schools. The Bais Yaakov school year revolved around production. Production was an annual theatrical event, typically a song and dance revue or a musical play. While various Bais Yaakov schools had varied extracurricular activities, the vast majority, if not all, put on a production, and that was the most important activity of the year. From the first few days of school, students already speculated about what play the school would choose to perform and which seniors would be chosen to lead the key committees. Indeed, students took active roles in every aspect of production, with seniors leading the efforts. Students ran the performance, arranging choirs and choreographing dances. They also ran the lights, organized the props, managed the box office, and sewed the costumes. School leaders made an effort to involve all students in production by matching students to committees based on their skills and interests. In the weeks leading up to production, almost no book-learning took place as classes were canceled for rehearsals and behind-the-scenes work, and countless students were excused from whatever classes were scheduled.

The promise of glory on the Bais Yaakov stage was one of the reasons I chose to attend a Bais Yaakov school, although I admit that I wished my school would have put on a Broadway play, as had been done in the past. But by the 1990s, rejection of secular popular culture in the yeshivish community led schools to eschew Broadway for scripts written specifically for Bais Yaakov schools. So instead of *Hello Dolly* or *Annie*, when I was a Freshman, my Bais Yaakov high school put on the melodrama *A Rose Among Thorns*, written by a Bais Yaakov teacher in New York.

When auditions were announced, there was quite a buzz in the hallways and many girls gathered to watch tryouts, even if they weren't trying out themselves. For my initial tryout, I sang "Part of Your World" from *The Little Mermaid*. I soon learned from the audience's reaction that Bais Yaakov girls did not typically audition with Disney songs. I chose a traditional Yiddish song for my callback audition.

I was thrilled to be cast as the titular Rose, or Raizel (Rose in Yiddish). Besides loving the stage, for a new kid coming from a different school than most other girls, getting cast for the junior lead put me on the map. Unlike the theater nerd stereotype so popular in shows like *Glee*, getting cast in a lead role in a Bais Yaakov production and having theatrical talent is a major source of social status. I played the

The author in costume for her role
in her high school production.

part of Raizel until intermission, when the character aged and was played by a popular junior instead.

Raizel starts the play as a teenage girl in Russia. She is convinced by a friend to attend a communist meeting, as a result of which she abandons Orthodoxy and becomes a communist. After a few years, she becomes disillusioned with communism, and in act two, her former comrades murder her parents. Raizel leaves Russia and moves to Israel to live on a secular Zionist kibbutz. Years pass and in act three, Raizel, now called Shoshana (Rose in Hebrew), becomes disillusioned with that lifestyle as well. She decides to move to Jerusalem and become religious again. However, her secular husband refuses to give her a *get* (Jewish divorce), so she ends the play tragically as an *agunah* (chained wife). The final note of the play is a voiceover by the actress who played Raizel's mother, raising awareness about the communal issue of *agunot*.

Being cast in a lead role, I thought the play was wonderful. I got to cry onstage and had many dramatic moments. However, some of the women in the all-female audience, my mother included, were perplexed. This was my mother's first exposure to a Bais Yaakov production, and she wondered why teenage girls were putting on such a depressing show. I saw their point, though caught up in the glory of having the final bow, it hadn't occurred to me before. Plotlines of Bais Yaakov plays often involved either physical danger from villains of Jewish history, spiritual danger, or both. Indeed, the authors of these scripts seemed not to have always given thought to the fact that the performers were teenage girls. In *A Rose Among the Thorns*, act one Raizel is the only character in the entire play who is a high-school-aged girl. Many of the characters are men and the other women are adults. Thinking back, Raizel's male friend, who exposes her to communism, could just as well have been another teenage girl. But these scripts did not seem tailored to the performers in this way.

In addition, unlike in Broadway shows, where song and dance numbers are woven organically into the storyline, drama in Bais Yaakov plays simply stopped, and the choir or dancers came on stage to perform. Scripts also required many different set and scenery changes as the action switched back and forth between locations. There seemed to be little thought given to how to stage the play to run more smoothly and require fewer behind-the-scenes changes. These elements of musical productions would be fairly obvious to someone well-versed in Broadway productions. However, in line with community norms, many of the women and girls involved in these productions did not have that exposure.

The "frum – not frum – frum again" plot line of *A Rose Among Thorns* was actually quite a common trope in Bais Yaakov productions. Students joked about how this was the second play in a row to have that narrative. Heavy, melodramatic, and moralizing messages were common as well. One school lampooned the scripts in their yearbook:

SYNOPSIS OF SCHOOL PLAY

SON: Father, I'm leaving.

FATHER: My son, you must go now. May Hashem (God) always be with you in all your endeavors. Do not forget for a moment what you have learned in your father's house. Let my teachings be with you on your journey. May you succeed B'Ezras Hashem (with God's help) to fulfill your goal, to accomplish your undertaking. Remember who you are and what you stand for. Go now in peace.

SON: Thank you for your blessing, Father. But was all that necessary when I was just going to the grocery store?[1]

Like high school students globally, girls in Bais Yaakov schools poked fun at their schools and its rules in yearbooks. In this example, students make fun of the heavy religious messaging typical of the plays, with a father giving a blessing appropriate for a major life event, which likely would have occurred in a play where the son is embarking on a religiously perilous journey, when the child in question (again, a father and son, not a mother and daughter) is merely running an errand.

The year after *A Rose Among Thorns*, my high school produced a song and dance revue. The theme of this production was the life cycle. The scenes included a bris, cheder, bar mitzvah, and wedding. I was in the cheder choir. My costume consisted of shiny black pantaloons, tzitzis, and a shtetl-style yarmulke cap, all made by the costume committee. My naturally curly hair stood in perfectly for ringlet *peyos*. I still remember the Yiddish song we sang as we ran through the theater aisles to stage, "In Cheder *Arein*," on our way to cheder. For the wedding scene, most of the students played grooms, while one lucky girl got to play the bride and wear a wedding gown on stage.

I thought the production was great. We took great pride in the professionalism of our work. Additionally, there was an element of competition between schools: our production had to be at least as

---

1. Bais Yaakov High School, *M'gama (Yearbook)*, Brooklyn, NY, 1980, n.p.

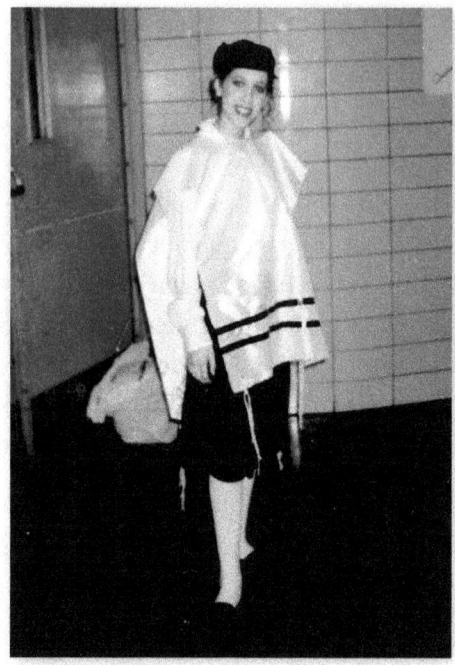

The author, age 15, in costume
for Cheder Choir. 1992.

good as our camp friends' school productions. But again, there were complaints from the audience. Why was an all-girls school focusing on the male lifecycle? Why are the girls playing boys for so much of the production? I saw their point, though it hadn't occurred to me before. Bais Yaakov girls always played boys, and within Jewish culture, the normative life cycle was the male experience. Boys and men have the famous milestones in Jewish life and the songs to go along with them. It didn't generally occur to the girls and women involved that an audience might think this odd. Apparently, many audience members did take issue, and the next year's production included an *Eishes Chayil* (Biblical Woman of Valor) scene.

In the late 1990s, my sister was hired to direct a Bais Yaakov play, but she did not like any of the scripts the school provided her as options. She and I co-write a script instead, which in a turn of events, I ended up directing. *The Goldeneh Medina,* set in the turn-of-the-century Lower

East Side, told the story of teenage Orthodox immigrant Soreleh, who befriends Rose, a secular Jewish girl from uptown. We tried to correct some of the issues we had seen in common scripts. The play had a clear, positive, religious message, but the storyline was light on drama and heavy on comedy. The characters who started the play religious remained religious throughout. The characters who started the play not religious remained not religious throughout. No one underwent any unrealistic changes, no one died in gruesome circumstances, and there were no Nazis or Cossaks. We strove for historical accuracy. In addition, unlike scripts that often jumped from set to set and back again, the script required one major set that remained throughout the play and allowed students to focus their energies on building this one set piece (it turned out spectacular). The main characters were all high-school-aged girls, and the vast majority of characters were girls and women. We wrote the dances and songs into the storyline of the script, replacing the trend at the time for dances and choirs to come out of nowhere and break into the drama artificially.

These changes did create some tension with students, particularly over the "marketplace" dance. When it was time for the dance during dress rehearsal, the dancers filed onto the stage, put down folding chairs backwards, and straddled the chairs, waiting for the music to start. I stopped the action and asked the dance heads why there were metal folding chairs in the middle of the Delancey Street market. They did not understand the question. I insisted, much to their very vocal chagrin, that the dancers needed to be on stage in the market scene from the beginning of the scene, and that they should sit on crates or some other object that one would naturally find there. The girls ultimately decided to sneak on stage during the scene and all pop out from behind crates and pushcarts when the music started. They did such a good job that during the actual show I didn't see them at all and had a moment of panic that they had missed their cue. But then they all popped out and the audience reacted with delight. No one, to my knowledge, objected to the changes I had introduced. Frankly, I don't think anyone really noticed them.

While Bais Yaakov schools had moved away from secular plays by the 1990s, summer camps were still borrowing scripts from Broadway for their summer productions. The camps kept most storylines intact, but lyrics and plot lines were rewritten as needed to remove overt sexual content, and of course, girls played all the roles, including men. I played Professor Higgins in a Camp Sternberg production of *My Fair Lady*. I was a little disappointed because I really wanted to play Eliza. I didn't mind playing a man, but Eliza's songs were better. Still, Higgins is quite a fun role, and I had no problem playing the domineering professor. My costume consisted of a cardigan sweater borrowed from a bunkmate and my black pajama pants. Even though the camp's dress code, in line with Bais Yaakov standards, required that girls wear skirts in public, camp leaders permitted me to wear pants when I was on stage playing a man. The camp left in the love triangle between Higgins, Freddy, and Eliza, but made a few lyrical edits. In the song "I could have danced all night," which follows Eliza's successful linguistic breakthrough, the words "I only know when he began to dance with me," were replaced with "I only know when he became so pleased with me." Indeed, the romantic dance between the two was removed from the script entirely. In the joyous "The Rain in Spain" scene, the actresses playing Eliza, Pickering, and I began dancing in a circle, like a hora, singing the famous song. The director approached us backstage in a panic, informing us that staff were complaining because male and female characters were touching, and we should take care not to touch anymore! The fact that we were all fourteen-year-old girls seemed irrelevant. We rolled our eyes and acquiesced.

In the ensuing years, productions have only increased in their production value and professionalism. Bais Yaakov high school students have mastered production tools and other recording software that I wish had existed when I was in high school. I would have had a lot of fun with them. I certainly miss the thrill of acting and being on stage. When I think back to high school, I think about production. When I reminisce with old high school friends, the conversation invariably turns to production. For me, as for many others, production created a lot of drama, both in front of and behind the curtain. It also provided opportunities for us to take leadership roles and hone skills we would go on to use in our professional lives. It gave us a social outlet and the chance to do something we loved. I'm grateful that the Bais Yaakov system provided and continues to provide this showcase for girls' talent and a significant opportunity for girls to build leadership skills.

Singing in the House of Jacob

Sarah Snider

Here is the story of a woman named Sarah Schenirer who lived in Krakow, Poland, at the turn of the twentieth century, as told in contemporary Bais Yaakov schools around the world.

Sarah Schenirer, a seamstress, noticed that while little Jewish boys got to go to little Jewish boy schools called cheders, little Jewish girls went to either 1) public schools or 2) no schools. This educational system caused a discrepancy between the little Jewish girls and little Jewish boys, because while the boys were able to absorb the knowledge and traditions of their long and glorious Ashkenazi Jewish heritage, the girls were not. Sarah Schenirer recognized this instructional gap as potentially destructive to the future of the Jewish people, since half of their numbers lacked any sort of informed understanding about their purpose in this intricate religious world. She decided to start a school for the little Jewish girls, which she called Bais Yaakov, often transliterated into English as Beth Jacob, or the House of Jacob. There was obviously some resistance among the rabbis of the time, because then – like today – men liked to think of themselves as the primary vessels for holy religious study, and women as inferior vessels. But then – also like today – there were some forward-looking men who agreed with Sarah Schenirer: in those difficult times of pogroms and persecution combined with a growing trend toward secular assimilation, the best answer to keeping the Jewish people from falling apart was educating the women. Pre-Holocaust Europe saw the growth of hundreds of

Jewish girls' schools due to the movement started by Sarah Schenirer. She directed her best students to go out and start schools of their own.

In the translated words of Sarah Schenirer, "The main goal of the Bais Yaakov school is to train the Jewish daughters so that they will serve the Lord with all their might and with all their hearts; so that they will fulfill the commandments of the Torah with sincere enthusiasm and will know that they are the children of a people whose existence does not depend upon a territory of its own, as do other nations of the world whose existence is predicated upon a territory and similar racial background."[1] This statement proved especially prescient in just a decade's time with the onset of World War II and the vast upheaval it brought upon the communities and territories of Western, Central, and Eastern Europe, home to Ashkenazi Jews for over one thousand years.

Sarah Schenirer, through foresight and determination, single-handedly changed the face of Jewish education and standardized what before had been seen as destructive and forbidden – the formal Jewish education of females. This proto-feminist movement as it existed in Europe was destroyed in the inferno of the Holocaust, but by that time it had spread across the ocean to the United States. Orthodox Jewish girls' schools called Bais Yaakov exist all over America today, connected through ideology and partnership embodied by the annual North American Bais Yaakov student conventions and Sarah Schenirer conferences.

* * *

A few months before I turned four, my parents enrolled me in nursery school. I would remain in the same school for the next fourteen years, in a class with largely the same twenty-five girls, and that school was Sally Allen Alexander Beth Jacob School for Girls: A Division of the Yeshiva Beth Yehuda of the Greater Metropolitan Detroit Area or, as we knew it, Bais Yaakov.

Bais Yaakov inevitably looks different today than it did back in

---

1. Kranzler, David. "An Orthodox Revolution: The Creation and Development of the Beth Jacob Seminary for Girls." *Yad Vashem*, Oct. 11, 1999, www.yadvashem.org/download/education/conf/Kranzler.pdf.

1900s Poland, even though no Bais Yaakov administrator worth her salt would ever admit to this. There is a distinct tendency in the Ashkenazi yeshivish Orthodox community to idealize the perceived spiritual purity of late European Jewry, to act as if thousands of years of Jewish history and custom can easily be tossed aside, or at least heavily filtered through the especially pious Eastern European perfection of the last two hundred years.[2] This sort of trend is exemplified in the chassidic movement, some of whose members truly believe that Moses wore a round furry hat perched atop his head as he descended from Mt. Sinai with the tablets three thousand years ago in the desert.

But unfortunately for those who might wish it to be, Bais Yaakov is not at all like it was in the days of old in one major and specific way: Sarah Schenirer's Bais Yaakov was nothing if not fluid and adaptable, whereas the modern-day ones are – in a word – rigid.

What does rigid look like? On the first day of first grade, when I was five, my mother dressed me up in an adorable sundress and drove me off to school. Before I even entered the building, I was turned around and sent home to change due to my immodestly bared arms.[3]

* * *

It's this sort of fundamentalism-tinged story that restrains me from telling people about my ultra-Orthodox schooling. I certainly spent a lot of time, especially in high school, getting called to the principal's office and berated for wearing eyeliner. I kept a pair of the ugliest, thickest, whitest knee socks I could find in my locker to change into when my ankle was caught flashing bare out of my long skirt, because if I had to wear knee socks, I wasn't going to bother trying to make them look good. But when people hear this, they think that I just barely escaped

---

2. See Yoel Finkelman, "Nostalgia, Inspiration, Ambivalence: Eastern Europe, Immigration, and the Construction of Collective Memory in Contemporary American Haredi Historiography," *Jewish History*, 23.1 (2009): 57–82.
3. For discussions of tznius in early Bais Yaakov schools, see Leslie Ginsparg Klein, "The Troubling Trend of Photoshopping History," *The Lehrhaus*, November 17, 2016; and Naomi Seidman, *Sarah Schenirer and the Bais Yaakov Movement: A Revolution in the Name of Tradition* (Liverpool: Littman Library of Jewish Civilization, 2019).

my crazy religious cultish upbringing. In truth, there's no escaping your crazy religious cultish upbringing. It happened, no matter what you think about it as an adult, no matter how much you've changed.

I have a number of friends and acquaintances who were raised in a much more modern and moderate Orthodox environment than I was – think Mennonites to the Amish – but still collect on the social currency of relaying the harrowing tale of their exit from the community to wide-eyed audiences. Others stay in the fold and capitalize on the opportunity to write the sort of popular "Look at My Bizarre Religious Lifestyle!" articles that all walks of secular persons, Jewish or otherwise, will read in order to assure themselves that they aren't crazy like Those People. And if that's the sort of thing you're looking for, there's a whole trending genre of ex-Orthodox content out there. Whatever my aim is, though, it's not to do that. I'm not here to feed the voyeurism beast or fight against my community. If anything, I'm fighting against myself.

* * *

A while ago, a video of two Bais Yaakov students[4] was leaked to YouTube without their permission. In this video, the girls are wearing nearly the same school uniform of a button-down Oxford blouse and ankle-length pleated skirt that I did for many years, and one of them has her hair in a long braid, maybe also for the same reason that I always did – long, loose hair is considered immodest, and I didn't want to cut mine off.

The video, which has over 120,000 views as of this writing, shows the girls rapping in front of their lockers about Dor Yeshorim, or "Upright Generation," an organization that goes to Orthodox Jewish high schools and gives the students blood tests to determine if they are carriers of any common Jewish genetic diseases. No names are ever recorded, and no one ever sees their results. A couple of years down the line, you just call the Dor Yeshorim offices with the number

---

4. "Dor Yeshorim Rap," *YouTube*, uploaded by Dor Yesharim, 18 May 2016, https://www.youtube.com/watch?v=JUFIBZwOccA.

you were assigned in high school and the number of the guy you're dating to see if you can get married, and Dor Yeshorim tells you *yes* or *no*. This way, you don't have to be sad when you enter the dating stage because you won't have to carry with you any definitive knowledge about whether your genes are uncontrollably trying to give your children Tay Sachs.

The secular Jewish media lost it. It was like a breath of life was suddenly discovered in the otherwise comatose body of teenage Orthodox Jewry. Despite the fact that the wet blanket of Orthodoxy was doing its darndest to smother the spirit out of its practitioners, these two heroic young women had somehow found out about rap and were using the medium to humorously sing about important aspects of their own lives, with lyrics like, "Doing this test to see if we're a match / And if it's a yes, well, I'm a really good catch / Going on a date to look for a connection / And under the chuppah, we'll express our affection." I read at least four different articles written in this breathless tone.

In the interest of realism, let me tell you a bit more about my own Bais Yaakov experience: Probably not a week of high school went by without someone making up a song about our lives, a tongue-in-cheek critique of our school or our community or our social structure, but one most often imbued with a sense of joy and absurdity, not a feeling of being trapped. We regularly performed and recorded the songs on digital cameras, but this was a time before smartphones and in the earlier days of YouTube, so no one ever saw our creations.

In fact, sometimes it feels like we didn't ever do anything but sing. We were frequently taught our lessons through song all throughout elementary and middle school, memorizing everything from the dates of Jewish holidays to Torah trivia to mathematical theories using tunes. ("THROUGHHHHHH EVERY TWO POINTS THERE'S EXACTLY ONE LINE, TWO POINTS DETERMINE A LINE!" shouted to the illicit tune of "Spongebob Squarepants.") We sat on the floor in circles and sang during recess. We sang after school in play practice and to elderly people in nursing homes on Sundays. We sang during class. We sang about which brand of deodorant was best. (For some reason, we thought it was Right Guard – "When you come back from the game / And you're feeling really lame / Use Right Guard / Use Right Guard.") We sang about the time the vending machine got Vitamin Water. We sang about the time a classmate accidentally said she was going to take off her shirt when she meant sweatshirt. We sang about the time the hallway ceiling collapsed because our school didn't have enough money to do necessary repairs. We sang about "Daring to learn, so that we won't burn" in hell. (It was a joke. We weren't in Catholic school.)

Sometimes we sang in protest. Instead of heading to class after singing our morning prayers, we would remain at our tables, singing about how we wanted to go to the Bais Yaakov Convention after our principal got into a disagreement with the principal of Bais Yaakov Montreal and decided that we wouldn't be participating that year. Sometimes the principal sang back, marching down the hall, chanting, "One detention, two detention, three detention, four! Who wants more?" as we scattered in all directions. The best image of this I can give you is that we lived in an episode of *Glee*, but instead of just the musical theater freaks and outcasts, we all sang, cool kids and nerds alike, because it was woven into the social fabric of our daily lives.

And so I reject the idea that those two rapping girls were breaking out of their communal shell or in any way subverting expectations of who they were and what they would become. This idea of Orthodox teenage girls as lifeless, uniformed dolls is an invention of those who opt to feel superior to them instead of merely different. Just because you aren't hearing Orthodox women sing, just because they don't sing in front of men, just because they aren't listening to the same secular music that you are and singing renditions of songs familiar to you, it doesn't mean they aren't doing it. Chances are, they will go off to seminary in Israel, as my classmates and I did, and have one last hurrah while preparing themselves to return to an immediate life of motherhood and responsibility. They'll come back changed, more demure, more serious, less likely to burst into song. But they'll send their daughters to Bais Yaakov, and their daughters will sing.

* * *

Here we see one of the key benefits of single-sex education for Orthodox girls. Certainly, you can argue that there are drawbacks, such as having a Judaic studies education that is non-equivalent to that of the boys. And this is true; ultra-Orthodox boys start learning Mishnah and Talmud in late elementary school, and the girls start learning it never. On the flip side, Orthodox girls tend to receive much stronger Biblical and secular educations since their time isn't totally eaten up by Talmudic study, whereas some boys never receive a high school diploma because they don't accomplish all of the state educational requirements.

In a world where women are restricted in what they can do, say, wear, and sing in front of men to whom they are not related (and even some to whom they are), single-sex education is the most liberating system possible within the confines of right-wing Orthodox religious practice. In all societies, religious or secular, women are taught to behave differently in front of men, to act *for* men. If you remove men from the equation, you create a women's realm where girls are free of those constraints (if not from the overarching Male Gaze), as demonstrated by all the singing as well as the countless other pranks and hijinks that we got up to. A few of my classmates once stole a couch and managed to sneak it across the school parking lot, through the auditorium, and up multiple staircases to a hidden closet of a room, where they created a secret lounge that went undiscovered by our principal for months. We switched uniforms with the Bais Yaakov in Cleveland, and another time we switched schools with another Orthodox girls' school in our neighborhood. We had personalities, I promise you.

* * *

During a class I took in college on Women, Culture, and Society in the Modern World, we read a text depicting the camaraderie that developed within the Victorian women's realm in the absence of men, and it felt very familiar to me. The text described a scenario in which a male suitor came to call upon a young woman, and, instead of accepting her visitor, she and her friends teased him and then ran away to her bedroom to have a wild sisterly romp. They were more concerned with their bond with one another than with pleasing a potential husband.

It reminded me of a story my mother told me about a time when my father came to pick her up for a date, and her younger sisters answered the door, giggled, and then slammed the door in his face. For me, the Victorian scene mirrored what it felt like to be in the environment of an all-girls' school where not only was there no one to date, but you would get kicked out if you did happen to be caught dating someone. You can argue that this strict system of gender segregation is sexually frustrating or to the detriment of the girls' process of maturing into adulthood. You can argue that it's madness that girls can't even talk to boys as seniors in high school but then are expected to find one and agree to marry him after knowing him for a matter of weeks at the age of nineteen. But even if those things are true, it doesn't erase the space that is created for girls to interact directly and organically with one another without worrying what the boy next to them will think.

The first time that I noticed that girls don't talk as much in class when boys are around was when I was sixteen and taking an SAT class at a local public school (since, of course, Bais Yaakov did not offer SAT prep). When my Bais Yaakov classmates and I got together, whether in class or out, it was nearly impossible to get a word in edgewise; no one felt too self-conscious to speak up. But in this SAT prep class, whenever the teacher, a graduate student at University of Michigan, would ask the group a question, I would look around and notice that the girls seemed to know all the answers and yet were just sitting there, silent and unmoving. Instead and inevitably, a boy would raise his hand and – not bothering to wait until he was called on – announce, "I don't know, man, but Jessica Alba is a fox." And all the other boys would nod and murmur in agreement, and the teacher would say, "Yes, that's true. I think we can all agree that Jessica Alba is a fox. But does anyone want to tell the class how they got C on this problem?"

* * *

As an adult, I feel torn. I want my daughters to have what I had, a place to develop their voices before they realize that they aren't supposed to. But do I want them to learn that knee socks are more important than their education? Should they come to understand that missing a math lesson is necessary if they need to spend the time in the bathroom with a tissue soaked in makeup remover wiping off their eyeliner instead?

* * *

When we were taught the story of Abraham and Sarah in Bais Yaakov, we learned that the greatness of Sarah lay in the fact that when asked by the three angelic visitors where she was, Abraham responded, "She's in the tent."[5] In the tent, where we know a woman belongs, because as Psalms 45:14 says, "All the glory of the daughter of a king is inside." In fact, this gender construct can be very reassuring for those women whose personalities don't fit in well with the American culture of career above all, who don't particularly want to spend their time working long hours to chase capitalist success and would rather stay home and form closer bonds with their families and children. For others, it feels like a trap.

I graduated from high school near the top of my class, but I received no awards. All of the honors given out were for exhibiting good behavior, positive community contributions, and kindness to others. None were for academic achievements. As each one of us crossed the stage, the principal announced our best attributes into the microphone. When I walked towards her, my long hair rolled up into a bun, she pointedly pronounced, "Intelligent and articulate, we hope that Sarah Snider will use her talents for Torah." All of my hours of studying were for nothing if I couldn't learn to behave.

I realize that the retelling of this story may hold more bitterness than I actually feel. I laughed it off both at the time and now; my classmates snickered and nudged me, and my ever-reliable brothers whooped and yelled, "Is that a threat?" from their seats in the audience. And yet, when I look back on it, I also realize how detrimental this attitude can be for the development of a woman who ultimately does want to seek success and recognition. I was such a woman, but it took me years to realize it and even admit it to myself, because seeking any

---

5. Genesis 18:9.

form of acknowledgement for one's work was possibly immodest, but definitely irrelevant.

* * *

When I was in graduate school for my MFA in Creative Writing, a television producer came to speak to a class I was taking on storytelling structure. I bumped into him later that day in the hallway and thanked him for his advice; he shook my hand and said to me, "Congratulations on being so ambitious." A number of my friends questioned why this man felt the need to bestow his good graces on me merely because I, a woman, was fighting to be ambitious. I have mixed feelings, though, because, on the one hand, they were right to point out that this compliment was almost certainly gendered. Conversely, having grown up in a society and culture that told me to be good, to be competent, and sometimes even to be smart, but never to be ambitious, receiving positive recognition of the fact that I found the courage to be ambitious was, to me, a reason to rejoice.

* * *

And maybe Sarah Schenirer is rolling over in her grave at the thought of me. Certainly, 1920s Sarah Schenirer probably wouldn't like many of the things about me, most of which I won't go into because I really have no desire to explain why people wouldn't like me. But it's possible that present-day Sarah Schenirer would tell me go to learn Talmud, to pick up some Aramaic, to try to take on a greater role in my community, to empower myself religiously and probably even career-wise. Those might not be the lessons that Bais Yaakov wanted me to absorb, but it's hard for me to imagine that progress stops in 1935.

* * *

In my year in a Modern Orthodox seminary in Israel, there was a girl named Beth who used to tease me because I went to such an ultra-Orthodox school. She would see me in the hallways and yell, "Look, it's Sarah Schenirer!" One time, a visiting rabbi came to speak to us, and she raised her hand and made a comment on the Torah text we were discussing.

"What's your name?" he asked.
"Beth," she responded.
"Hmm," he said thoughtfully. "Beth. Beth Jacob!"
 And, for once, I got the last laugh.

A Zine Called *The Heresy*: Angst and *Apikorsus* in a Modern Orthodox Day School

Sara Feldman, Abby Glogower, Sarah Gray

> We exist to penetrate and educate (if that is at all possible). If we fail in this venture, then at least we will be able to reflect on *The Heresy* and know that we were able to speak out intelligently in our dissent.
>
> We are capable of thought and capable of sharing it.
>
> – Editors' introduction to *The Heresy*, Vol. 1 (Fall 1994)

1. Growing Up Heretical

The Heresy was a literary zine (underground, self-published magazine) produced by adolescent authors Sara Feldman, Abby Glogower, and Sarah (Schreiber) Gray between the fall of 1994 and the spring of 1995 – our sophomore year at Akiva Hebrew Day School, a Modern Orthodox Jewish day school in Southfield, Michigan. Its five eight- to ten-page volumes were assembled with scissors and glue on our bedroom floors, xeroxed with our babysitting money in batches of up to twenty-five, and distributed surreptitiously to our friends.[1] In *The*

---

1. For a history of the zine medium and zine culture, see Stephen Duncombe, *Notes from Underground: Zines and the Politics of Alternative Culture*, 3rd ed. (Portland, OR: Microcosm 2017). For works on zines and feminism, see Alison

Heresy, we leveraged and satirized the teen magazine tropes of advice columns, top ten lists, and cartoons, which we printed alongside our attempts at serious fiction and commentary – writings that the authors now find both cringy and compelling (fig. 1).[2] A product of its time and place, *The Heresy*'s critique of power structures – including teachers and principals, capitalism, and social stratification – reflected the prevailing attitudes and concerns of disaffected youth culture of the mid-1990s. Yet the publication was unique in its exploration of a profoundly niche American identity: adolescent girls struggling with gender, class, and religion in the context of Modern Orthodoxy, a particular strain of Orthodox Judaism that provided enough intellectual stimulation to produce inquiry but was sufficiently stringent to confuse those who asked too many questions. At Modern Orthodox day schools such as Akiva, boys and girls studied secular subjects together but learned Hebrew and Torah separately and according to different curricula. Secular culture was alternately embraced and shunned on the basis of a seemingly inscrutable logic. Humility and piety vied with money and power in the establishment and maintenance of communal order.

In the early 1990s, the Orthodox community of Detroit was mostly spread between two adjacent suburbs: Oak Park and Southfield. The Oak Park community included more traditional Orthodox families, including the majority of the yeshivish community. Modern Orthodoxy was based in Southfield, the next urban-flight ring out from Detroit's urban core. While the affluent lived in both cities, those with lower incomes tended to reside in Oak Park or near its border.[3] At a farther

---

Piepmeier, *Girl Zines: Making Media, Doing Feminism* (New York: New York University Press 2009); and Rebekah J. Buchanan, *Writing a Riot: Riot Grrrl Zines and Feminist Rhetorics* (New York: Peter Lang 2018). Although there are zines by Jewish authors and about Jewish topics, the literature on them is very limited. For a list of notable Jewish zines, see Rena Yehuda Newman, "Eight Nights of Jewish Zines," *New Voices*, December 10, 2020, https://newvoices.org/2020/12/10/eight-nights-of-jewish-zines. In 2019, Chava Shapiro founded the Jewish Zine Archive, which is based in Tucson, Arizona (https://www.instagram.com/jewishzinearchive/).

2. Most creative content was generated by the author-editors, but *The Heresy* did feature some submissions from like-minded classmates.

3. Metro Detroit's Orthodox Jews lived alongside Black and Chaldean neigh-

Figure 1 "The psyche of the typical Yeshivat Akiva Hi skuwel stoodant." The front page of *The Heresy 4* is a chaotic pastiche from the minds of its fifteen-year-old authors in early 1995.

bors. These populations were viewed as threats, and Jewish day schools provided an effective means of ensuring that Orthodox children did not mingle with their non-Jewish neighbors. White Anglo-Saxon Protestants had their own exclusive suburbs. Ours were places where these three outsider populations could safely migrate in pursuit of suburban prosperity. Relations were begrudgingly tolerant but certainly not warm.

geographic distance from the shifting epicenter of Orthodox Jewish money, Oak Park kids were rarely seen at Southfield Shabbos tables or afternoon hangouts – unless they made the five-mile trek or got invited to sleep over. Shabbos afternoon hangouts in Southfield comprised social life outside of school, characterized by walks, games, basketball, and gossip – especially about the Oak Park kids, their smaller houses, and their cheaper clothes.

By age fifteen, we understood that we were mismatched with our environment. Friends since middle school, we were (each in her own way) weird, bookish, creative, curious, and troubled by injustice. Significantly, we all came from families that could not afford full tuition for their multiple children at Akiva. Sarah – the daughter of Deadheads, one of whom converted to Judaism – had been at Akiva the longest but lived in the more affordable and religiously observant adjacent suburb of Oak Park. She had been excluded and bullied at Akiva for her entire life as teachers and principals – reluctant to discipline cruel children of wealthy parents – consistently looked the other way.

The daughter of educated professionals who were *baalei teshuva*, Sara joined the fifth-grade class at Akiva after Bais Yaakov administrators had explained to her parents that they could not stop children with *yichus* from bullying her.[4] Leaving the atmosphere of Bais Yaakov worsened Sara's situation; living in Southfield did not spare her from becoming an instant outcast at Akiva.

Abby was the daughter of a University of Michigan Hillel rabbi, and in seventh grade she began the fifty-minute commute from Ann Arbor to Southfield. Blessed with an out-of-town cachet, Abby found

---

4. Sarah and Sara also suffered the misfortune of sharing a name not only with each other, but with a number of wealthy and more popular Sara(h)s. We were thus rarely called by our own names at Akiva. Sarah was called "Schreiber" so constantly and derisively that she pursued a legal name change in adulthood. For context, the boys at Akiva often called each other by their last names, but Sarah was "Schreiber" to everyone, boys and girls alike. Sara, intending to have more control over what Akiva classmates would call her, periodically announced new nicknames for herself. Until we graduated, only family and close friends called us by our first name. Dear reader, rather than distinguishing ourselves again in the same manner, we direct your attention to the spelling of our names as a way of telling us apart in this essay.

more social success with Akiva students but clashed regularly with teachers and administration. Our parents found meaning, safety, and beauty in Orthodox Judaism and believed that a Modern Orthodox day school would provide those things to us as well. But despite their loving intentions and financial sacrifice, we didn't belong there and longed for a world where we did.

In the pages of *The Heresy*, we see three misfits painfully and defiantly searching for authentic political, intellectual, and ethical life inside a financially secure, suburban Modern Orthodox Jewish community. By turns vulgar and cliché, and occasionally luminous, *The Heresy* functioned not only as a mirror of the culture and communities around us, but also as an attempt to imagine ourselves in other worlds, worlds we continue struggling to build even now. In this essay, the authors return after twenty-five years to the awkward but impassioned creation of our adolescence, approaching the magazine with the benefit of some academic training to explore people in place and time, but also with the painful intimacy of lived experience forever inscribed on the walls of our interior worlds. Ultimately, we find that in *The Heresy* our younger selves began articulating the values that guide our adult lives. It contained the seeds of the surprisingly durable, non-normative connections to our Jewishness that we would maintain into adulthood and our professional lives at the margins of Jewish institutional life.

II. Between and Beyond Torah Umadda

How did the concept of the *apikores* enter our lexicon? Possibly through the crumbs of Talmud study that fell to us from the men's side of the table, where we saw the serious study and vaunted intellectual life of Judaism happening. Alternately translated for us by our teachers as an apostate and a heretic, the *apikores* was an Epicurean, someone like the Talmudic figure Rabbi Elisha ben Avuya, a great Torah scholar who opted to Hellenize, his outsider status reflected in his nickname "*Acher*" (Other). Curious, rebellious, impassioned skeptics, we found the *apikores* (as fun for adolescents to pronounce as "epidermis") tremendously appealing. Still too young to imagine ourselves outside our Modern Orthodox milieu, we grasped at the world beyond it through bits and snatches of the popular culture permitted to us by Modern Orthodoxy's bargain: access to the non-Jewish world was cautiously permitted, so long as we remained inside the community, accepting its mandates and values. This Judaism was "Modern," but it was also "Orthodox," and so could only permit so much elasticity. Thus, to be non-Orthodox was simply to be irrelevant or disdained. In our world, Jewish sects not based on halakhic observance were regarded as illegitimate failures, their adherents were barely more Jewish than non-Jews, and association with them was strongly discouraged. One Akiva rabbi explained to us that the Holocaust was divine punishment for Reform Judaism, whose adherents were currently delaying the coming of *Moshiach*.

We found this post-Holocaust theodicy and many other of our Torah teachings to be morally unacceptable and ignorant of the non-Jewish world. In turn, we began to question the *madda* (secular knowledge) our community embraced. Where did it come from? What values did it espouse? Perhaps most importantly, was there more we were missing? Our school's motto, "The Best of Both Worlds," begged the question: by what and whose measurement? As it was becoming increasingly clear, not ours. We began to wonder if *apikorsim* had an important duty: to learn about the outside world in order to destabilize orthodoxies by questioning commonly accepted beliefs and working to resolve their inconsistencies and hypocrisies. In naming our paper *The Heresy* we were not renouncing our Judaism so much as wrestling with it, searching for what resonated as meaningful, ethical, and interesting. We yearned for other ethical Jewish models. Socialism and atheism were de facto apostate positions, so profoundly had the memory of the Jewish Left – another rebellious child of halakhic Judaism – been erased from our contemporary community's collective consciousness together with Yiddish. Along with folk religion, women's traditions, and other trappings of our "ghetto" heritage, we sensed there were righteous ghosts waiting to be reclaimed as part of our Jewish birthright, conveying to us a usable past.

Textual production, we were beginning to discover, provided a means of working through problems, and a vehicle of communication across generations, culture, and distance. If the debates of the rabbis, immortalized in the Talmud (that we were not permitted to study), were a guide to critical thinking, how could we devise reckonings of our own? A pair of Abby's poetic contributions to *The Heresy* provide a window into our fraught desire to live ethical lives beyond the dictates of halakhah. "Magic in the Middle" and "The Boy with 2 Heads" both seem, at first glance, like adolescent literary trash. But together they express the impossible moral and intellectual position of the Modern Orthodox teenager (fig. 2). The Boy is a "magnetically hideous" freak who, "born still" and "encased in glass," never had the chance at life. One head is of course the Orthodox one, and the other is secular American. It would seem that two heads would provide four eyes and greater insight (as either the greater ability to see, or the trope of the bespectacled prolific reader). Instead of enabling this creature to study its world and its own predicament, these eyes are "vacuous," trained "eternally upward" towards the heavens, repeating an unquestioning

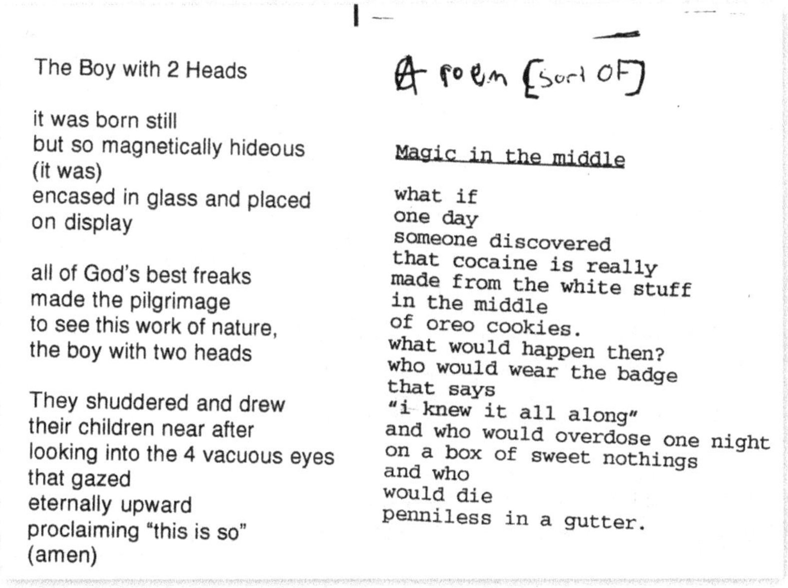

The Boy with 2 Heads

it was born still
but so magnetically hideous
(it was)
encased in glass and placed
on display

all of God's best freaks
made the pilgrimage
to see this work of nature,
the boy with two heads

They shuddered and drew
their children near after
looking into the 4 vacuous eyes
that gazed
eternally upward
proclaiming "this is so"
(amen)

A poem (sort of)

Magic in the middle

what if
one day
someone discovered
that cocaine is really
made from the white stuff
in the middle
of oreo cookies.
what would happen then?
who would wear the badge
that says
"i knew it all along"
and who would overdose one night
on a box of sweet nothings
and who
would die
penniless in a gutter.

Figure 2 Abby's teenage poetry in *The Heresy* 3 (left) and 2 (right).

"amen." Like an educated woman saying *"amen"* every morning to *"shelo asani isha,"* "The Boy" accepts an eternity of marginalization and silence.

How might we escape this fate? Little epicureans, we had begun studying, questioning, and critiquing the world around us, longing for intellectual engagement, sensual pleasures, just causes, and above all the freedom they signified. But we also feared that world and worried whether we were equipped to navigate it responsibly. This uncertainty appears in "Magic in the Middle," a poem conflating the consumption of hard drugs and nonkosher confections, specifically cocaine and Oreo cookies, a staple of American childhood which was not yet kosher.[5] We knew that both these things were forbidden, but we needed to know why and what distinguished them so that we could develop our own authentic moral and ethical codes. Was it measurement or mindset that distinguished the baring of knees from the wearing of a miniskirt? What about mixed dancing versus sexual adventures; opening mail on Shabbos versus drunk driving; sneaking food on Yom Kippur versus chemical dependency on tobacco? What tools equipped us to navigate dangerous excesses and murky moral territory? If drugs and Oreos were revealed to be one and the same, the poet posits, some might fail the test and "overdose one night / on a box of sweet nothings" or "die penniless in a gutter," the excessive rules of their childhood education having deprived them of the ability to respect danger and make reasonable distinctions. A more noble fate awaits those who "knew it all along," who had developed strong character and internal moral compasses. Frustrated, we experimented in speaking back to our world, poking fingers in its fallacies and failings, knowing there was nowhere else we could be except marginal, or *acher*.

The editors' introduction in the first volume of the Heresy established our embattled religious, social, and intellectual positions by recognizing that an "underground paper" came with "dangers...both

---

5. Oreo cookies became certified kosher in 1997. Julia Langer, "Getting the Lard Out: The Koshering of the Oreo Cookie," *Cornell Chronicle*, February 26, 2008, https://news.cornell.edu/stories/2008/02/getting-lard-out-koshering-oreo-cookie.

Volume #1

~The Heresy~

Wowee! free match with every issue

Introduction

The idea of an underground newspaper has long been toyed with at the school. Upon deciding to actually get off our butts and create the Heresy, we recognized the dangers involved both external and from within. We are no strangers to the evils of a publication if not managed properly and considerately. We would never think of openly slandering individuals at Akiva, niether students nor faculty, as we do not wish to be insolent aggravators. We view this paper as an offshoot of the infamous slam book era. (The slam book suffered at the hands of one student who found the concept of truth to be too disturbing.)

We exist to penetrate and educate (if that is at all possible). If we fail in this venture, then atleast we will be able to reflect on the Heresy and know that were able to speak out intelligently in our dissent.

We are capable of thought and capable of sharing it.

-The Heresy

Contents

Intro... p.1
Short Story... p.1
Question/Answer... p.5
Fads et Akiva... p.4
Movie Commercial Reviews... p.4

hi KIDS!

Hans and Grethel

Once upon a time, there was a little blond German girl who lived in the woods, hundreds of years before all the village's Jews would be lined up and shot there.

The little German girl, named Grethel, spent all her days combing lemon juice into her hair and singing bawdy songs. She dreamed that someday a king would find her, be blinded by her blondness, and change the country's religion so he could divorce his wife and marry Grethel.

One day, an old peasant woman came to the river, where Grethel sang and added bleach to a shampoo. Grethel had instincts to turn the hag away, but even in her isolation she was familiar with the local folklore about heroes whose kindness to freaks payed for itself in the end.

"Oh, have a glass of water, Grandmother, and sit down that we may talk awhile." The tired old woman accepted, and joined Grethel at the riverbank.

"Thank you, dear child. I am so weary. Would you like to buy an apple?"

"Oh, no. I never eat food offered by strangers, even by those as kindly-appearing as you."

"Then may I offer you a magic potion that turns hair a much more natural shade of platinum than does your well-intended attempt?"

-1-

(continued on p.2)

Figure 3 The introduction to *The Heresy* and its first literary piece. Composed by Sara Feldman, "Hans and Grethel" exhibits a snarky mistrust of the non-Jewish world. Here, texts collected by the Grimm Brothers are parodied as bigoted, shallow, and sexist. Holocaust memory overwhelms the outward gaze, but the piece also displays a typical flattening of Holocaust history and ancestral European geography common in Jewish education, situating the Einsatzgruppen in German-speaking lands rather than Slavic ones. "Ukraine" was a word we had never encountered in school or through Orthodox media.

external and from within" (fig. 3). Outside threats were obvious: censure, discipline, or expulsion from school administrators. But perhaps more significantly, we grappled with the ethics of our critique, wanting to be absolutely honest about ideas without heaping cruelty on individuals. Thus, in grasping prose, our introduction pledged not to slander particular faculty or students as we sought to hold a mirror to our environment. "We exist to penetrate and educate (if that is at all possible)," we averred, "If we fail in this venture, then at least we will be able to reflect on *The Heresy* and know that we were able to speak out intelligently in our dissent." Already at age fifteen, we sensed the futility of attempting to reorder our world, but also a profound moral imperative to at least try. Submitting to an inconsistent logic of halakhah was confounding enough, but we also witnessed daily the scholastic and other advantages afforded our well-to-do peers and the struggles the less privileged among us faced. The Torah we were taught neither explained nor offered any solutions for the troubling social stratification of our communities, igniting a fierce egalitarianism and bent towards social and economic justice that has remained with us ever since.

III. Derekh Eretz: Defying Class and Gender

Today, we have the benefit of hindsight and a more academic understanding of North American Judaism in historical context. Our teenage selves, chafing strenuously at practices a Jewish community had developed in response to historical and economic stresses, only saw the Modern Orthodox community of Southeast Michigan as hypocritical and unfair. Taught to be vigilant against the pressure of antisemitism, we were also wholly uneducated about, for example, economic factors: their role in stoking and suppressing antisemitism, their pressure on United States immigrant communities, and their implications for nongovernmental institutions. We did not know then that Modern Orthodoxy was a still young substrain of American Judaism that had pronounced its distinction from the traditional, immigrant cultures of Jews more recently landed in the United States. By the time we arrived at Akiva in the early 90s, Modern Orthodoxy had solidified its pride in its elite education, class manners, and embrace of mainstream American capitalism. We lived in the crosshairs of a "model minority" strategy: alongside its other contradictions, the community wanted to secure political and economic protection for fidelity to Torah and halakhah while evading the antisemitism directed at more conservative and conspicuously cloistered strains of Orthodoxy.

We did not know the history, but we were becoming curious and skeptical observers, troubled by exclusionary practices our community upheld in its effort to cultivate a successful and modern American Jewish identity. We worried that in the process, we were being (mis)educated in the prevailing ways and values of the land. Just as Modern Orthodoxy struggled to classify the status of non-Orthodox Jews, it also strained to name and acknowledge gaps in economic class endemic to (but so often willfully ignored within) American culture. We observed that community leadership consisted of doctors, lawyers, and businessmen who drove new cars, traveled regularly to Israel, and sent their teenagers to the mall with hundreds in pocket money. Community standing was earned through conspicuous philanthropy, sponsored kiddush luncheons, and paying full price for day school tuition. The *gemach* (communal chest) and food aid[6] found in other Orthodox communities did not exist in ours because its members were not supposed to need them. Genuine *chesed* seemed to be in short supply; Zionism was militant, even though Israel was considered still a bit shabby to live in; political debates oscillated vaguely between Democrats and Republicans but never passionately enough to divide a shul; Shabbos lunch conversations often turned to discussions of home remodeling, US–Israel relations, and the perceived scourge of (middle-class) Black people moving into Jewish neighborhoods. Rolling our eyes at the adults, we were also infuriated by how socioeconomics seemed to impact the elasticity of halakhic observance. For instance,

---

6. In 1990, a kosher food pantry serving the region opened its doors in Berkley, MI. Some Akiva students were known to volunteer a little at this charity; needing the food was another story.

we noticed that the wealthier a family was, the more its members could socially afford halakhic laxity such as Triangle K (or sometimes no *hechsher* at all) in the cupboards, immodest dress, and wearing a toupee to work "instead" of a yarmulke. Torah devotion was expected, but just as important was fealty to American capitalism: a successful career (for men), a large, well-appointed house, and a smartly dressed, college-educated family that vacationed often in Israel and Florida.

Akiva groomed us to join these ranks of an Orthodox Jewish elite of polished and educated doctors, lawyers, and businesspeople deftly mixing with the secular world, but only so far as it suited their financial advancement. Ours was a world steeped in the promise of United States exceptionalism: an infallible democracy where a hard-working off-white minority could participate and succeed. But this devotion carried a dark ethical fallacy, asserting that our country was a place where those who had money deserved it and those who did not were some combination of lazy or unwise. Like the claim that Reform Jews had caused the Holocaust, this, too, we could not accept. We felt moral outrage at an orientation to the world which we struggled to square with our own emerging values of creativity, equality, personal liberty, and feminism.

Using the pastiche of material and intellectual tools available to us, *The Heresy* questioned not just the halakhic underpinnings of our Orthodox world but the *derekh eretz* of the later-stage capitalism on which it was premised. We chose a masthead font that lent an air of elegance and legitimacy. A tongue-in-cheek *Beis-Samech-Daled* (the initials for "with God's help" common in Orthodox writing practice) graced the upper right-hand corner of every page, signaling our erudition in *limudei kodesh* and the earnestness of our moral position. The first volume introduced readers to two recurring cartoon characters. One (the work of Abby) was "Stickie," an androgynous, uninhibited id-figure who spoke without restraint (fig 4). Irascible, nonsensical and crude, Stickie was a mere assemblage of slapdash lines, free from both the oppressively heteronormative order governing our day school existence and the clothing that ordered our subjugation by gender, class, and school administration.

Figure 4 The Heresy 1 introduces Avana and Stickie. We knew nothing about the Chinese Communist leader Mao Zedong. But growing up in an environment thoroughly scrubbed of the shameful stain of communism, the mere name was enough to inspire curiosity.

In contrast, Sara created Avana, a characterless naïf, whose Hebrew-sounding portmanteau of familiar Modern Orthodox day school names (Ilana, Avi, Aviva, etc.), made her a kind of Akiva everygirl: bland, pliable, unquestioning (fig. 4). In her deadpan debut she is indistinguishable from her retinue, carbon copies in the preppy GAP clothing that was de rigueur in affluent, early 90s suburbia: skirts covering girls' knees, and boys' heads yarmulka'ed. The distance separating the boys and girls is marked with a mandate posed as a question: *"Shomrei negiah?"*[7] – noting the hypocrisy of pieties that were publicly performed but privately breached. The figures' mouths curl downward in sour, contemptuous haughtiness, a cartoonish reflection of the tormentor peers whose ranks we could not afford to join. In subsequent cartoons, Avana would experiment with rebellious behaviors: smoking cigarettes, getting suspended, and – in true mid-90s American fashion – dancing in a concert mosh pit. But Avana's escapades are all empty posturing. Throughout, she remains simpering,

---

7. "Do they observe the laws forbidding physical contact between genders?"

insubstantial, a stuffed flannel shirt. Her noncommittal attempts to trade JAP (Jewish American Princess) existence for alternative cachet fall flat. She is the archetypal poseur whose aspirational coolness is not subversive but surface. In essence, she is the model Akiva student, one who might sample noncommittally from the buffet of popular culture in the secular world but will ultimately recede back into the environment from whence she came, assuming the materialistic circumscribed life of mitzvot and maternity – or at the very least, the performance thereof.

Avana was but one expression of the twin crises of gender and class we struggled to navigate in our Akiva world. How were we to enact American adolescence as Modern Orthodox teens, and what kind of adulthood awaited us on the other side of this passage? Alienated from Christian models of gender and sexuality, we could glimpse the secular teenage world of dates and dances in popular culture, but it was not ours to inhabit. A collective pining for that unrealized life became an act of social cohesion for Akiva girls, fixating on the teenagers in magazines and TV shows, obsessing over makeup, clothing, and boys. On Shabbos mornings on the women's side of the *mechitza* (partition) at Young Israel of Southfield, heads rose in turn as one walked the gauntlet of sartorial scrutiny shared by mothers and daughters. There was no logical place for these women, either. College-educated (Stern and Touro), they studied teaching, social work, even medicine, and sometimes maintained careers after marriage. Yet, it seemed to us that they could never be respected for their intellect within their religious community. But for procreating, cooking, decorating, and chauffeuring, they were somehow extraneous. However beautiful or smart a young Akiva girl might be, dowdy invisibility in a roomy, beaded sweaterdress was ultimately her ideal fate. We worried increasingly that what we would now call gender normativity and cis-heterosexuality – a necessary condition for a respected identity – also spelled the destruction of identity.

Family was truly destiny, both in that our lives were meant to culminate in marriage and motherhood but also in the economic hierarchy governing our school. To be a "poor" weirdo from Oak Park was to occupy a precipitous position in the social order, and consequently Sarah suffered tremendously. One of the smartest students in the class, her intellectual gifts were always apparent but undervalued. She was bullied constantly by wealthy students for her modest lunches, ill-fitting clothes, and lack of social graces – and the teachers knew whose side they were required to take. During high school, when grades started to count for college, her intelligence was finally appreciated, but by wealthy students who wanted help boosting their grades. She found herself provisionally invited to hangouts with short-term friends only in exchange for tutoring or paper writing.

Sarah's first-person narrative piece in Volume 3, "TNT Holland & Silver Bic," painfully expresses her anguished conflict between self-worth (or even superiority) and self-hatred as she endures the humiliations of having a female body, lower economic class, and powerful mind at Akiva in this moment (fig. 5). Outcast and victimized, she recounts the tutoring sessions paid for not with cash but with a few hours of friendship and the opportunity to "stay for dinner." She describes the rare luxury of having a new dress and the struggles to conform her body to biologically impossible standards. She narrates not-so-accidentally cutting the skin of her legs while attempting to fulfill the social mitzvah of hairlessness. Decorating her body, she muses "at school they all think shes nothing, but she dont care because she's like, superwoman, and she giggles and laughs and makes a fool of herself." Eschewing the grammar, spelling, and typographical conventions she had long before mastered, Sarah also intentionally misspells the word "friend," inverting the "i" and "e" to show the artificial nature of social relationships in her unfriendly world. Torn between pride in her own intellect and shame at social rejection, the narrator cries in the shower, then seeks a self-destructive solace in the forbidden act of smoking cigarettes, though it "cuts her throat. because she wants to." She finds some hope and comfort in music: "not doing her math homework, instead playing guitar, but not very well. but she'll be good."

Smoking as destructive agency and music as escape also appear in Sarah's later piece, "Supermart." Unlike the tortured, insecure girl of

Figure 5 "TNT Holland & Silver Bic" (excerpt), *The Heresy 3*. We don't remember consciously pairing the story with a clipping from a Victoria's Secret catalog, but the juxtaposition is perfect.

"TNT," the protagonist-narrator of "Supermart" is comfortable in his body and social position. Tellingly, he is also a non-Jewish boy named Kevin. Free from both the pressures of appearance that stalked Akiva girls and the lucrative career mandates for the Akiva boys, Kevin is free and self-assured, despite his mediocrity. He knows his band is terrible at playing music, but they persist joyfully in this pastime. He contemplates love but rejects the possibility of romance with a fellow cashier, believing he might be better off alone. Kevin is far less talented than the protagonist of "TNT," but he also suffers less. For Kevin, smoking cigarettes and drinking serve his pleasure impulse, not the self-harm and escapism that drive the narrator of "TNT." He lives for his own enjoyment without worrying for the future, casually accepting that it is likely without promise. Whereas the narrator of "TNT" often wishes to be like the rich people she tutors, Kevin reflects matter-of-factly on his job as a cashier in the supermart and the system in which he is imbricated: "These stupid people give me money – lots of it – and lucky me! I get to put it in a machine, where I don't get any of it (stupid me)." Kevin is a fantasy of freedom whose existential ease only seemed possible outside the rigid class and gender structures of Modern Orthodoxy. Kevin also nods at the masculine misfit archetypes of individualistic rebels and learned truth speakers filtering down to us through popular culture – in essence, secular *apikorsim*. But our escape into these cultural realms was fraught, for the world of our literary heroes – like the rabbinic world – was largely a space for men.

IV. Curiosity and Conformity in the Grunge Age

Just as the extra-Talmudic culture of our foremothers had been erased as the shameful trappings of a primordial, non-Zionist ghetto, so, too, was the rest of secular Jewish culture (except for some of the streams which focused upon the Holocaust and Zionism). We knew that the Torah belonged to the men, but we did not yet know that secular Torahs had long ago emerged from Jewish culture, that there was a world of letters more inclusive of women, more inquisitive about achieving a just *olam hazeh*, and very interested in the contours of Jewish identity in a secular world. Jewish American literature was rare in our curriculum and Yiddish literature was nonexistent. Deprived of this line of access to our own culture along with expressions of any other marginal or hybrid identities, we were left grasping at white, Christian, male models. While they taught us much about individualism, intellectualism and worldly experience, they failed to help us find our footing in a racist, capitalist, patriarchal, theocratic society.

Academically, Akiva Hebrew Day School's "The Best of Both Worlds" meant a dedicated "Torah True" Jewish education (*limudei kodesh*) and (supposedly) college-preparatory secular studies (*limudei chol*). Colloquially, students called these simply "Hebrew" and "English" classes. Our Hebrew teachers, who typically hailed from a more traditional Orthodoxy (except for the Israelis), were expected to teach as strict a reading of halakhah as they saw fit in exchange for allowing extensive classroom discussion instead of mere drilling. Teachers of secular subjects were usually nonobservant Jews or not Jewish at all, offering us the smallest and safest glimpses at real-life extra-Jewish existence. Because our particular strain of Judaism maintained a liberal romance, at least a surface one, with the world of ideas, we existed in a fragile intellectual and cultural space wherein access to popular culture was somewhat limited but not explicitly forbidden. Students like us could choose, in effect, how much we wanted to engage with the secular world: no one stopped us from being curious, but the environment also made genuine curiosity into an act of rebellion. For instance, while our "Hebrew" teachers entertained debates on a wide range of topics, from the finer points of food preparation halakhah to the sources of rabbinic authority, "English" teachers shrugged off our questions about "gays in the military" (a major subject in the news at the time) as inappropriate for class discussion.

Our growing feeling of being silenced and controlled is decried explicitly on the cover of Volume 3 (fig. 6). A picture scavenged from some magazine depicts a young victim being restrained by grown men as they cut out his tongue, with the attendant caption "The Akiva Police at Work," adding: "Could this be happening to you or someone

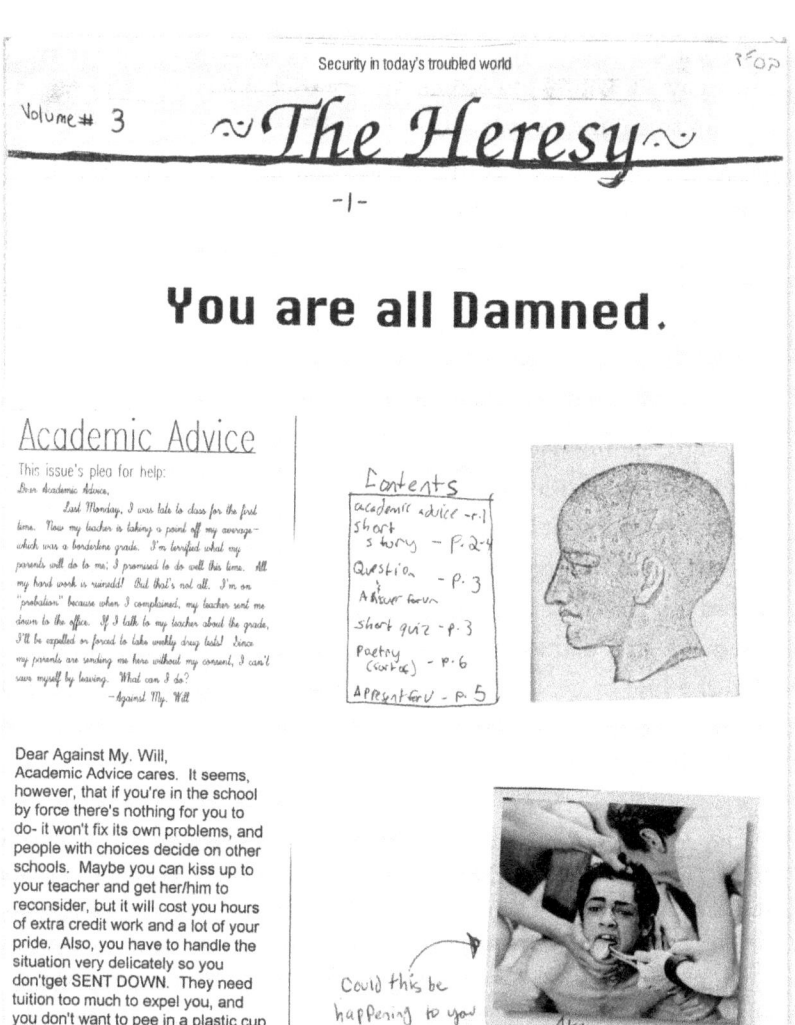

Figure 6 "The Akiva Police at Work," *The Heresy 3*.

you know?" The original magazine caption, "The Cincinnati Police at Work," and its context were things we barely grasped at the time. We knew only that the image was shocking and therefore appealing. In fact, it was a still from Pier Paolo Pasolini's controversial antifascist film *Salò* (1975), which was in the news as part of an ongoing First Amendment and gay rights case.⁸ In 1994, Cincinnati police had arrested the staff of the gay bookstore Pink Pyramid on obscenity charges for renting the film to an undercover officer fishing for pornographic material.⁹ Largely clueless about the culture wars raging in U.S. discourse at the time, we were barely beginning to understand that censorship and homophobia also existed outside our Akiva bubble, aided by police and state oppression.¹⁰ (Certainly, we were not being educated about the connections between American racism and European fascism.¹¹) Lacking nuance or a sense of scale, "The Akiva Police at Work" is at least indicative of how trapped we felt. The forcible cutting out of the tongue signified to our teen selves the stifling of the overpowered individual, the unfreedom of our existence.

Our environment did feel totalitarian, and we lived in fear at school. When the rabbi charged with enforcing morning minyan attendance figured out that we had skipped davening, we had to flee our hiding spot in the girls' bathroom for foliage near the playground or scramble onto the higher ground of toilet seats when he eventually barged through the door to apprehend us. Special humiliation rewarded

---

8. *Salò, or The 120 Days of Sodom* is a film adaptation of the Marquis de Sade's *The 120 Days of Sodom* with the setting moved to the Nazi puppet state in Italy (the fascist Italian Social Republic, also known as the Republic of Salò), thus – like the photo captions – mismatching levels of cruelty from different contexts.
9. The pink triangle was a Nazi concentration camp badge marking prisoners as "homosexual." (A pink triangle superimposed on a yellow triangle to make a six-pointed star indicated a "Jewish homosexual.") To commemorate the victims of persecution and the homophobia prolonging the AIDS epidemic, gay rights activist groups have used the pink triangle as a positive symbol, sometimes visually reversing the Nazi version by inverting it into the pink pyramid.
10. Unfortunately, we have not been able to recall or find the print source of this clipping. For a glimpse of the national conversation about the Pink Pyramid case in 1995, see Wray Herbert, "Is Porn Un-American?" *U.S. News & World Report* (July 3, 1995), 51.
11. See, for example, James Q. Whitman, *Hitler's American Model: The United States and the Making of Nazi Race Law* (Princeton, NJ: Princeton University Press 2017).

our nonconformity to the formal and informal expectations set for clothing. For scholarship students such as us, uniform violations could result in being "sent down" (to the principal's office); periodically, an entire classroom of girls had to line up against the wall so a rabbi could check skirt length.[12] This discipline, combined with our classmates' mockery of off-brand or home-sewn clothing, turned our vestments into a daily source of struggle to delineate and preserve our identities against conformist erasure. We feared being teased and persecuted for clothing that deviated from the Akiva norm, but we did not concede to adopt it.

Sara's story "Beige" (Volume 4) transports readers directly into the physical and psychic spaces of our Akiva classrooms. By 1995, the facilities of the former Annie Lathrup School were already in sorry disrepair, and everything inside was shabby, uninspired, and devoid of decoration or cheer. The narrator of "Beige" recounts being reprimanded for violating the school dress code two ways at once: her oversized and fuzzy cream shirt has no collar and is neither white nor light blue. But this small act of rebellion is a trap and the narrator's efforts to stand out ultimately subsume her within the dilapidated beige walls and furnishings of her classroom. Over four short, synesthetic paragraphs, the narrator becomes physically and emotionally overwhelmed by the dullness of the sensory environment – the clanging of the broken heaters, the monochrome room, its preponderance of rules whose arbitrariness, becoming – like the color beige – inscrutable, exasperating, and even violent. The mounting pressure eventually tumbles down a slippery slope of panic:

> The teacher's sharp voice cut into the sound as my closest friends in the class were asked to answer questions they didn't understand, a shortcoming for which they were punished with points off their report-card grades, which could destroy their hopes for lives:

---

12. The poorly made, polyester uniform skirts worn by our classmates cost an extravagant forty dollars, but we were permitted to wear navy or gray skirts of suitable length instead. Sarah and Sara's mothers, both of whom sewed clothes, spoke out against the institution of these uniforms.

keeping them from college admission or rendering them unworthy of scholarships, which would guarantee that they became blue-collar workers, homeless people or trapped in marriages in which they have to submit in order to get financial support and not bruises.

The closest friends were clearly *us*: adolescent girls desperate to forge our own independent paths but who depended desperately on education beyond Akiva to fulfill that destiny. Recognizing she is trapped, that if she has any hope of escape she must temporarily submit to the entire system around her, the narrator collapses into her monochromatic surroundings, concluding "my shirt matched my desk, the sleeves blending in so well that I might have been a dismembered head resting on fatty vanilla ice cream with no toppings." The fuzzy shirt is the fraught camouflage worn to unwinnable battle. Sara was determined that her exit be in the form of a serious education, a leap to the life of the cosmopolitan, international mind. But to secure some passage to that next stage, she had, for the time being, to blend in just enough to be left alone.

Where could we learn to be who we wanted to become? Two extraordinary adults at Akiva looked past children's places in social hierarchies to treat everyone with equal kindness: a taciturn Black custodian who cared for us with grandfatherly love and exhausting labor, even going so far as to supply the school with toilet paper himself when it ran out, and a yeshivish Oak Park rabbi who taught academic skills through his rigorous approach to Torah study.[13] An energetic woman teacher introduced us to joyful literary analysis of *Navi*. We lacked extracurriculars such as art, music, social clubs, and sports (beyond boys' basketball), but one Modern Orthodox English teacher with a personal passion for literature and writing led creative writing and drama groups – spaces that became a small salvation. In a bizarre Orthodox Jewish version of the Dead Poets Society, this one

---

13. This was also the one rabbi who tried to teach Gemara to girls who wanted to learn, hosting a free weekly class after school and – for over a decade – one for the adult women in the community. In the course of his decades-long career at Akiva, this unconventional rabbi was fired and rehired twice.

English classroom functioned as an anomalous reversal space at Akiva, where nerds and weirdos were encouraged and praised, and wealth could not spare a less talented student from belittling and mockery. This was not an egalitarian space, but for once we were on top: here, intellectually-inclined misfits such as us found our "rebbe," one who acknowledged our talents and introduced us to the (masculine, western, Christian, and white) literary canon. In the pages of Eliot, Hemingway, Salinger, Updike, and Vonnegut, we were encouraged to study a world where anger, dejection, passion, and hate cultivated rich and textured interiority, and where sex and intoxication were not just sins but part of this great thing called "experience" – a thing permitted to non-Jewish boys like Sarah's alter-ego narrator "Kevin" or even Modern Orthodox ones as long as they upheld the unspoken bargain to incorporate any and all of it back into a bourgeois life of halakhic theism.

Already readers, we realized that we too could be writers, and like typical adolescents, we began fumbling with feelings through language, parroting the writers who were now furnishing our interior worlds. Our literary aspirations, we imagined, ennobled *The Heresy* with valuable creative substance above and beyond humor, satire, and critique. These textual models, however, championed a kind of individualistic freedom that was impossible for girls to achieve: we would never be free to roam the world doing whatever we wanted, safely and without a sense of responsibility for the wellbeing of other people. (To wit, for whatever combination of fear and collective solidarity, our stories and poems in *The Heresy* were almost always published anonymously). Yet we imbibed this passion for individualism both to help us maintain a sense of self in a world where we didn't fit, and to imagine our exit.

Thus the masculine literary canon became our warped container in which to fashion our senses of self. We were not supposed to know about sex, yet heteronormativity saturated everything. Lacking a viable strategy to solve the problem of being girls, we invariably turned our hopes and attention to the vexing realm of masculinity, for in the world of boys and men we found the basis of both our greatest threats of oppression and hopes for freedom. Thus, *The Heresy* regularly explored and satirized what was, as far as we could tell, the ideal young man in our world – painted ironically, for instance, in a mock advice column (fig. 7). All messages indicated that he was not a studious *talmid chacham* but rather a Modern Orthodox "All-American Boy:" charming, okay at basketball, with wealthy parents and good career prospects. It mattered not whether he was kind or cruel, curious or complacent – the goal was merely to marry, have Jewish children, and then donate generously to the same institutions that raised us, a perpetuation of individual and communal existence that seemed to us unfulfilling. Without any serious investment in intellectualism, liberational politics, or expressions of creativity (no one was an artist, hardly anyone played an instrument), there seemed no avenues (besides money) to distinguish oneself.

We worked off of whatever else was readily available and accessible in the popular culture cautiously permitted to us. Grunge band front men of the early 90s, such as Kurt Cobain and Eddie Vedder, appealed to Sarah and Abby. These misfit bards and reluctant stars' rare expressions of feminist masculinity proudly championed the subaltern: queers, women, and the working class. There can be no question that "alternative" music sprang into the mainstream at just the right moment for us. Newly accessible through the radio, this particular pop culture ethos resonated perfectly. Bands and styles formerly relegated to the underground were now delivered into homes via mainstream MTV and magazines such as *Rolling Stone* and *Spin*.[14] In sharp contrast to the pompous arena rock of the 1980s, the breakthrough alternative music of the early 1990s had an aesthetics of sincerity: down-to-earth, self-effacing, emotional, cerebral, tormented anthems for noble losers and misfits. In an ironic reversal similar to

---

14. There is a prodigious literature on grunge music and culture of the early 90s. For an accessible essay that illuminates the powerful effects of grunge's cultural mainstreaming, see Steven Hyden's ten-part essay "Whatever Happened to Alternative Nation?," especially "Part 1: 1990: 'Once Upon a Time, I Could Love You,'" *A.V. Club*, October 5, 2010, https://www.avclub.com/part-1–1990-once-upon-a-time-i-could-love-you-1798221947.

our tenth-grade Akiva English classroom, the worlds of grunge and alternative offered us sanction, the promise of righteousness through nonconformity. But just as we longed for an authentic Judaism, we longed for authentic experiences of counterculture, desperate to rise above the consumption of fads (fig. 8).

Sara's uneasy relationship with North American whiteness led her elsewhere, toward the culture of her Black neighbors and immigrant friends. Her uncontrollable mane bore no resemblance to the silky ideals in ubiquitous advertisements for products whose desperate application only made her hair more detestable; seeing the ingenuity and beauty of Black hairstyles proudly worn around the neighborhood gave her hope of someday learning to care for her textured hair. All she knew of Black cultural production was what she heard on Black radio stations and television programs, since Black writers were not acknowledged by our school curriculum. Our classes did offer an occasional glimpse of Russian literature and, as Russian-speaking immigrants typically joined our school upon their arrival in Detroit (until eventually their parents realized that public schools offered a better education), Sara befriended these fellow outsiders. The prevailing teleologies of Americanism and Zionism dismissed their culture and history as irrelevant to modern Jewish identity, but Sara – losing hopelessly to them at chess, marveling at their lever-back earrings, lacquered wood gifts, and alphabet – was intrigued. Ignorant of how our short-term classmates had come to be called "Russians," Sara imagined some kind of "Russian" Jewish ancestors who, having also grown up Orthodox, became literary and political radicals.

Thus, it was Sara who, in the course of her cultural peregrinations, discovered Karl Marx at the Southfield Public Library and began educating us to possible economic and social orders beyond what we saw at Akiva. One of the most powerful artifacts in *The Heresy* appears in the form of an "advertisement" for a fictitious aspirational "Young Socialists' Club" spread across three pages in Volume 5 (the final volume) of *The Heresy* (fig. 9). Confronting readers with a moral imperative not to "ignore the poverty – and greed – that scourge American capitalist society," the fiery ad asserts that poverty was not

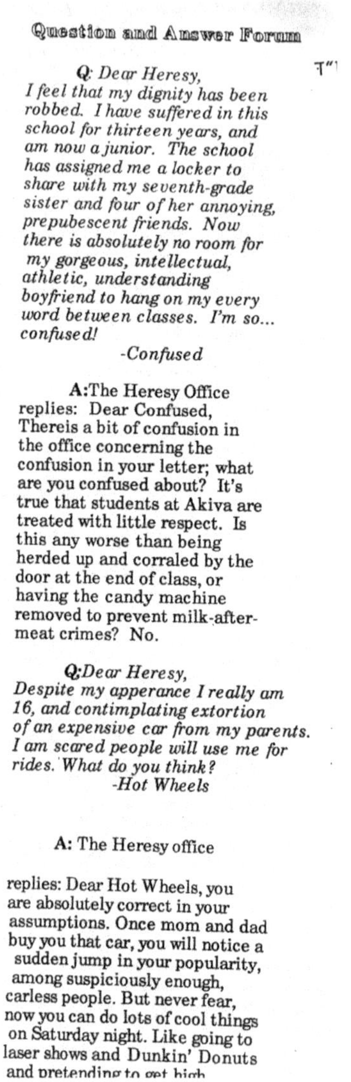

Question and Answer Forum

Q: Dear Heresy,
I feel that my dignity has been robbed. I have suffered in this school for thirteen years, and am now a junior. The school has assigned me a locker to share with my seventh-grade sister and four of her annoying, prepubescent friends. Now there is absolutely no room for my gorgeous, intellectual, athletic, understanding boyfriend to hang on my every word between classes. I'm so... confused!
    —Confused

A: The Heresy Office replies: Dear Confused, There is a bit of confusion in the office concerning the confusion in your letter; what are you confused about? It's true that students at Akiva are treated with little respect. Is this any worse than being herded up and corraled by the door at the end of class, or having the candy machine removed to prevent milk-after-meat crimes? No.

Q: Dear Heresy,
Despite my apperance I really am 16, and contimplating extortion of an expensive car from my parents. I am scared people will use me for rides. What do you think?
    —Hot Wheels

A: The Heresy office replies: Dear Hot Wheels, you are absolutely correct in your assumptions. Once mom and dad buy you that car, you will notice a sudden jump in your popularity, among suspiciously enough, carless people. But never fear, now you can do lots of cool things on Saturday night. Like going to laser shows and Dunkin' Donuts and pretending to get high

Figure 7 Our advice columns regularly played with and subverted the classic format, using absurdity, sarcasm, and editorial critique to explore issues of gender, school authority, economic class, and popularity.

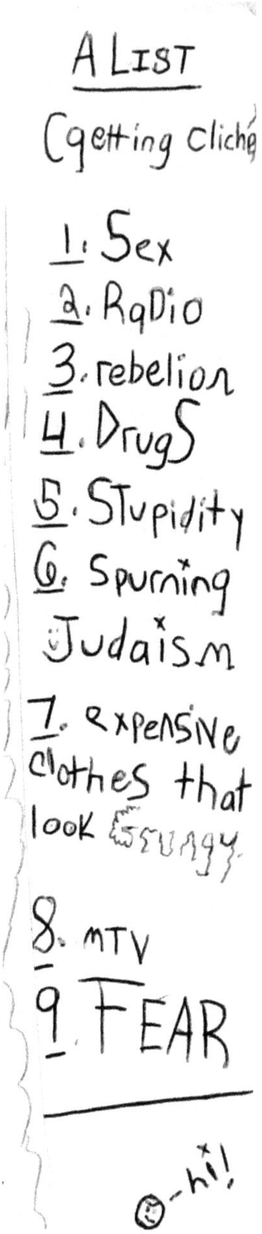

A LIST
(getting Cliché)

1. Sex
2. Radio
3. rebelion
4. Drugs
5. Stupidity
6. Spurning Judaism
7. expensive clothes that look grungy
8. MTV
9. FEAR

☺ -hi!

Figure 8 "A List (Getting Cliché)," *The Heresy 1*.

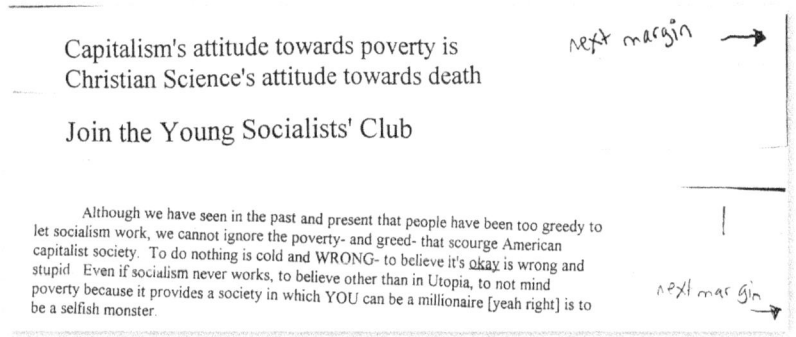

Figure 9 There was, of course, no actual Young Socialists' Club at Akiva outside of our own minds. It is worth noting a rhetorical strategy here based on emunah (belief), the exhortation to feel and know in one's heart both what is right and what is possible.

an individual moral failing but a cruel, systemic and collective one that condemned adults and children alike to unnecessary suffering and death through lack of health care and housing, and concludes with the famous socialist credo "From each according to ability, to each according to need." In our ongoing search for resonant and meaningful Torah and *derekh eretz*, such concepts were a precious find.

Conclusion: The Hard Work of Heresy

There was no final goodbye issue of *The Heresy* wherein we formally ended the publication experiment. A combination of factors contributed to its demise: The excitement of the project wore off. Abby succeeded in petitioning her parents to let her transfer to public school in Ann Arbor. The class of 1997 shrank every year, graduating as a group of ten. Combined with their newfound status as upperclassmen, this improved the social dynamic for Sarah and Sara. Towards the end, we were slipping anyway. Abby sloppily gendered Stickie with a "he" pronoun, accidentally betraying the extent to which we had internalized the relationship between gender and freedom. We also worried about our own learned snobbery, that we were becoming the assholes we didn't want to become. For instance, the Avana cartoon

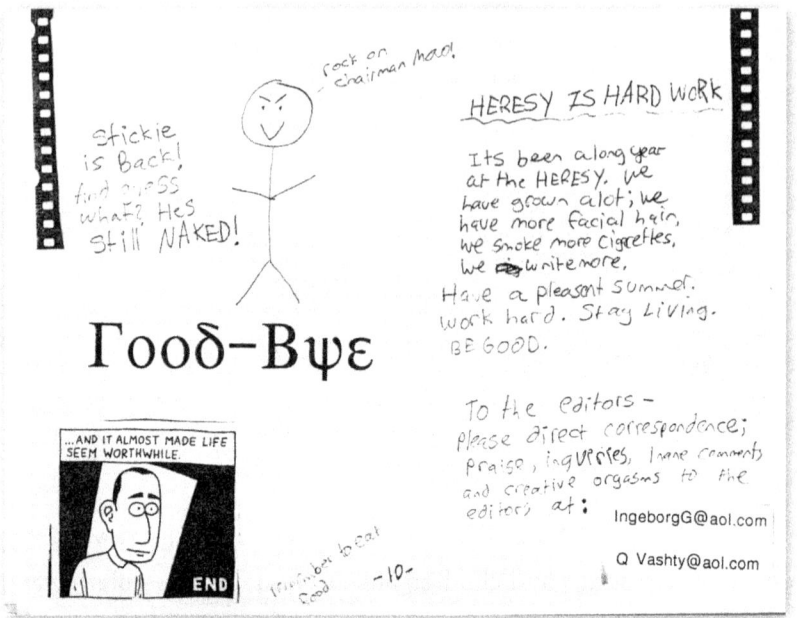

Figure 10 "Heresy is Hard Work": The last page of *The Heresy 5*, the last issue, circa May 1995.

eventually made transparent reference to one of our classmates and mocked their attempts at being cool.

Consciously or not, the last issue of *The Heresy* does conclude with a farewell, if not forever then at least for the academic year (fig. 10). In an ongoing nod to our romantic rediscovery of our lost cultural past, "Good bye" is spelled out in Cyrillic-looking letters.[15] Beneath it, we pasted in an excised cartoon character reflecting dolorously on an experience that "almost made life seem worthwhile." A missive titled "Heresy Is Hard Work" recounts our growth and change over our nine-month experiment ("We have grown alot, we have more facial hair, we smoke more cigarettes, we write more") and concludes with a sendoff that proves prescient: "Have a pleasant summer. Work Hard. Stay Living. BE GOOD." In the plainest language, this farewell

---

15. Including some Greek, since we could not tell the difference at the time.

uncannily managed to encapsulate the emerging worldview and guiding principles we carry into adulthood.

Our quest to become *apikorsim* has, in a way, come full circle. Heresy is hard work, not least of all because it is unending. The frustrations of our teen years have matured into perspectives enabling us to understand both the contours of and pressures on the Modern Orthodoxy that molded us. To make sense of our world and who it made of us, was, after all, the purpose of *The Heresy* – an endeavor that began in the rabbinical era and continues today on the OTD (Off the *Derech*) internet. Despite being outcasts, we did find aspects of Jewishness we love, appreciate, and integrate into our adult and professional lives. Some former classmates have come forward to apologize for cruelties they exhibited in our youth, a comforting reminder that we are all works in progress. Despite our ongoing fear of retribution, the outsider perspectives gained in our teenage years still drive us to interrogate all orthodoxies in an effort to illuminate their histories, motivations, and full consequences, and to consider alternatives. Ultimately, *The Heresy* was a fundamental part of our education, preparing us to strive towards outspoken but compassionate irritation in the blind spots of complacency and inconsistency that affect every community, Jewish and otherwise. If we fail in this venture, then at least we will be able to reflect on our efforts and know that we tried to speak out in our dissent.

The Heresy is being preserved in the Special Collections Research Center at the University of Michigan.

My Shul, My Place

Miriam L.

My mother grew up on top of the shul we called by the name of the street it was on, not knowing its real name, where she and her parents lived solely because of the cheap rent. She heard the pounding footsteps of the bearded, black-hatted, suited men every morning as they came for davening, watched them going in and out from her bedroom window. She smelled the chlorine coming from the basement mikva that the men would use Shabbos morning, and she didn't have the option to sleep through Shabbos davening because the noise from downstairs ensured that she woke up. Every Shabbos when she was a young child, she would walk down the middle staircase of the three-story townhouse with her father, straight into the men's section. Because the community did not have an Eiruv and nobody else could bring their children, she was the only little kid there. She quickly became a regular part of the shul, sitting under the table watching the men's pressed black suit pants and matching dress shoes move in sync, standing next to her father as he *leined* every week, and peering over to see the Torah. She became the "girl in the men's section" and the "girl in the sukkah," among the sea of men and boys; when all the other girls stayed home, she had a sense of familiarity with shul that none of her other peers had.

I grew up going to that shul when we visited my grandmother, who had moved years ago to a house a few blocks away from my mother's childhood home. My mother often reminded me that it was my grandfather's shul, who had passed away when I was one year old. The once white and speckled floor had been worn out from the decades of shoes walking over it, past the point of ever being able to be cleaned. The walls were lined with multi-colored *seforim* (books) with gold and silver letters, and one small shelf of kid's books like *Yossi and Laibel*, with missing covers and pages ripped out from years of use.

As a child, I dreaded going to that shul, where I knew that because I had grown up in a different neighborhood, I didn't fit in. "Different communities do different things," my mother would tell me as I kicked and screamed, refusing to put on the itchy, uncomfortable white tights to match all the other girls in the shul. She reminded me that she also had to respect the community, pointing to her equally itchy and uncomfortable sheitel from the hat box in the back of her closet, which was chosen to be as close as possible to her natural red curly hair and replaced her usual colorful, simpler scarf. "It's not the same, you're making me do this," I cried, but each time, I would eventually surrender to her ultimatum, reluctantly put on the tights, and follow her to shul. I knew that the members of the shul were all my grandfather's friends, and my mother had the opportunity to feel connected to her father here, right below the place she grew up in. So, despite putting up a fuss every time, I always went along with her.

The small, crowded women's section had hard uncomfortable wooden benches that had the permanent smell of what I called "grandma perfume." As women, we weren't really there for the davening, or at least we didn't have to come on time, so we usually made it there just in time for the end. Despite the shul not being big enough for more than fifty people, only the women closest to the thick wooden *mechitza* (partition) with a movable white curtain covering the small open squares at the top could hear anything that was going on from the men's side. My cries of "I'm hungry, Imma, when is this going to be over" were always met with indignant shushing from the women who were standing as close as they could to the *mechitza* to try to make out what was going on.

"Are they at Musaf yet?" women would ask worriedly as they entered the shul hurriedly from the women's entrance at the back of the building, at the end of a long alleyway that was crowded by children meticulously dressed in matching clothing, playing and screaming while their parents prayed inside. *Why does it matter,* I wondered at the women's questions, *we can't hear anything over the colossal* mechitza *anyways.*

At home, in our Modern Orthodox community, the Friday nights of my elementary school years were filled with me and my mother sitting down on our white leather couch, opening up my first grade siddur with large Hebrew writing and a maroon velvet cover with pearled buttons sewn on by my mother. Like most young kids, I preferred playing with toys over davening, so we negotiated which *tefillot* I would have to say from the Friday night davening they were saying at shul, and slowly my mother taught me all of them until they became second nature and easy for me to recite alone. Soon after then, it was decided I was old enough to go with my father to shul. I was the only little girl in our house-turned-into-shul that couldn't fit more than thirty people, and my parents were the youngest members. For Shabbos day, my mother, who needed everyone out of the house to clean up and get ready for the meal, insisted that we all go to shul with my father during the day. To make sure that we went along, the kids were rewarded with a trip to Baskin Robbins every Thursday night for their "one dollar a scoop" night, where we could choose any flavors we wanted.

A few years into elementary school, the rabbi of our small shul-in-a-house moved away, and we switched to the larger one where all of my friends went. However, while all the other kids my age went to the kids' program, where they davened with a group leader for prizes, played games like Red Rover, Steal the Salami, and Boxes, I stayed with my parents. "You're almost Bat Mitzvah, you need to stay in shul and daven," my parents instructed, but all I wanted to do was run out and play with my friends. So we compromised and agreed that I would stay in shul for Shacharis and leave after the Torah reading. I'd sit in shul, swinging my feet back and forth, impatiently counting the pages left until after Torah reading, when I'd quickly run out and join my friends. In this shul, sitting in the women's balcony ten feet above the men's section, I could hear everything over the short *mechitza* with wide spaces in between.

For one of my birthdays I begged my parents to have a "professional birthday party at a real place" like some of my friends were having in locations like Pump It Up, laser tag, or a gymnastics place. After a lot of lobbying my parents agreed – on one condition. I had to give a *dvar* Torah at my shul during kiddush in front of everyone, both men and women. I'm not sure why that was the condition, because while it was commonplace for one of the shul members to give a *dvar* Torah, nobody else my age ever did. But I was determined to have the birthday party of my dreams, so I followed through. I was a proud but nervous ten-year-old, standing up straight in front of the entire shul, in a sparkly black dress with pleats on the bottom half, reading from a paper and feeling everyone's eyes on me. The message I got was this: *You are a part of the congregation, you matter, and you deserve to be here.*

The following year, my family moved a few states away and we started going to a new shul. I had gotten older and was no longer incentivized with ice cream to attend. I didn't really have a desire to go to shul Friday nights until one of my friends invited me to go with her older sister, and we went every week feeling grown-up and mature. For Shabbos days, I was asked to run the children's program at my family's shul, and I ended up spending my time organizing games, snacks, and children's davening instead of praying upstairs with the minyan. I organized a program to teach girls the Shabbos davening that they didn't learn in school, as my mother did for me so many years earlier. I fell into the habit of not really caring about shul attendance. It became normal for me that my father and brother would go and I wouldn't.

After spending my post-high school year in Israel grappling with Orthodoxy and feminism, I returned to my family, and I announced to my parents that I would be going to shul every morning. I can't really identify why I chose to take this drastic, life-changing decision upon myself that day, but I did.

My parents looked at each other, surprised. "Even during the week?"

I nodded fervently, internally trying to convince myself that waking up at 6:50 AM before a long day of work at my summer internship was a good idea, but putting on a strong face for them. They pointed out that my father had planned to go to shul some days and I needed to be home while my siblings slept. They did not understand why I was trying to switch things up, but I insisted that I was not responsible for my father's religious obligation and put my foot down: I was going to go to shul three times a day every day that entire summer.

Rain or shine, I sleepily turned off my blaring phone alarm in my dark basement room with wooden walls from the 1950s, hurriedly got dressed, and made my way to shul every morning of that summer. My presence was so unexpected that the first morning, when I drove into the parking lot, one of the men saw my car and called out, "We have a tenth," and they began to pray in anticipation of the tenth man walking in. When a man didn't walk into the sanctuary, the rabbi started looking for him. Was he in the bathroom? In the library? They needed to start praying and he needed to come inside. But I was the tenth man, in my bright pink raincoat and denim dress, standing on the women's balcony looking over at the men who had no idea I was there. After some time, another man came inside and they started praying, but it wasn't until a few days later when a man noticed me walking into the building and put it all together that they realized that there never had been a tenth man that day.

"The men don't even acknowledge my presence," I complained to my mother, who sympathetically hugged me but had no response. The only words that the rabbi, in all black and white except for his long grey beard, ever uttered to me were the one day that I brought my brother to shul and the rabbi shook his hand, then turned to me and said, "You have a better shul attendance than him. You would've done us much more use if you were a boy." I didn't respond to him, and just kept on going to shul, every day, three times a day.

I started school at Yeshiva University in Manhattan, and I found a friend who also valued going to shul as much as I did. We'd wake up before anyone else on the twelfth floor of Stern's all-female Brookdale Hall in Midtown Manhattan, get dressed in the dark so as not to bother our roommates, and walk ten minutes to shul, no matter the weather, catching up on the day before and building a meaningful friendship around the crazy lengths we went to for going to shul. As the sun slowly began to rise over the still-asleep city during the winter, we would walk together complaining about the frigid weather and marveling at how still and empty the city felt. Over the months, as we walked down Lexington Avenue, passing 33rd street, 32nd, 31st, 30th, until 29th, to Congregation Talmud Torah Adereth El, one of the oldest shuls in the United States, we began to recognize the few early-risers that we passed every morning, all starting their day: the runners in their bright workout clothes and sneakers, the business folks in their freshly-pressed meticulous suits. We walked past the same restaurants as the workers entered to start their day, mopping the floors and turning on the coffee machines, until our feet memorized the way and we didn't really need to pay attention to where we were going to end up at shul.

During a summer break from college, I ended up in a new shul with equally-sized men's and women's sections, with a short, simple wooden *mechitza* down the middle and the bimah smack in the middle of that. I was surprised when a woman with dark curly hair and a colorful headband, who I found out later was part of the shul's clergy, approached me and asked me if I wanted to hold the Torah after it was taken out of the *aron*. I nervously agreed and listened to her instructions attentively.

When it was time, she nodded to me, and I followed her as we slowly walked up to the bimah in front of the shul, to the tall wooden *aron* with subtle lighting. We stopped at the dark blue velvet curtain with multicolored squares while another woman pulled open the drapery and opened the wooden doors to the Torah scrolls clothed in velvet with embroidered gold letters and heavy, shiny silver crowns. We stood together as I was handed the Torah, trembling and not believing that I was actually doing this. I turned around to face the shul, and everyone's eyes were on me, the one holding the Torah that they were about to read from, and I realized I was going to be able to hear every word loudly and clearly. "*Deracheha Darchei Noam*," the ways of the Torah really, truly are pleasant.

My Yechi Yarmulke

Chanan Maister

I couldn't actually tell you when I started wearing the Yechi yarmulke, and I don't remember when I stopped wearing it either. All I know is that I started wearing it when I was living in a somewhat *meshichist*[1] community (though I went to a community Orthodox school), continued wearing it when I moved to an anti-*meshichist* community a state over (and attended a Lubavitch cheder), and was still sporting it a couple years later at a Torah Umesorah school, which is when I finally stopped wearing it. I attended three different elementary schools in three years, and at each school the yarmulke signified different things to both staff and my fellow students, though at the time I didn't recognize how my wearing it affected how I was treated by them – in fact, I didn't understand its significance in any way until many years later, religiously, politically, or socially.

A Yechi yarmulke is embroidered or adorned with the words "*Yechi Adoneinu Moreinu V'Rabbeinu Melech HaMoshiach L'olam Vaed*," which translates loosely to "Long Live our Master, our Teacher, our Rebbe, the King Messiah Forever." This phrase or idea has been used in Chabad Lubavitch since well before I was born in 1987, representing the belief most Lubavitchers held that the Rebbe was the long-awaited Messiah, which gained mass currency in the mid-eighties. When

---

1. Someone who believes that Rabbi Menachem Mendel Schneerson, the Rebbe of Chabad Hasidism, is the Messiah.

the Rebbe died in 1994, many Lubavitchers continued to believe he was the Messiah and many of these people are uncomfortable acknowledging his death. Some Lubavitchers even believed he had never died in the first place. In the following years, there developed a schism in the movement between those who accepted the Rebbe's death as proof that he is not the Messiah (the "antis") and those who continue to believe he will redeem the Jews from exile (the *meshichists*). The tension between the two factions has since mostly died down, though at the time it seemed possible that Chabad would no longer be considered part of normative Orthodox Judaism.

I was living in Mequon, Wisconsin, when the Rebbe died in 1994. I remember my mother attending a *shloshim* (mourning on the thirtieth day) event for him held in our local Chabad Shul. Though I didn't know it at the time, our local *shluchim* (Chabad emissaries, who had started the shul) identified as *meshichists*. Nevertheless, even they, who believed he was the messiah, publicly acknowledged he had died. I have no doubt that it was due to the influence of these same local *shluchim* that my mother had me wear the yarmulke – in fact, it's entirely possible they gave it to her for me to wear.

At the time, I was attending what I would best describe as a community Orthodox Zionist school in Milwaukee – there were several other Lubavitchers in my class, but most of the kids were Modern Orthodox, and it was co-ed. If you had asked me what it meant to be a Lubavitcher at the time, I would have known that we davened with a different siddur, were more strict with kashrus, had a rebbe, and were against land for peace in Israel – not only did I not understand what Yechi/*meshichism* was, I don't even know that I was at all aware of its existence, even if it was literally on my head. I doubt most of the other kids knew either, but I'm sure my Hebrew-subject teachers did. Some of them were Lubavitch, too, and they must have had opinions of their own. Nevertheless, I don't remember anyone ever saying anything to me on the subject. Maybe they were all wise enough to keep their mouths shut – after all, what's to be accomplished by saying anything to an eight-year-old about their possible controversial religious beliefs?

We moved to Saint Paul, Minnesota, in the fall of 1996, literally the day before school started. That year I attended a Lubavitch Cheder, and it was the first time I truly learned what exactly it meant to be Chabad. It was really a culture shock. I was coming from a community where we were one of very few frum families, and the new community, while small, was mostly made up of Lubavitch lifers. In addition, the community was uniformly "anti," against the idea of the Rebbe's being *Moshiach*. I imagine that when we showed up, with me in a Yechi yarmulke, people had eyebrows raised. Nevertheless, I don't recall anyone ever saying anything about it to me. At the time, only a few years after the Rebbe's death, beliefs and the public exhibition thereof were much more fluid. Some still secretly hoped, and it took a long time to give up the dream. In our new community, only on holidays like Simchas Torah, when the alcohol flowed and people's inhibitions disappeared, would some community members express their (otherwise hidden) *meshichist* belief.

My new class had only seven or eight kids, made up of two grades, and it was partially taught in Yiddish, which I didn't know at all. Coming from a class of twenty kids, whose religious identities were all over the place, to a school where nearly all the kids specifically identified as Lubavitch, was very different. There was no Zionism in the school, I could eat pretty much anything any kid brought, and we learned a lot about the Rebbe and Lubavitch. While in my previous school, my teachers had undoubtedly known what my yarmulke represented, though most of my classmates didn't, in Minnesota the kids knew too, and must have treated me differently because of it. Or perhaps it was only a cause of great confusion – here was a kid who came in not knowing much of anything about Chabad, yet wearing a yarmulke that represented, at least in that community, radical Chabad thought, and this in a time when the Chabad community as a whole was riven by internal strife. Perhaps someone did say something to me, and yet because I really didn't know anything about it I simply didn't register it.

I also recognize that my situation is a cliché. There are plenty of (generally non-American) people whose first experience with Chabad is with a *meshichist* who plops a Yechi yarmulke on their heads, and they really have only the vaguest sense of what it means. If my situation was different than that, it's because I grew up Lubavitch, in America, in a time when *meshichism* wasn't only on the fringe.

After a year spent in Lubavitch Cheder in Saint Paul, my parents decided to send me to the local Torah Umesorah school in Saint Louis Park. Though the school then was what would now be considered fairly centrist, even then it was noticeably more yeshivish than the day school I had attended in Milwaukee two years before, and it was certainly very different *hashkafically* (philosophically) from the Chabad school I was coming from. From the start, I had a chip on my shoulder; I was picked on for being Chabad, for being a bit of a nerd, for having a stutter, and for coming from Wisconsin and being a Green Bay Packers fan. While I didn't actually know anything about football, it didn't really matter to those kids. In response, I became an avid Packers fan. Similarly, though I had always been well aware that I was Lubavitch and somewhat different, I never took pride in it until I was made fun of for it.

As an example of my ignorance when it came to messianic matters, I remember once writing a piece for a class Haggada that quoted "the Rebbe Shlita." Up to that point, I thought that, just like there was an Alter Rebbe, a Mitteler Rebbe, etc., the name of the most current Rebbe was "Shlita." I had no idea what that title meant. My teacher at the time told me I couldn't write that, because he wasn't alive anymore (it stands for: "*Sheyikhye Le'orech Yamim Tovim Amen*," "May he live a good long life, Amen,"), and I recall being annoyed by that, because it somehow felt disrespectful to me; in the end I simply referred to him as the "Lubavitcher Rebbe."

At some point before my Bar Mitzvah, one kid decided to pick on me and during recess kept on grabbing my Yechi yarmulke and making fun of me for wearing it. It was only around then that it first dawned on me that what it said wasn't just some Lubavitch slogan, but a very specific message, proclaiming that I believed that the Rebbe was not only *Moshiach*, but that he was alive, and that this marked me out as someone who believed something which many people thought was not only wrong, but most probably heretical.

The school administration didn't say anything to me about the yarmulke, which in retrospect I appreciate. Perhaps they realized I was just a kid who didn't know anything; perhaps they wouldn't have said anything regardless, because they didn't think it was their place. Of course, kids will be kids, and they made plenty of fun of me for things other than my yarmulke, but there's no doubt it provided an easy target. I'm sure the message they heard at home about Lubavitch wasn't a particularly positive one.

By the time I entered high school, an "anti" Lubavitch Yeshiva, I wasn't wearing that yarmulke anymore. Not only because it didn't fit, but because I finally knew and understood what it represented. Ironically, I'm not even sure I would have been allowed to wear it – when I went on to post-high-school yeshiva in Los Angeles, the wearing of Yechi yarmulkes was expressly forbidden. By that point, I had also learned that Lubavitch messianism was something to keep under wraps – we visited the Rebbe's grave in Queens, and we publicly marked his Yahrtzeit on the third of Tammuz, all acknowledging his death. But at the same time, when we had a little bit of l'chaim at a *farbrengen*,[2] in the privacy of our classrooms, our teachers would talk about the Rebbe's redeeming us from exile.

I never lived up to the promise of that yarmulke, never was the person it proclaimed me to be. But there's no doubt it made me a stronger Lubavitcher, if only because I was forced to defend myself as one because of it, even if I didn't realize the messaging it broadcast to those around me, and the way they treated me in turn.

I wouldn't wear such a yarmulke now, and my beliefs are a lot more fluid than they once were, but I don't have any regrets about wearing it. I'm more amused than anything at the thought of the impression I must have made in my peripatetic schooling, and at the thought of a naive little kid with a big political and religious statement placed prominently on his head, oblivious but proud.

---

2. A Chabad-Lubavitch festive gathering.

The Golem, Goyim, and the Hasidic Imagination

Schneur Zalman Newfield

The stories from my childhood that made the deepest impression on me were the ones my father read out loud after Shabbos lunch. When I was in the second grade, he started reading the books from the Prophets section of the Bible in English translation: Joshua, Judges, Samuel, and Kings. I remember the scene when the high priest Eli is informed that the Ark of the Covenant has been captured by their enemies and he falls backwards in shock and breaks his neck and dies. I remember David endlessly evading the wrath of King Saul who tries to kill him out of murderous jealousy. But mostly I remember the constant threat the ancient Israelites faced from the no-good Philistines who attacked them at every turn. I cheered every time Samson smote the Philistines, including in his last heroic act after Delilah cut his hair, the Philistines gouged out his eyes and imprisoned him, and Samson stood in the temple of Dagon and prayed to God for strength to pull apart the pillars supporting the entire structure. I celebrated when Samson managed to topple the temple, killing three thousand of the enemy.

Once we finished the book of Kings, we shifted to a somewhat more recent saga of Jewish danger and deliverance, to that of the sixteenth-century Golem of Prague. My father read to me the cartoon Golem stories written by Arnold Fine and illustrated by Howard S.

Speilman, serialized in the children's section of *The Jewish Press* each week.

Even before my father read these stories to me, I knew (and believed with complete faith) the story of the Golem's creation by the mystic Rabbi Judah Loew. I acquired my knowledge of the Golem during recess at school when my friends and I would gather around a bulky tape recorder and listen repeatedly (incessantly?) to a dramatized narrative called *The Mysterious Golem of Prague* directed by Simcha Gottlieb and Chaim Clorfene. The audiotape grippingly described how, in order to shield his community from blood libels and other heinous plots, Rabbi Loew fashioned an animated creature as a protector. Using his walking stick, Rabbi Loew drew a life-size human form in soft clay, around which he and his followers made seven circuits while chanting a ten-word kabbalistic formula. At the end of this ritual, a non-verbal being with superhuman strength emerged.

The Golem cartoons my father read to me in *The Jewish Press* only reinforced the reality of the Golem and his exploits. The main villain was a wicked Catholic priest named Father Thaddeus who was consumed by a burning hatred against the Jews. Thaddeus was always creeping along the cavernous labyrinth beneath his church, meeting with his henchmen and devising schemes to ensnare the innocent Jews. And each week, just as calamity was about to envelop the Jews, the grunting and snorting Golem would rush on the scene to prevent it and protect the Jews from the evil Catholic priest. Speilman's minimalist cartoons effectively conveyed the deviousness of Thaddeus and the brutal strength of the Golem. Thaddeus was depicted sporting shoulder-length hair and wild eyes. The Golem was depicted as a head taller than everyone else, possessed of a chiseled face and bulging muscles. With a cascade of "Whack!" "Boom!" and "Thud!" the young reader was mesmerized by the Golem's ability to always disrupt the evil plots and protect his Jewish charges (fig. 1).

In my pre-adolescent mind, the stories of the Philistines and those of Father Thaddeus merged with the messages I received in school about non-Jews. We were taught that Jews possess two souls, a divine and animal one, while non-Jews only possess an animal soul. The

The Golem, Goyim, and the Hasidic Imagination · 233

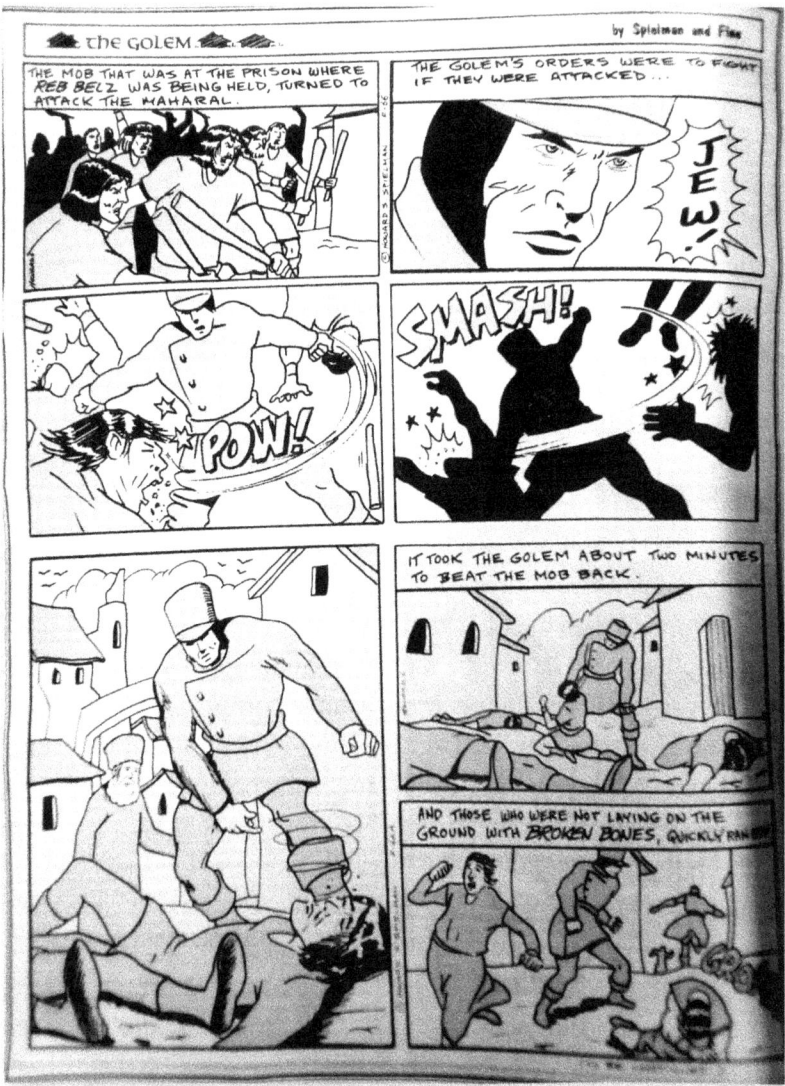

Figure 1 A page from the long-running weekly *Golem* cartoon in *The Jewish Press*.

animal soul gave its possessor vitality to stay alive but not the ability to transcend base animalistic instincts.

This message of Jewish superiority contributed to a feeling of separation from our Afro-Caribbean neighbors, which matched the parallel universes we inhabited. The Golem stories with the villainous

Father Thaddeus made me terrified of the massive Tudor gothic style brown brick Episcopal Church of St. Mark, with its bright red windows and spire topped with a crucifix, located across the street from my yeshiva, Oholie Torah, the Tent of Torah. Every time I passed the church, I shuddered because I associated this church with the one Father Thaddeus used to plot against the Jews of Prague. In my immature mind, the wicked "goyim" from the Golem stories melded with the Afro-Caribbean youth in the neighborhood who threw eggs and rocks at our yeshiva buses on Halloween as they transported us to and from yeshiva. I had no idea that the church ran a food pantry for needy parishioners and that it was adorned with stained glass windows celebrating Dr. Martin Luther King Jr. and Harriet Tubman and the struggle for African-American freedom.

I routinely watched Black families in suits and dresses, holding Bibles, going off to church on Sundays. In the summertime, young Rastafari men with dreadlocks carried large boom boxes and played reggae music until late in the night. On hot days, little Black girls in tank tops and shorts, their hair made up in cornrows, played double Dutch jump rope and licked large blue-and-red ice popsicles, and little Black boys turned on the fire hydrants and cooled off in the jetting water. I observed all this but never interacted with any of it, as if I was living behind a clear glass wall. I didn't know the first or last name of a single one of my Black neighbors and doubtless they didn't know mine. We lived, attended school, worshipped, and played in two completely disconnected worlds that just happened to occupy the same crowded city blocks. Not only did most Lubavitchers not interact with their Black neighbors, but there was intense negativity aimed at them. It was common to refer to them as *shvartzes*, a derogatory Yiddish word for Black people. I often heard hateful "jokes" at school playing on racist stereotypes in line with the idea of non-Jews being akin to animals.

In the past few years, I have heard stories from Lubavitchers about how the Rebbe, Rabbi Menachem Mendel Schneerson, the spiritual leader of Lubavitch, met in 1968 with Shirley Chisholm, the first Black woman elected to Congress, and encouraged her to use her position on the House Agricultural Committee to help the inner-city poor receive food assistance from the federal government, and that Chisholm went on to champion the federal food assistance program known as WIC. This may all be true, but when I was growing up in the 1980s and 1990s, we were never told about the Rebbe meeting any Black politicians or about his concern for our Black neighbors. All I heard about Black people was, "Hey! That's the *shvartza* that stole my cousin's bike."

Although I can now look back on this from an anti-racist perspective, I was not immune from this prejudiced view of our Black neighbors as a child. When I was seven years old, my non-Orthodox Aunt Marta, a successful businesswoman, brought me an armful of drawing books, colored pencils, and toy soldiers for me to start a small business selling them on the street in front of my house. My first response was, "The *shvartzes* are gonna steal them!"

For me, and many other Jews in Crown Heights, the connection between our Black neighbors and violent anti-Semitism was only strengthened tenfold after the racial tensions that flared up in 1991. The immediate cause of the rise in tension occurred when Yosef Lifsh, a young Lubavitcher, accidentally drove his car into and killed Gavin Cato, the seven-year-old son of Guyanese immigrants, and the following day a group of Black teens stabbed and killed Yankel Rosenbaum, a twenty-nine-year-old Lubavitcher. But tensions simmered for decades, fed on a steady diet of mutual disregard and negative stereotypes. Years later, I would learn that this negative attitude that views non-Jews as an ever-present threat to Jewish survival was part of a broader perspective on the Jewish past that the noted twentieth-century Polish-born American historian Salo Baron criticized in the 1960s as "the lachrymose conception of Jewish history." This conception views all of Jewish history as an unrelenting catalogue of tragedies.

On a personal level, after much reading of secular books on my own as well as meeting and befriending non-Jews in college, I came to realize how misguided and hurtful this view of non-Jews was, and how the stereotypical view of our Black neighbors as particularly violent was racist and unfounded. As a child, the message I took away from the Golem stories, which fit with many Hasidic tales I absorbed from my yeshiva days featuring evil Eastern European noblemen who immiserated the lives of their Jewish subjects, was that it was necessary to fear the "goyim" among whom we lived. I accepted that there would always be wicked characters like Father Thaddeus who forever schemed to hurt the Jews, and that the Jews always need a protector, whether in the shape of Samson, the Golem, or the Lubavitcher Rebbe.

As the Talmud (Shabbos 21b) notes, "*girsa diyankusa*," the knowledge we acquire at a young age, makes a deep impression on us. This is the power of ultra-Orthodox children's literature, such as the Golem cartoons in *The Jewish Press*, absorbed at a tender age when we are so impressionable and before our critical thinking skills are fully developed, to influence so tremendously the trajectory of a community and its interactions with others.

Torah Shebe'al Peh

Devora Steinmetz[1]

I knew what was going to happen. The youngest of three girls, I knew that next year a day would come when the boys would get their black-and-white marbled-cover Gemaras, and I would not. And I wanted nothing more than to learn Gemara too.

Our fourth-grade teacher, warm, enthusiastic, and full of love for Torah and for his students, was absent for a week in the spring. The substitute, like my teacher, a young follower of Chabad, didn't teach us much, as I recall, but she did tell us about the Rebbe. He knows all seventy languages, she told us, and he responds to every letter he gets, in whatever language it's written!

Now I knew what I had to do. I would write to the Rebbe, and he would no doubt agree that girls should be allowed to learn Gemara, and I would show his letter to the principal, and he would let me learn along with the boys. This seemed like a better plan than waiting for the *bas qol*[2] that I had been hoping for. I knew that the principal would have to listen to a *bas qol*, and I was sure that he would listen to the Rebbe as well.

Though the Rebbe understood every language, and certainly English, I felt it only appropriate to write him in Hebrew. My Hebrew

---

1. Note: The author's recollection is of her experience in an Orthodox yeshiva day school in Manhattan in 1969–70.
2. A heavenly proclamation.

was good – we spoke only Hebrew all morning at school beginning in first grade – but not quite good enough to articulate exactly what I wanted to say. I lay on my bed, with a yellow pad and paperback Ben-Yehuda dictionary, and looked up the word that I needed. To deprive – *limno'a*. I know it can't be, I told the Rebbe, that *chazal* would deprive anyone of the opportunity to learn Torah.

I copied over the letter neatly and mailed it, and I waited eagerly for the reply. Weeks went by, summer came, and my mother took my sisters and me to visit my aunt in Toronto for a few days. I called my father every night – Did a letter come for me in the mail?

Fifth grade started with neither letter nor *bas qol*. I was deeply engaged in my studies. Rabbi Gold told us, one day when we were learning Chumash, that any idea that any of us offered in class was *torah shebe'al peh*, part of the Oral Torah. Rabbi Gold told us that the Selichot prayer in which we ask God, over and over, to act for the sake of one thing and then another, ends with *aseh lema'an tinoqos shel beis rabban* – act for the sake of schoolchildren. When all else fails, we ask God to remember the children who are learning in school, because spending our day learning Torah is the most precious thing in the world. Rabbi Gold told us that if a child misbehaved and distracted the class for one minute, that was twenty-two minutes of *bitul torah*,[3] because there were twenty-two children in the class. And Rabbi Gold was absent from school one day to protest the shootings at Kent State. Torah was everything, and sometimes you had to take time from learning Torah to do what Torah teaches you to do.

And then one day, in the middle of the morning, Rabbi Gold told the girls to move their desks to the back of the room. We could do our homework, he said, or anything else we wanted to do. Next year, and the year after, and the year after that, the boys and girls would be in separate classes, but in fifth grade we were still together. We learned Hebrew and Chumash and Mishna together all year, but now, in the

---

3. Wasting time on frivolous activities that could otherwise be spent learning Torah.

Devora's yellow notebook and a black-and-white-marbled-cover Gemara.

spring, the boys were about to start learning Gemara, and the girls were not to be a part of this.

I made my way toward the back of the room, passing Rabbi Gold's large wooden desk. "But Devora," he said quietly, "Nobody stops you from listening."

So listen I did. I didn't get the black-and-white marbled-cover Gemara, but I had a little yellow memo book that I held in my lap, under my desk. Every day, on the bus home from school, my classmates Michael and Seth would lend me one of their Gemaras, and I would copy the text into my memo book. I copied carefully, not wanting to miss a thing, down to the little block-print and Rashi-script letters that I would come to learn only later indicate marginal cross-references. This was my text from which I followed along as Rabbi Gold taught the opening lines of Berakhot – *tana heikha qa'i deqatani me'eimasai.*

Ephemeral Memories of Childhood Ephemera

Shamma Boyarin

Growing up, our small Orthodox synagogue in a mostly-secular small community just south of Be'er Sheva was frequently the target of the educational efforts of a couple of chassidic groups that were active in the area, specifically Chabad and Gur. For example, two young chassidim from Gur organized a weekly Torah portion group for us kids (aged approximately five to seven) and if we came to it, we got a popsicle. The group kind of fell apart after a few weeks because they wouldn't answer our questions. These questions weren't cheeky or blasphemous. They were questions that one could find being asked and answered when looking at a Chumash with *Mikra'ot Gedolot*,[1] which many of us had been doing already. But the chassidim weren't there for that kind of learning, and we realized that a free popsicle wasn't worth an hour of boredom, so we stopped going. But this wasn't the only way chassidic groups tried to educate the kids in our synagogue, and the thing that I remember most now, almost forty years later, was a small weekly pamphlet.

    I don't remember its name or who was behind it, though I'm certain it came from one of these chassidic groups. I remember that

---

1. The major commentaries most often included in printed editions of the Torah (Aramaic Targum Onkelos, Rashi, Rambam, Ohr HaChaim, etc.).

these pamphlets included a short something about the weekly Torah portions, a few lessons about *mussar* (Jewish ethics), and stories. The stories were of outstanding rabbis from the Talmud and the Middle Ages though the early modern period, though of course they weren't given in any such historical or contextual manner. A story about a third-century rabbi from the Galilee was presented in the same way as a story about an eighteenth-century German rabbi. I remember only one thing from these pamphlets in more detail than this: a story about the Rambam (Maimonides). Part of why this story stuck with me was its message but also its (for me as kid) gruesome details.

The story was that a rumor had gone out that the Rambam had abandoned Judaism and was no longer keeping halakha, so a few rabbis went to test him. When the Rambam greeted them, he served them a human hand for the first course, and a young goat in its mother's milk: dishes that are not only not kosher but brazenly not kosher. When the rabbis, who thought these actions confirmed the rumors, angrily accused the Rambam of abandoning halakha, he laughed at them and explained they were wrong. The "human hand" he served them was just an artichoke, a vegetable whose appearance resembled a human hand. And the baby goat cooked in its mother milk had a complicated halakhic justification that shocked me at the time and is part of why I remember this story.

According to the story, the Rambam told the rabbis that the mother and the goat had died during childbirth (or something like this) and so it was OK for him to serve it this way, milk and meat together. I remember that even at the time I wasn't sure if this halakhic rule was just made up for the story or could actually be found in some halakhic source. I have never checked because I don't want to know. The upshot of the story is that that the rabbis realized that they had not only misjudged the Rambam, but that he was a greater halakhic authority than they were.

I am not sure what lesson they expected a tween boy to take from this story. As far as I remember, none of these stories were presented with specific morals explaining their point. They were meant simply to provide exemplars of prominent figures from the past. I do think there was some aspect of chassidic subversiveness, an attempt at subtle (or not so subtle) critique of a viewpoint that sees chassidus as a kind of a heresy. This would fit with my other strong memory that these pamphlets introduced me to: the figure of Jonathan Eybeschutz, a controversial figure who was accused of being a neo-Sabbatean. In any case, as I've gone through my own personal and scholarly transformations regarding Jewish tradition, this story about the Rambam has frequently floated in mind. And so, probably not in the way the authors intended, they have made a lasting impact on me. I think the Rambam, at least the version they told me about in that story, would approve.

Bibliography

"A Portrait of Jewish Americans." *Pew Research Center.* October 1, 2013. https://www.pewforum.org/wp-content/uploads/sites/7/2013/10/jewish-american-full-report-for-web.pdf.

Abate, Michelle Ann. *Tomboys: A Literary and Cultural History.* Temple University Press, 2008.

Abramson, Shayna. "Faceless: Do Extreme Tznius Codes Perpetuate Rape Culture?" *The New York Jewish Week: JOFA Blog.* August 16, 2017. http://jewishweek.timesofisrael.com/faceless/.

Attfield, Judy. "Barbie and Action Man: Adult Toys for Girls and Boys." *The Gendered Object,* ed. Pat Kirkham. Manchester University Press, 1996: 80–90.

Bado-Fralick, Nikki and Rebecca Sachs Norris. *Toying with God: The World of Religious Games and Dolls.* Baylor University Press, 2010.

Bais Yaakov High School. *M'gama (Yearbook).* Brooklyn, NY, 1980.

Baker, George. "Una Paloma Blanca." Warner Bros., 1975.

Bare, Bobby. "Detroit City." *Detroit City and Other Hits.* RCA Victor, 1963.

Begun, Yerachmiel. "B'siyata D'shmaya." *Miami Boys Choir: B'Siyata D'Shamaya.* Yerachmiel Begun and the Miami Boys Choir, 1984.

———. "It's Min Hashomayim." *Miami Boys Choir: It's Min Hashomayim.* Yerachmiel Begun and the Miami Boys Choir, 1992.

———. "Light up the Nights." *Chanukah: Light up the Nights.* Yerachmiel Begun and the Miami Boys Choir, 1997.

———. "We Need You." *Shabbos Yerushalayim.* Yerachmiel Begun and the Miami Boys Choir, 1989.

Ben Shimon, Yoel. *Mahzor Minhag Roma Le-Chol Hashanah.* 1450.

Held in the National Library of Israel, JER. NLI. 8° 4450. Accessed April 2021. https://www.nli.org.il/en/books/NNL_ALEPH000042898/NLI.

Benjamin, Walter. *Berlin Childhood around 1900,* trans. Howard Eiland. Harvard University Press, 2006.

———. *Berlin Childhood around 1990.* Harvard University Press, 2006.

———. *Correspondences,* eds. Gershom Scholem and Theodor W. Adorno. Trans. Manfred R. Jacobson and Evelyn M. Jacobson. University of Chicago Press, 1994.

———. *Selected Writings Vol. 2.* Harvard University Press, 1993.

Ben-Uri, Galila. *The Missing Crown.* Bristol, Rhein & Englander, 1988.

———. *The Mysterious Cargo.* C.I.S. Publishers, 1989, third printing 2007.

Bernstein, Dainy. *Reading the World: American Haredi Children's Literature, 1980–2000.* Diss. City University of New York, 2021.

Biale, David. *Hasidism: A New History.* Princeton University Press, 2020.

Bilu, Yoram. "From Milah (Circumcision) to Milah (Word): Male Identity and Rituals of Childhood in the Ultraorthodox Community. *Ethos* 31.2 (2003): 172–203.

Bloch, Emmanuel. "Immodest Modesty: The Emergence of Halakhic Dress Codes." *Studies in Judaism, Humanities, and the Social Sciences* 1.2 (2018): 25–32.

Bloch, Marci Lavine. "The Devora Doresh Mysteries 2: Review." *Jewish Book Council*, March 2, 2012. https://www.jewishbookcouncil.org/book/the-devora-doresh-mysteries-2

"Bp upsherin cookies. Not too expensive." Imamother.com. May 23, 2021. https://www.imamother.com/forum/viewtopic.php?t=430250. Last Accessed July 1, 2021.

Brandt, Deborah. "Sponsors of Literacy." *College Composition and Communication* 49.2 (1998): 168.

Brauner, Reuven, trans. *Dress in Accordance with the Halochoh.* The Rabbinical Committee to Uphold the Honor of Jewish Sanctity, n.d.

Brener, Tali (טלי, ברנר). "Children in the Synagogue and in Life Rituals in Early Modern Ashkenaz: Childhood Studies Contribution to Israel's History." ("ילדים בבית הכנסת ובטקסי החיים בראשית העת החדשה באשכנז: תרומתו של חקר הילדות לתולדות ישראל"). *Zion* 78:B (ציון, שנה ע"ח כרך ב', תשע"ג) (2012): 183–207.

Brookshaw, Sharon. "The Material Culture of Children and Childhood: Understanding Childhood Objects in the Museum Context." *Journal of Material Culture* 14.3 (2009): 365–383.

Brown, Francis., S.R. Driver, and Charles A. Briggs. *The Brown-Driver-Briggs Hebrew and English Lexicon.* Hendrickson Publishers Marketing, Sixteenth Printing, 2015.

Buchanan, Rebekah J. *Writing a Riot: Riot Grrrl Zines and Feminist Rhetorics.* Peter Lang, 2018.

Cash, Johnny. "A Boy Named Sue." *At San Quentin.* Columbia Records, 1969.

———. "I Walk the Line." *Johnny Cash with his Hot and Blue Guitar.* Sun Records, 1956.

Chait, Baruch. *The Katz Passover Haggadah: The Art of Faith and Redemption.* Illustr. Gadi Pollack. B&B Septimus Educational Materials, 2003.

Clarke, Alison J. "Making Sameness: Mothering, Commerce and the Culture of Children's Birthday Parties." *Gender and Consumption: Domestic Cultures and the Commercialisation of Everyday Life*, eds. Lydia Marten and Emma Casey. Ashgate, 2007: 79–96.

Cohen, Floreva G. *A Hanukkiyah for Dina.* Board of Jewish Education, 1980.

Cohen, Moshe (Rabbi). (כהן, משה, רב). "Doll Toys and Landscape Pictures Depicting Astronomical Objects." ("בובות משחק ותמונות נוף המכילות גרמי שמיים"). *Tehumin* 33 (תחומין כרך 33) (2012): pp. 464–472.

Cross, Gary S. *Kids' Stuff: Toys and the Changing World of American Childhood.* Harvard University Press, 1997.

Cypress, Rebecca. "The Community as Ethnographer: Views of Classical Music in the English-Speaking Orthodox Jewish Community." *International Review of the Aesthetics and Sociology of Music* 41 (2010): 117–139.

Dale, Gordon. A. *Music in Haredi Jewish Life: Liquid Modernity and the Negotiation of Boundaries in Greater New York*. Diss. City University of New York, 2017.

Dean, Jimmy. "Big Bad John." *Big Bad Jock and Other Fabulous Songs and Tales*. Columbia Records, 1961.

Derevenski, Joanna Sofaer. *Children and Material Culture*. Routledge, 2000.

Deutsch, Barry. *How Mirka Got Her Sword*. Amulet Paperbacks, 2012.

Dion, Celine. "Donna the Prima Donna." *Donna the Prima Donna*. Columbia Records, 1963

Dixon, Franklin W. *The Hardy Boys Mystery Stories*. Stratemeyer Syndicate and Simon & Schuster, 1927–2005.

"Dor Yeshorim Rap." *YouTube*. Uploaded by Dor Yesharim, 18 May 2016. https://www.youtube.com/watch?v=JUFIBZwOccA.

Duncombe, Stephen. *Notes from Underground: Zines and the Politics of Alternative Culture*, 3rd ed. Microcosm, 2017.

Eli Gerstner. "Daddy Come Home." *YBC 5: Chanukah*. EG Productions, 2010.

———. "Those Were the Nights." *YBC 5: Chanukah*. EG Productions, 2010.

Fader, Ayala. *Mitzvah Girls: Bringing Up the Next Generation of Hasidic Jews in Brooklyn*. Princeton University Press, 2009.

Falk, Pesach Eliyahu. *Oz Vehadar Levusha*. Feldheim Publishers, 1998.

———. *The Tznius Handbook: Educational Diagrams for Women and Girls*. Third Edition. Feldheim Publishers, 2010.

———. *The Tznius Handbook: Educational Diagrams for Women and Girls (Pamphlet)*. n.p., 2010.

"Feeding and Eating Disorders." *Diagnostic and Statistical Manual of Mental Disorders*. American Psychiatric Association, 2013.

Finkelman, Yoel. "Nostalgia, Inspiration, Ambivalence: Eastern Europe, Immigration, and the Construction of Collective Memory in Contemporary American Haredi Historiography." *Jewish History*, 23.1 (2009): 57–82.

———. *Strictly Kosher Reading: Popular Literature and the Condition of Contemporary Orthodoxy*. Academic Studies Press, 2011.

Fleming, Dan. *Powerplay: Toys as Popular Culture*. Manchester University Press, 1996.

Forman-Brunell, Miriam, and Whitney, Jenifer Dawn, eds. *Dolls Studies: the Many Meanings of Girls' Toys and Play*. Peter Lang Publishing, 2015.

Gabay, Dovid. "The Letter." *Omar Dovid*. Sameach Music, 2008.

Ganz, Yaffa. *Savta Simcha and the Incredible Shabbos Bag*. Feldheim Publishers, 1980.

Garner, Ruth, Mark G. Gillingham, and White C. Stephen. "Effects of 'Seductive Details' on Macroprocessing and Microprocessing in Adults and Children." *Cognition and Instruction* 6.1 (1989): 41–57.

Geddes, David. "The Last Game of the Season (A Blind Man in the Bleachers)." Big Tree Records, 1975.

Gess, Nicola. "Gaining Sovereignty: On the Figure of the Child in Walter Benjamin's Writing. *MLN* 125.3 (2010): 682–708.

Ginsparg Klein, Leslie. "'No Candy Store, No Pizza Shops, No Maxi-Skirt, No Makeup': Socializing Orthodox Jewish Girls Through Schooling." *The Journal of the History of Childhood and Youth* 9.1 (2016): 140–158.

———. "The Troubling Trend of Photoshopping History." *The Lehrhaus*, November 17, 2016. https://www.thelehrhaus.com/scholarship/the-troubling-trend-of-photoshopping-history/.

Glaser, Tompall. "Put Another Log on the Fire (The Male Chauvinist National Anthem)." *Tompall (Sings the Songs of Shel Silverstein)*. Evil Eye Music Inc, 1975.

Goldin, Simha. "Jewish Society Under Pressure: The Concept of Childhood. *Youth in the Middle Ages*, eds. P.J.P Goldberg and Felicity Riddy. York Medieval Press, 2004: 25–43.

Gormé, Eydie. "Blame it on the Bossa Nova." *Blame it on the Bossa Nova*. Columbia Records, 1963.

Greene, Lorne. "Ringo." RCA Victor, 1964.

Grout, Donald Jay. *A History of Western Music*. W.W. Norton and Company, 1960.

Harp, Shannon F., and Richard E. Mayer. "The Role of Interest in Learning from Scientific Text and Illustrations: On the Distinction between Emotional Interest and Cognitive Interest." *Journal of Educational Psychology* 89.1 (1997): 92–102. https://doi.org/10.1037/0022–0663.89.1.92.

———. "How Seductive Details Do Their Damage: A Theory of Cognitive Interest in Science Learning." *Journal of Educational Psychology* 90.3 (1998): 414–34. https://doi.org/10.1037/0022–0663.90.3.414.

Hartman, Tova. *Feminism Encounters Traditional Judaism: Resistance and Accommodation*. Brandeis University Press, 2007.

Herbert, Wray. "Is Porn Un-American?" *U.S. News & World Report*. July 3, 1995.

Hidi, Suzanne, and William Baird. "Strategies for Increasing Text-Based Interest and Students' Recall of Expository Texts." *Reading Research Quarterly* 23. 4 (1988): 465–83. https://doi.org/10.2307/747644.

Hodder, Ian. "Human-thing Entanglement: Towards an Integrated Archaeological Perspective." *Journal of the Royal Anthropological Institute* 17 (2011A): 154–177.

———. "Wheels of Time: Some Aspects of Entanglement Theory and the Secondary Products Revolution." *Springer Science+Business* 24 (2011B): 175–187.

Horton, Johnny. "The Battle of New Orleans." Columbia Records, 1959.

Hubner, Carol Korb. Personal communication. June 2021.

———. *The Devora Doresh Mysteries*. The Judaica Press, 2006.

———. *The Devora Doresh Mysteries 2*. The Judaica Press, 2007.

———. *The Twisted Menora and Other Devora Doresh Mysteries*. The Judaica Press, 1981.

Hyden, Steven. "Whatever Happened to Alternative Nation?" *A.V. Club*. October 5, 2010. https://www.avclub.com/part-1–1990-once-upon-a-time-i-could-love-you-1798221947

Keene, Carolyn. *Nancy Drew Mysteries*. Simon & Schuster. 1930–2003.

Klein, Leah. *The B.Y. Times: Shani's Scoop*. Targum Press, 1991; repr. by Menucha Publishers, 2019.

———. *The B.Y. Times #4: War!* Targum Press, 1991; repr. by Menucha Publishers, 2019.

Kligman, Mark. "Contemporary Jewish Music in America." *The American Jewish Year Book* 101 (2001): 88–141.

Koenig, Harold G. "Research on Religion, Spirituality, and Mental Health: A Review." *The Canadian Journal of Psychiatry* 54.5 (2009): 283–91. https://doi.org/10.1177/070674370905400502.

Koppel, Moshe. *Judaism Straight Up: Why Real Religion Endures.* Koren, 2020.

Kranzler, David. "An Orthodox Revolution: The Creation and Development of the Beth Jacob Seminary for Girls." *Yad Vashem*, 11 Oct. 1999, www.yadvashem.org/download/education/conf/Kranzler.pdf.

Langer, Julia. "Getting the Lard Out: The Koshering of the Oreo Cookie." *Cornell Chronicle*. February 26, 2008. https://news.cornell.edu/stories/2008/02/getting-lard-out-koshering-oreo-cookie.

Leavitt, June. *The Flight to Seven Swan Bay.* Feldheim Publishers, 1985, repr. 2011.

Leibman, Laura. "Children, Toys, and Judaism." *The Bloomsbury Reader in Religion and Childhood*. Bloomsbury, 2017: 299–306.

Levine, Dov. "Yisroel." Composed by Chumi Berry. *Kumzitz Classics*. Suki and Ding Productions, 1992.

Linzer, Dov. "Tzniut, Halakha and the Male Gaze: Lecture and Sources." *YC Torah Library*, August 10, 2016. https://library.yctorah.org/2016/08/tzniut-halakha-and-the-male-gaze-lecture-and-sources.

Loketch-Fischer, Minna. *The Relationship Among Modesty, Self Objectivication, Body Shame and Eating Disorder Symptoms in Jewish Women*. Diss. Hofstra University, 2016.

Mallul, Chen. "The Haggadah That Brought the Nazis to the Seder." *National Library of Israel*. March 21, 2018. https://blog.nli.org.il/en/exodus-from-europe/. Last Accessed April 2021.

Marcus, Ivan G. "Honey Cakes and Torah." *Judaism in Practice: From the Middle Ages through the Early Modern Period*, ed. Lawrence Fine. Princeton University Press, 2011: 122–123.

———. *Rituals of Childhood: Jewish Acculturation in Medieval Europe*. Yale University Press, 1996.

Marx, Ursula, Gudrun Schwarz, Michael Schwarz, and Erdmut Wizisla, eds. *Walter Benjamin's Archive*. Trans. Esther Leslie. Verso, 2007.

Mayer, Richard E., ed. *Cambridge Handbook of Multimedia Learning*. 1st edition. Cambridge University Press, 2005.

Mickey Katz and His Kosher Jammers. "Haim afen Range." *Yiddish Square Dance*. RCA Victor, 1947.

Miller, Korin. "40 Things Only '90s Kids Will Remember." *Women's Health Magazine*. August 2, 2019. https://www.womenshealthmag.com/life/g28471716/things-only-90s-kids-remember/. Last Accessed July 1, 2021.

Miller, William R., and Carl E. Thoresen. "Spirituality, Religion, and Health: An Emerging Research Field." *American Psychologist* 58.1 (2003): 24–35. https://doi.org/10.1037/0003-066X.58.1.24.

Milligan, Amy K. "Hair Today, Gone Tomorrow: Upsherin, Alef-Bet, and the Childhood Navigation of Jewish Gender Identity Symbol Sets." *Children's Folklore Review* 38 (2017): 7–26.

———. *Jewish Bodylore: Feminist and Queer Ethnographies of Folk Practices*. Lexington Books, 2019.

Mohr, Patricia, John A. Glover, and Royce R. Ronning. "The Effect of Related and Unrelated Details on the Recall of Major Ideas in Prose." *Journal of Reading Behavior* 16.2 (1984): 97–108. https://doi.org/10.1080/10862968409547507.

Nathan, Eli. "Colored Candles." *Destiny I*. Aderet, 1985.

Nelson, Willie. "On the Road Again." *Honeysuckle Rose*. Columbia Records, 1980.

Neusner, Jacob. *The Idea of History in Rabbinic Judaism*. Brill, 2003.

Newman, Rena Yehuda. "Eight Nights of Jewish Zines." *New Voices*. December 10, 2020. https://newvoices.org/2020/12/10/eight-nights-of-jewish-zines.

Oorah. *Shmorg 8: Marvelous Middos Machine*. n.d. https://www.youtube.com/watch?v=wuh-gl498-c.

Oring, Elliot. "Rechnitzer Rejects: An Unorthodox Humor of Modern Orthodoxy." *Jokes and their Relations*. University of Kentucky Press, 1992: 68–82.

Pardue, Rivkah Avins. *Renewing Tradition Through Text: Tznius in 20th-Century America*. Thesis, Barnard College, 2021.
Pasolini, Pier P, Sade, et al. *Salo: 120 Days of Sodom*. Water Bearer Films, 1990.
Pickett, Bobby "Boris" & The Crypt Kicker. "Monster Mash." *The Original Monster Mash*. Garpax, 1962.
Piepmeier, Alison. *Girl Zines: Making Media, Doing Feminism*. New York University Press, 2009.
Plato. *The Republic*. The Gutenberg Project. https://www.gutenberg.org/files/1497/1497-h/1497-h.htm.
Preston, Johnny. "Running Bear." Mercury Records, 1959.
"Remember that AT&T Jingle, 'Reach Out – Reach Out and Touch Someone? Hear It Again & Find Out more," *Click Americana: Vintage & Retro Memories*, n.d. https://clickamericana.com/media/advertisements/reach-out-reach-out-and-touch-someone-1979-1982.
Rogers, Kenny. "Coward of the County." *Kenny*. United Artists, 1979.
———. "The Gambler." *The Gambler*. United Artists, 1978.
Rotenberg, Abie and Moshe Yess. *Marvelous Middos Machine: Episode 1: Up Up and Away*. M&M Enterprises, 1986.
———. *Marvelous Middos Machine: Episode 2: Shnooky to the Rescue*. M&M Enterprises, 1987.
———. *Marvelous Middos Machine: Episode 3: Does Anyone Have the Time?* M&M Enterprises, 1988.
———. *Marvelous Middos Machine: Episode 4: Shnooky's Bar Mitzvah*. M&M Enterprises, 2011.
Rotenberg, Abie. *Journeys Vol. 1*. M&M Enterprises, 1985.
———. *Journeys Vol. 2*. M&M Enterprises, 1989.
———. *Journeys Vol. 3*. M&M Enterprises, 1993.
———. *Journeys Vol. 4*. M&M Enterprises, 2003.
Sade. *The 120 Days of Sodom and Other Writings*. eds. Austryn Wainhouse, Richard Seaver, Simone Beauvoir, and Pierre Klossowski. Grove Press, 1987.
Seidman, Naomi. *Sarah Schenirer and the Bais Yaakov Movement: A*

Revolution in the Name of Tradition. Littman Library of Jewish Civilization, 2019.

Serra, Michael J., and John Dunlosky. "Metacomprehension Judgements Reflect the Belief That Diagrams Improve Learning from Text." *Memory (Hove, England)* 18.7 (October 2010): 698–711. https://doi.org/10.1080/09658211.2010.506441.

Shapiro, Chava. *The Jewish Zine Archive.* Tucson, AZ. https://www.instagram.com/jewishzinearchive/.

Sheinson, Yosef David, and Zvi Miklos Adler. *Mosaf LeHaggadah Shel Pesach.* HaHistadrut HaTzionit Ahidaj VeNahem Be Germaniah, 1946.

Sherman, Alla. "Hello Muddah, Hello Fadduh (A Letter from Camp)." *My Son, the Nut.* Warner Bors. Records, 1963.

Shiezoli. "Eli Gerstner CBS, FOX, Universal & YBC Live 4 Part 2 (of 3)." YouTube Video, 10:37. December 22, 2011. https://www.youtube.com/watch?v=IoOdoGFdOh4

Shirey, Larry L., and Ralph E. Reynolds. "Effect of Interest on Attention and Learning." *Journal of Educational Psychology* 80.2 (1988): 159–66. https://doi.org/10.1037/0022-0663.80.2.159.

Siegel, Malky. *The Baker's Dozen, Book 2: Ghosthunters!* Targum Press, 1992, repr. by Menucha Publishers, 2017.

Silton, Nava R., and Joshua Fogel. "Religiosity, Empathy, and Psychopathology among Young Adult Children of Rabbis." *Archive for the Psychology of Religion* 32.3 (September 2010): 277–91. https://journals.sagepub.com/doi/abs/10.1163/157361210X532040.

Sleepwalking. "Daddy Come Home...YBC Speechless!!" *Imamother.* November 27, 2012. https://www.imamother.com/forum/viewtopic.php?t=200361. Last Accessed July 1, 2021.

Sovine, Red. "Phantom 309." Starday Records, 1967.

Stark, T, Miriam. "Technical Choice in Kalinga Ceramic Traditions." *Material Meanings: Critical Approaches to the Interpretation of Material Culture,* ed. Elizabeth S. Chilton. University of Utah Press, 1999: 24–43.

Stearns, Peter N. "The Impact of Religious Change." *Childhood in World History.* Routledge, 2006: 33–42.

———. *Anxious Parents: A History of Modern Childrearing in America*. New York University Press, 2003.

Ta-Shema, Israel M. "On Birthdays in Israel." ("על ימי הולדת בישראל"). *Zion*, 2001 (ציון, תשס"ב): 19–24.

The Beach Boys. "Kokomo." *Still Cruisin'*. Elektra, 1988.

The Coasters. "Charlie Brown." Atco 6132. Sony, 1958.

———. "Along Came Jones." Atco. Sony, 1959.

The Crystals. "Then He Kissed Me." *Philles Records Presents Today's Hits*. Philles, 1963.

The Shirelles. "Soldier Boy." *Baby It's You*. Scepter, 1962.

Toiv, Yossi. *Country Yossi & The Shteeble-Hoppers Volume 1: Wanted!* CY Productions, 1983.

———. *Country Yossi & The Shteeble-Hoppers Volume 2: Strike Again*. CY Productions, 1984.

———. *Country Yossi & The Shteeble-Hoppers Volume 3: Still On the Loose*. CY Productions, 1985.

———. *Country Yossi & The Shteeble-Hoppers Volume 4: Captured*. CY Productions, 1987.

———. *Country Yossi & The Shteeble-Hoppers Volume 5: Break Out*. CY Productions, 1987.

———. *Country Yossi & The Shteeble-Hoppers Volume 6: Ride Again*. CY Productions, 2010.

———. "Who Did a Mitzva?" *Kivi & Tuki Volume 3: Boker Tov, Layla Tov*. CY Productions, 1987.

Wade, Suzanne E., and Robert B. Adams. "Effects of Importance and Interest on Recall of Biographical Text." *Journal of Reading Behavior* 22.4 (December 1990): 331–53. https://doi.org/10.1080/10862969009547717.

Wells, Helen. *Cherry Ames* Series. Grosset & Dunlap, 1943–1968.

"Where can I get *upsherin* cookie cutters in Monsey?" Imamother.com. December 18, 2010. https://www.imamother.com/forum/viewtopic.php?t=135988. Last Accessed July 1, 2021.

Whitman, James Q. *Hitler's American Model: The United States and the Making of Nazi Race Law*. Princeton University Press, 2017.

Williams, Matt. Personal communication. April 2021.

———. Untitled Manuscript.

Wilson, Mara. "The B.Y. Times: The Orthodox Jewish Answer to The Baby-Sitters Club." *The Toast*. March 5, 2015. https://the-toast.net/2015/03/05/the-b-y-times-jewish-answer-baby-sitters-club/. Last Accessed July 1, 2021.

Wobst, H, Martin. "Style in Archaeology or Archaeologists in Style." *Material Meanings: Critical Approaches to the Interpretation of Material Culture*, ed Elizabeth S. Chilton. University of Utah Press, 1999: 118–132.

Wood, Abigail. "Pop, Piety and Modernity: The Changing Spaces of Orthodox Culture." *The Routledge Handbook of Contemporary Jewish Cultures*, eds. Roth, L. and Valman, N. Routledge, 2014.

Zager and Evans. *Exordium & Terminus*. RCA, 1969.

Zakon, Miriam Stark. *Gemarakup Super Sleuth Series, Book 1: Meet Gemarakup*. Mesorah Publications, 1990, Second Edition 2012.

Zikherman, Haim (זיכרמן, חיים). *Black Blue-White: a Journey to Israeli Haredi Society* (שחור כחול לבן: מסע אל תוך החברה החרדית בישראל). תל־אביב: ידיעות אחרונות; ספרי) Yedioth Ahronoth; Sifrei Hemed חמד), 2014.

About the Authors

Dr. Wendy Love Anderson teaches and writes about bodies and religious identity as they occupy the discursive space between Judaism and Christianity, especially during the Middle Ages. She is Assistant Director of Academic Programs in the Center for the Humanities and affiliate faculty in Religious Studies at Washington University in St. Louis. She received her M.A. in Religious Studies and her Ph.D. in History of Christianity from the University of Chicago. She is currently finishing a bonus M.A. in Jewish Studies and pursuing rabbinic ordination at the Academy for Jewish Religion in New York.

Dr. Dainy Bernstein, who uses ey/eir pronouns, holds a Ph.D. in English and a Certificate in Medieval Studies from the CUNY Graduate Center. Eir work focuses primarily on contemporary Haredi children's texts and materials, and ey also studies medieval British and Ashkenazic children and childhood in literature. Dainy was born and raised in Boro Park, Brooklyn, and attended Bais Yaakov schools from pre-school through high school. Ey then attended Yavne Seminary in Cleveland and taught English at Bais Yaakov of Boro Park before pursuing higher education. Dainy teaches college composition, medieval literature, and children's and Young Adult literature at Lehman College, CUNY. Eir current projects include a book on the beginnings of Haredi children's literature and an online database of Haredi children's texts, songs, and material culture.

Miriam Bernstein grew up in Boro Park and went to Bais Yaakov High School. She recently graduated with her Bachelors in Classics and Religious Studies from Brooklyn College, CUNY. She's interested in how the needs of a religious community shape the religious laws governing the community, and she plans to pursue graduate study in this area.

Dr. Shamma Boyarin comes from a Modern Orthodox household where learning in the traditional Jewish sense was a central component of Jewish identity. This love of traditional learning was also mirrored by a passion for the academic study of Judaism (of course, the borders between these two are not sharply delineated). Although he has grown up to be sharply critical and ambivalent of both Modern Orthodox Judaism and the academy, one of the central places where he contends with both is through his scholarship. The contribution to this volume is at least in part a small personal meditation on how childhood encounters can shape adult ideas. His areas of scholarship include Comparative Medieval Literature (Hebrew and Arabic), the Relationship between Religion and Literature, and aspects of Religion and Pop Culture (with a special focus on Heavy Metal).

Dr. Hillel Broder currently serves as the General Studies Principal at DRS Yeshiva High School for Boys of the Hebrew Academy of Long Beach in Woodmere, NY. Previously, he taught and served in various leadership roles at Fordham University, SAR High School, and Yeshiva University High School for Boys. Hillel has inaugurated educational innovations such as co-founding the Yeshiva Poetry Society, coaching performance poetry teams, and leading a regular Orthodox high school meditation *tefilla*.

He holds a Ph.D. in English from the Graduate Center, CUNY, and is a graduate of Yeshiva University's Yeshiva College. He has published academic articles in diverse publications, including *Hakira, Journal of Jewish Educational Leadership, Journal of the Kafka Society, Philosophy and Literature,* and *Journal of Medical Humanities*. Hillel has written music reviews for *The Lehrhaus, The Forward,* and *Tablet Magazine*. He is also an active writer of poetry and has published poems in *Typehouse Literary Magazine, Modern Poetry Quarterly Review, Leaves of Ink, East*

Coast Literary Review, Eunoia Review, and *Front Porch Review.* His first book of poems, *Counting Spheres,* offers a poem for each day of Sefirat Ha'Omer, synthesizing his interest in mysticism and poetry. His second book of poems, *Daily Blessings,* is forthcoming from Ben Yehuda Press's poetry imprint; it offers a poem corresponding to each page of *Brachot,* the first tractate of the Babylonian Talmud.

Shlomi Eiger is a practicing toy designer and researcher of childhood through toys and children's material culture, based in Tel Aviv, Israel. He is a graduate of the Department of Industrial Design at the Bezalel Academy of Art and Design in Jerusalem, Israel, with a B.Des. He has been working for over a decade as a toy designer and consultant for big brands such as Rummikub, Taf Toys, Halilit, the Ruth Youth Wing in the Israel Museum in Jerusalem, Space IL, and private entrepreneurs in the local and international toy industry. His experience as a practitioner, his familiarity with the inner industry processes, and his curiosity about the different meanings of the objects he creates led him to study for his M.A. in Child and Youth Culture Research at Tel Aviv University. His research on the material culture of children focuses on the role of toys and the processes for creating them in cultural construction and the ways toys reflect culture and society. His research intertwines methodologies of material culture research with his knowledge of the industrial toy industry.

Eiger has taught about toys and toy design at the Toy Invention Program (TIP) at Shenkar College of Engineering, Design and Art in Ramat Gan, Israel, and in Holon Institute of Technology (HIT), Israel. Besides his academic and design work, he runs the About Toys blog, where he discusses the cultural and historical aspects of the world of toys. See his toy design portfolio shlomieiger.com. Find his blog at aboutoys.com.

Dr. Sara Feldman is Preceptor in Yiddish at Harvard University. As a University of Michigan student, Feldman was unaware that exiting Orthodoxy could be a viable topic of academic research and instead wrote a doctoral dissertation that explored intersections between modern Yiddish, Hebrew, and Russian culture. Later, while a faculty member at the University of Illinois teaching both free and incarcerated students, Feldman began in earnest to investigate the threads that connect the contemporary OTD world with predecessors in Eastern Europe and the Americas. Adjacent passions include languages, studying and practicing various dance forms including Argentine tango, discovering Yiddish tangos and watching every Yiddish film available, and activism, whether in solidarity actions or labor organizing.

Dr. Yoel Finkelman is curator of the Haim and Hannah Salomon Judaica Collection at the National Library of Israel. He is the author of *Strictly Kosher Reading: Popular Literature and the Condition of Contemporary Orthodoxy* (2011).

Rabbi Elli Fischer is an independent writer, translator, and editor. He is editor of Rabbi Eliezer Melamed's *Peninei Halakha* series in English and cofounder of HaMapah, a project that applies quantitative analysis to rabbinic literature. He is a founding editor of *The Lehrhaus*, a web magazine of contemporary Jewish thought, and his writing has appeared in numerous Jewish publications. He holds degrees from Yeshiva University, rabbinical ordination from Israel's Chief Rabbinate, and is working toward a doctorate in Jewish History at Tel Aviv University.

Dr. Abigail Glogower is the founding curator of Jewish Collections at the Filson Historical Society in Louisville, Kentucky. A multidisciplinary scholar, curator, and educator, she earned her doctorate in visual and cultural studies from the University of Rochester with a focus on group portraiture in nineteenth-century America. She has traveled the country as a poet and singer-songwriter, and is a member of artist and musician collectives. She and her partner (a Reform turned Reconstructionist Jewish scholar of comparative religion) spend their time outside of work and activism with their rescue dogs and DIY restoring their home in a wonderfully diverse neighborhood on Louisville's South End.

About the Authors

Lonna Gordon grew up humming *The Marvelous Midos Machine* throughout her Brooklyn Bais Yaakov career. She has since moved to Philadelphia where she works as an engineer, putters around in the garden, and raises three little boys on *Daniel Tiger*, which is like *Marvelous Midos Machine* for toddlers. She looks forward to introducing them to Jewish story tapes in the future.

Sarah Gray is an accomplished home cook, fervent Groucho Marxist, and admin of over 900 Facebook tag groups. When not working the deli counter at a kosher supermarket, she spends her time hiking and camping with her fiancée, enjoying works of science fiction, and dancing with wild abandon whenever the mood hits. During the frigid Michigan winter months, she hibernates indoors playing video games and occasionally creates visual art. She has proudly raised a frei daughter.

Goldie Gross was born and raised Chabad in the Crown Heights section of Brooklyn. Currently, she is a student at the Institute of Fine Arts at New York University, where she is pursuing a master's degree in the History of Art and Archaeology. Her research interests are in modern and contemporary Jewish art (particularly the politically radical and outsider variety) and the visual representation of women in the ultra-Orthodox media. She organized an art exhibition on the latter topic titled *The Invisible Jew* (2018) and conducted further research on the issue as a Gilda Slifka Intern at the Hadassah-Brandeis Institute. She received her bachelor's degree in Art & Business from Baruch College, and her undergraduate thesis, titled "A Study of *Der hammer*: Aesthetic Influences on Art and Culture in the Communist Yiddish Press," received the Kanner Prize for Outstanding Thesis. She is a volunteer curator with the Jewish Art Salon, a member of The Met Collective, and creates and exhibits her own art in her free time.

Yehudis Keller was born and raised as Chabad-Lubavitch in Crown Heights, Brooklyn. She received her B.A. in Psychology and Fine Arts from Brooklyn College in 2020 and is continuing on to pursue an M.A. in Experimental Psychology. Under the guidance of research faculty in the psychology department, Yehudis volunteered at a research lab studying childhood psychopathic traits. She also assisted research on racial and ethnic disparities in counseling in urban colleges. She is currently focusing on mental health and other psychological research among current and former members of the ultra-Orthodox community.

Dr. Leslie Ginsparg Klein is the Academic Dean of Women's Institute of Torah Seminary & College in Baltimore. She was formerly an assistant professor of history and Jewish studies at Touro College. Leslie received her Ph.D. in Education and Jewish Studies from New York University. Her dissertation on the history of Bais Yaakov in America combined her interests in American Jewish history, history of education, gender history, and history of childhood. She is currently working on a book on the culture and development of Bais Yaakov schools in America.

Miriam L. is a senior at Yeshiva University studying Biology and Women's Studies in the S. Daniel Abraham Honors Program with plans to go to medical school and pursue a career in women's health. She spent a year learning at Michlelet Mevaseret Yerushalayim (MMY) in Israel before college, where she became passionate about Jewish Orthodox Feminism. Miriam is passionate about making shuls safe spaces for all members of the community regardless of gender identity, sexual orientation, or denomination.

Dr. Hannah Lebovits is an assistant professor of public affairs at the University of Texas-Arlington where she researches topics related to socially sustainable community development and governance. Hannah's academic work has appeared in several peer reviewed journals and books, and her public scholarship has appeared in local, national, and international media publications. She currently lives in Dallas, TX with her husband and two children.

Dr. Meira Levinson holds a Ph.D. in English Literature from the CUNY Graduate Center. She currently works as an education and writing consultant and an independent scholar. Her research focuses on the intersections of children's literature, speculative fiction, Jewish literature/poetics, and feminist theologies. Meira has presented her work at forums such as the Children's Literature Association, Modern Language Association, and the American Academy of Religion.

Chanan Maister grew up all over the Midwest, and after spending a decade in Crown Heights he's back there, living with his family in Michigan. He spends most of his free time reading.

Miriam Moster is a doctoral student in sociology at The Graduate Center, CUNY. She is a Mellon Humanities Public Fellow and Wexner Graduate Fellow. Her research focuses on ultra-Orthodoxy and the experiences of parents who leave strict religious marriages and communities. Her paper on the educational outcomes of former Hasidim was published as a chapter in *Off the Derech: Leaving Orthodox Judaism* (SUNY Press 2020). Alongside her research, Miriam founded Right to Parent, an organization working to support and advocate for parents who leave strict religious marriages and communities. (Learn more about this work at righttoparent.org)

Dr. Schneur Zalman Newfield was raised Lubavitch and attended Lubavitch yeshivas in Chicago, Miami, and Buenos Aires, Argentina. He participated in Lubavitch outreach activities in Russia, China, and Singapore. After completing the Lubavitch educational system, he earned a bachelor's degree in Psychology from Brooklyn College and a Ph.D. in Sociology from New York University. He then taught sociology courses for two years in six medium- and maximum-security New Jersey state prisons through Rutgers University-Newark's New Jersey Scholarship and Transformative Education in Prisons (NJ-STEP) consortium. He is now Assistant Professor of Sociology at Borough of Manhattan Community College (CUNY), and the author of *Degrees of*

Separation: Identity Formation While Leaving Ultra-Orthodox Judaism (Temple University Press 2020). Newfield is also a host on the Jewish Studies channel of the New Books Network podcast. Visit him online at ZalmanNewfield.com.

Jessica Russak-Hoffman graduated from Stern College for Women with a degree in English literature and worked as an editorial assistant in library trade and publishing before shifting into freelance writing and magazine editorial, but mostly uses her degree to enjoy SparkNotes memes. Jessica wrote pieces for BBC News and *JOFA Journal* about her post-9/11 Jewish chaplaincy, and her publishing credits include pieces for *Kveller, Lady Mamale, Jewneric,* and *NW Beauty*. Jessica lives in Seattle with her husband and three children. When she is not obsessively listening to Dave Matthews Band, Mumford and Sons, and the History Chicks podcast, she is tweeting about being Jewish @HoffmanJess, working on her next novel, and co-hosting the Kiddush Book Club podcast.

Sarah Snider is a professor of creative and academic writing and a practicing writer whose work touches on themes of community, family, gender, place, illness, and self. "Singing in the House of Jacob" is part of her essay collection-in-progress, generously supported by a Dorot Fellowship and a Hadassah Brandeis Institute Research Award. Sarah received her MFA in Prose from the University of Notre Dame, where she was awarded the La Vie de Bohème Award for Literary Excellence and William Mitchell Award for Distinguished Achievement in the Graduate Creative Writing Program. In addition to her creative and academic work, Sarah is involved in local Jewish and interfaith community-building initiatives, serves on the board of the Michiana Jewish Film Festival, and plays rec league ice hockey.

Dr. Devora Steinmetz is on the faculty of the Hebrew College Rabbinical School and of the Mandel Executive Leadership Program. She has served on the leadership team of Drisha, helping to establish Drisha's summer kollel and Israeli *beit midrash* as well as Yeshivat

Drisha in Israel, and has taught at the Jewish Theological Seminary, Yeshivat Hadar, and Havruta: a Beit Midrash at Hebrew University. She is the founder of Beit Rabban, a Jewish day school profiled in Daniel Pekarsky's *Vision at Work: The Theory and Practice of Beit Rabban*. She is the author of scholarly articles on Talmud, Midrash, and Bible, and of two books, *From Father to Son: Kinship, Conflict, and Continuity in Genesis* and *Punishment and Freedom: The Rabbinic Construction of Criminal Law*. She has a bachelor's degree in Biology from Barnard College, a master's degree in English Literature from Fordham University, and a doctorate in Comparative Literature from Columbia University.

Frieda Vizel was raised in the Satmar village of Kiryas Joel, which she left with her son. She now lives in Brooklyn, where she gives tours of the Jewish neighborhoods. You can find her at friedavizel.com.

Talia Weisberg is originally from New York, NY, where she attended a Modern Orthodox day school and Bais Yaakov high school. She earned her Bachelor of Arts degree at Harvard University in the Comparative Study of Religion with a secondary field in Women, Gender, and Sexuality. Her senior honors thesis explored the past and present of the Bais Yaakov movement and its role in the evolution of Orthodox women's formal religious education. She is currently a student at Yeshivat Maharat, the first Orthodox institution to ordain women as clergy. She previously served as the Director of Academic Affairs at the Consulate General of Israel to New England. Her writing has appeared in the *Forward*, *Alma*, the *Ms. Magazine* blog, and as a letter to the editor in the *New York Times*, and she has spoken or taught Torah for organizations including the Jewish Orthodox Feminist Alliance (JOFA), LimmudBoston, and the Camberville Open Beit Midrash.

Talia believes in the value of giving back and is involved with several community organizations, including LimmudBoston, the Crohn's and Colitis Foundation, and the Harvard alumni community; she also runs Greater Boston's only active gown *gemach* and volunteers as a matchmaker on the Jewish dating website SawYouAtSinai. She serves as the co-ritual chair on the board of the Orthodox Minyan at Harvard Hillel, a minyan that caters to students, young professionals, and young families. In 2013, she was named as one of the Jewish Week's "36 Under 36" young visionaries reshaping and broadening the Jewish community. She lives in Cambridge, MA, with her husband and rescue dog.

Anthologies from *Ben Yehuda Press*

Torah in a Time of Plague: Historical and Contemporary Jewish Responses. Edited by Erin Leib Smokler. **Winner of the 2021 National Jewish Book Award for Modern Jewish Thought and Experience.** A collection of essays using Torah – broadly understood to include any canonical Jewish text or tradition – to illuminate, explore, bemoan, or grapple with our current moment of plague.

Strange Fire: Jewish Voices from the Pandemic. Edited by T S Mendola. In this anthology, award-winning essayist and cultural critic T.S. Mendola presents a collection of previously unpublished art, poetry, essays, and short stories that explore our more-or-less heretical relationship to Judaism in times of crisis.

Liberating Your Passover Seder: An Anthology Beyond The Freedom Seder. Edited by Rabbi Arthur O. Waskow and Rabbi Phyllis O. Berman. This volume tells the history of the Freedom Seder and retells the origin of subsequent new haggadahs, including those focusing on Jewish-Palestinian reconciliation, environmental concerns, feminist and LGBT struggles, and the Covid-19 pandemic of 2020.

Studies in Judaism and Pluralism Honoring the 60th Anniversary of the Academy for Jewish Religion. Edited by Leonard Levin. From questions of philosophy and law to matters of liturgy and practice, this volume explores how Jewish communities can live with co-existing commitments to non-negotiable, contradicting beliefs.

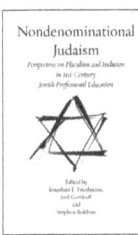

Nondenominational Judaism: Perspectives on Pluralism and Inclusion in 21st-Century Jewish Professional Education. Edited by Jonathan L. Friedmann, Joel Gereboff, and Stephen Robbins. This volume collects personal, academic, and philosophical reflections on learning, teaching, administrating, and leading in pluralistic Jewish settings; the unique roles of pluralism vis-à-vis denominational models; and the benefits and challenges of nondenominational Jewish education.

Ra'u Or: Essays in Honor of Dr. Ora Horn Prouser. Edited by Joseph Prouser. A collection of scholarly essays in celebration of Dr. Ora Horn Prouser on her 60th birthday. Dr. Prouser is CEO and Academic Dean at The Academy for Jewish Religion, a pluralistic rabbinical, cantorial and graduate school.

Voices of Orthodox women from *Ben Yehuda Press*

Monologues from the Makom: Intertwined Narratives of Sexuality, Gender, Body Image, and Jewish Identity. Edited by Rivka Cohen, Sara Rozner Lawrence, Sarah Ricklan, Rebecca Zimilover, and Naima Hirsch. A collection of first-person poetry and prose designed to break the observant Jewish community's taboo against open discussion of female sexuality

Life on the Fringes A Feminist Journey Toward Traditional Rabbinic Ordination by Haviva Ner-David. Part memoir, part commentary, this volume charts a startling Jewish feminist journey both solitary and engaging.

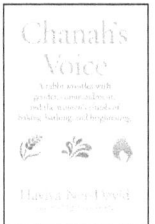

Chanah's Voice: A Rabbi Wrestles With Gender, Commandment, and The Women's Mitzvot of Baking, Bathing and Brightening by Haviva Ner-David. In this memoir, Rabbi Ner-David explores the spirituality of domestic life while struggling with the strictures of systematized Jewish law. Combining soul-searching honesty and deep Jewish knowledge, Chanah's Voice is the compelling voice of a new generation of Jewish feminism.

Reaching for Comfort: What I Saw, What I Learned, and How I Blew it Training as a Pastoral Counselor by Sherri Mandell. In 2004, Sherri Mandell won the National Jewish Book award for The Blessing of the Broken Heart, which told of her grief and initial mourning after her 13-year-old son Koby was brutally murdered. Years later, with her pain still undiminished, Sherri trains to help others as a pastoral counselor, one of the first in Israel's hospitals.

Life in the Present Tense: Reflections on family and faith by Rifka Rosenwein. Publishers Weekly called it "A treasure trove of wisdom from one of American Judaism's most beloved and lamented voices."

With an Outstretched Arm: A Memoir of Love and Loss, Family and Faith by B. J. Yudelson. This memoir recounts the author's journey from the liberal, southern Reform Judaism of the 1940s and '50s to the warm embrace of a more traditional Orthodox Jewish life. It relates how chance encounters propelled her, people and books inspired her, and tragedy tested her, challenging her to ask difficult questions.

www.ingramcontent.com/pod-product-compliance
Lightning Source LLC
Chambersburg PA
CBHW050549160426
43199CB00015B/2587